VISION OF TRANSFORMATION

The Territorial Rhetoric of Ezekiel 40-48

SOCIETY OF BIBLICAL LITERATURE

DISSERTATION SERIES

Michael V. Fox, Old Testament Editor
Pheme Perkins, New Testament Editor

Number 154

THE VISION OF TRANSFORMATION
The Territorial Rhetoric of Ezekiel 40–48

by
Kalinda Rose Stevenson

VISION OF TRANSFORMATION

The Territorial Rhetoric of Ezekiel 40-48

by
Kalinda Rose Stevenson

Scholars Press
Atlanta, Georgia

THE VISION OF TRANSFORMATION
The Territorial Rhetoric of Ezekiel 40–48

Kalinda Rose Stevenson

Library of Congress Cataloging in Publication Data
Stevenson, Kalinda Rose, 1943–
    The vision of transformation : the territorial rhetoric of Ezekiel
40–48 / Kalinda Rose Stevenson.
       p.   cm. — (Dissertation series / Society of Biblical
Literature ; no. 154)
    "Slightly revised version of my Graduate Theological Union
doctoral dissertation"—Acknowledgements.
    Includes bibliographical references.
    ISBN 0-7885-0242-5 (alk. paper). — ISBN 0-7885-0243-3 (pbk. :
alk. paper)
    1. Bible. O.T. Ezekiel XL–XLVIII—Criticism, interpretation,
etc.   I. Title. II. Series: Dissertation series (Society of
Biblical Literature) ; no. 154.
BS1545.2.S74   1996
224'.406—dc20   96-7000
                                       CIP

Printed in the United States of America
on acid-free paper

For Jim, Eric, and Darlene

Table of Contents

Table of Figures

Acknowledgments

This work is a slightly revised version of my Graduate Theological Union doctoral dissertation. Completion of the dissertation was the endpoint of a long journey made possible by family, friends, mentors, and guides. I am grateful to my excellent dissertation committee, who shaped my work in particular ways: my director, Marvin Chaney, of San Francisco Theological Seminary and the Graduate Theological Union; Arthur Quinn, of the Rhetoric Department of the University of California at Berkeley; Allan Pred, of the Geography Department of the University of California at Berkeley; John Endres, S.J. of the Jesuit School of Theology at Berkeley and the Graduate Theological Union; and Clare Fischer, of Starr King School for the Ministry and the Graduate Theological Union. Each of these people contributed a unique perspective and specific help to my work.

I am truly grateful for the friends and guides who supported me on my way, especially Kim McCourt, Barbara Williams, SNJM, Jason Mixter, and Lois Lively.

My greatest appreciation is for my husband and children, Jim, Eric, and Darlene. My husband Jim—my resident computer consultant—prepared the diagrams, and has been a source of unfailing love, support and encouragement. More than anyone else, he made it all possible. I dedicate this study to these three people who mean so much to me, with love and gratitude for who they are and who I am because of them.

Finally, I acknowledge the gracious call of God to this journey with the prophet Ezekiel. I am grateful for the journey—even for the painful parts—because I am not the person I was when I began. Truly, God has been there.

Abbreviations

AB *Anchor Bible*
AnBib *Analecta Biblica*
BA *Biblical Archaeologist*
BAR *Biblical Archaeology Reader*
BHS *Biblica Hebraica Stuttgartensia*
BJRL *Bulletin of the John Rylands Library of Manchester*
CahRB *Cahiers de la Revue Biblique*
CBQ *Catholic Biblical Quarterly*
CHG *Cambridge Human Geography*
FOTL *Forms of the Old Testament Literature*
HeyJ *Heythrop Journal*
HR *History of Religions*
HSM *Harvard Semitic Monographs*
IBC *Interpretation: A Bible Commentary for Teaching and Preaching*
ICC *International Critical Commentary*
IDB *Interpreter's Dictionary of the Bible*
IEJ *Israel Exploration Journal*
JAAR *Journal of the American Academy of Religion*
JBL *Journal of Biblical Literature*
JETS *Journal of the Evangelical Theological Society*
JOAS *Journal of the American Oriental Society*
JR *Journal of Religion*
JSNTSup *Journal for the Study of the New Testament—Supplement Series*

JSOT *Journal for the Study of the Old Testament*
JSOTSup *Journal for the Study of the Old Testament—Supplement Series*
MHCHG *Making Histories and Constructing Human Geographies*
NTS *New Testament Studies*
OBT *Overtures to Biblical Theology*
OTG *Old Testament Guides*
OTL *Old Testament Library*
OTM *Old Testament Message*
PEQ *Palestine Exploration Quarterly*
PMG *Postmodern Geographies*
RB *Revue Biblique*
RSV *Revised Standard Version*
SBLDS *Society of Biblical Literature Dissertation Series*
SEA *Svensk Exegetisk Arsbok*
Sem *Semeia*
SJOT *Scandinavian Journal of the Old Testament*
SWBA *Social World of Biblical Antiquity*
TS *Theological Studies*
TynBul *Tyndale Bulletin*
VT *Vetus Testamentum*
VTSup *Vetus Testamentum— Supplement Series*
WBC *Word Biblical Commentary*
ZAW *Zeitschrift für die alttestamentliche Wissenschaft*

Preface

This preface is a brief discussion of six studies published since the completion of my doctoral dissertation in 1992. It is also an opportunity to give priority to the geographical perspective which shaped my study of Ezekiel 40–48. Human geography is a broad division in the discipline of geography which deals with the spatial aspects of societies. In recent years, a number of human geographers have asserted that a significant change is underway in social theory. One of the strongest voices has been that of Edward Soja. He argues that history has been privileged over geography for the last hundred years.

> For at least the past century, time and history have occupied a privileged position in the practical and theoretical consciousness of Western Marxism and critical social science. Understanding how history is made has been the primary source of emancipatory insight and practical political consciousness, the great variable container for a critical interpretation of social life and practice. Today, however, it may be space more than time that hides consequences from us, the 'making of geography' more than the 'making of history' that provides the most revealing tactical and theoretical world. This is the insistent premise and promise of postmodern geographies.[1]

A second proponent of the same premise is Allan Pred. Pred's study, *Making Histories and Constructing Human Geographies*, insists on the inseparable interrelationship between the historical, geographical, and social. Pred's work is a critique of social theory which ignores the constraints of time and space.[2]

If these human geographers are right, then scholarship across the disciplines has tended to think in historical terms without seeing the importance of spatial categories. It is significant that the dominant critical method of biblical studies which arose during the nineteenth century was the "Historical Critical Method." There was no corresponding "Geographical Critical Method." It is true that biblical scholars have always paid attention to geography, but it has been physical geography rather than human geography.

Scholars have long recognized that access to space is a central concern of Ezekiel 40–48, and have discussed areas, boundaries, and access. However, to my knowledge, no one has used the language of human geography to show that the fundamental intention of these chapters is to create a new human geography by changing access to space. Human geography shows that every society is organized in space. Changing the spatial organization of the society changes the society. Ezekiel 40–48 is a vision of a new society organized according to a new set of spatial rules. It is a temple society with controlled access to sacred space, based on a spatial theology of holiness. The perspectives and vocabulary of human geography clarifies aspects of the text which scholars have found problematic, and allows us to see the rhetorical point of the vision. This Rhetor wants nothing less than to create a transformed world.

This transformed world is one arranged according to the categories of a priestly worldview. In his book, *Raising Up a Faithful Priest,* Richard Nelson has presented a superb and profoundly respectful discussion of the theology of priesthood. Three chapters are particularly pertinent here. In his chapter, "Israel's Culture Map," Nelson explains the two basic classifications which lie at the ideological core of the book of Ezekiel: the holy in opposition to the profane and the clean in opposition to the unclean.[3] It is significant to note that Nelson uses spatial language to define these categories. That which is clean is *in its proper place* with the boundaries established by God in creation.[4] That which is unclean is something *out of place.* The *sphere* of the ordinary is the common, while the *realm* of the divine is

---

[1.] Edward W. Soja, *Postmodern Geographies: The Reassertion of Space in Critical Social Theory* [London: Verso, 1989], 1).

[2.] Allan Pred, *MHCHG* (Boulder: Westview Press, 1990).

[3.] Richard D. Nelson, *Raising Up a Faithful Priest: Community and Priesthood in Biblical Theology* (Louisville: Kentucky, Westminster/John Knox, 1993), 17–38.

[4.] Emphasis added.

the holy. The quality of holiness was objectively dangerous and ordinary people had to *keep their distance.*[5] The priests were "boundary setters" who defined and separated these categories and taught these distinctions to the people.[6] In the chapter, "Priesthood and Theology," Nelson shows that the priests were "boundary crossers" who had access to the *sphere* of the holy for the well-being of the community.[7] In "Restoration and Utopian Vision," Nelson then shows very clearly how this concern for boundaries lies at the heart of Ezekiel 40–48.[8]

In *Jerusalem in the Book of Ezekiel,* Julie Galambush studies the metaphorical depiction of Jerusalem as YHWH's wife.[9] The aspect of her work that is most immediately relevant here is that the significance of the metaphor comes from the same priestly worldview. While the clean and the profane are neutral, both holiness and uncleanness are dangerous states. The uncleanness of the woman Jerusalem threatens the holiness of YHWH. Ezekiel uses the metaphor of the city as unclean and faithless wife to justify YHWH's anger as the shamed husband. The solution for this female impurity is removal of the city. Galambush also makes clear that the new temple of Ezekiel 40–48 is designed to ensure purity. In this new creation, YHWH has no wife. Contrary to earlier prophetic tradition, and even contrary to Ezekiel's earlier prophecies, Jerusalem has no place in the new Israel.[10]

In *Graded Holiness,* Philip Peter Jenson focuses on the "Holiness Spectrum" (holy, profane, clean, and unclean) in the Pentateuchal priestly texts.[11] Although the entire work has implications for any study of Ezekiel 40–48, three chapters in particular relate to the emphases of my work. In the chapter, "Concepts of Holiness and Purity," Jenson discusses these concepts and the idea of degrees of holiness and uncleanness.[12] In his chapter on the "Holiness Spectrum," he considers a structural anthropological perspective on how "an organized world-view links the individual, the community and the natural world. This world-view is generally reflected and sustained by the ritual and social life of the group."[13] Jenson devotes

---

[5] Nelson, 25–26.

[6] Nelson, 20.

[7] Nelson, 83–110.

[8] Nelson, 112–119.

[9] Julie Galambush, *Jerusalem in the Book of Ezekiel: The City as Yahweh's Wife,* SBLDS, 130 (Atlanta: Scholars Press, 1992.)

[10] Galambush, 147–157.

[11] Philip Peter Jenson, *Graded Holiness: A Key to the Priestly Conception of the World,* JSOTSup, no. 106 (Sheffield: JSOT, 1992).

[12] Jenson, 40–55.

[13] Jenson, 58.

an entire chapter to "The Spatial Dimension" in which he shows how the grading of holiness was expressed in zones separated by distinct boundaries.[14] As part of this chapter, he also notes the use of the numbers 5 and 10 (and the multiples 20, 50, 100) and number 4 and the use of the rectangle and the square. He suggests that there is a structural relationship between numbers and figures as part of the concern for order and unity.[15] I am particularly intrigued by Jenson's comments on the use of the square shape in the design of the Priestly Tabernacle. The same set of numbers and shapes is also significant in the temple design in Ezekiel. Although neither of us has concentrated on these matters, both Jenson and I have arrived at similar conclusions about the importance of the numbers and shapes in the worldview of holiness.

Graded Holiness is an excellent study which approaches the priestly cultic material as a theological worldview based on a view of holiness. Jenson notes that Ezekiel 40–48, The Temple Scroll, the Epistle to the Hebrews, and the Mishnah share with the P materials "the principle of graded holiness."[16] Since both P and Ezekiel 40:48 share the same principle, it is not surprising that Jenson's study of the Pentateuchal materials has considerable overlap with my study of Ezekiel. The differences between our studies come from the distinctions between structural anthropology which studies a community's worldview and human geography which studies the way a society is organized in space. Human geography would ask structural anthropology, How does the community's theological worldview lead to a particular organization of social space?

A further difference in our approaches is that Jenson is developing "a conceptual approach" to priestly theology which differs from my rhetorical approach.[17] In his Conclusion, Jenson notes that one of the limitations of his method is that "relatively little attention has been paid to the historical and social realities to which the texts bear witness."[18] He then goes on to discuss the various approaches to developing a theology of the cultic texts, and his choice to focus upon the Priestly writing.[19] In contrast, a rhetorical approach focuses on questions of historical, social, *and* human geographical realities to understand how a text is a response to a particular rhetorical context. It is precisely here that a work published since the com-

---

14. Jenson, 89–114.
15. Jenson, 96–98.
16. Jenson, 215.
17. Jenson, 214.
18. Jenson, 210.
19. Jenson, 212–215.

pletion of my dissertation has challenged one of the important assumptions of my argument. Steven Shawn Tuell's, *The Law of the Temple in Ezekiel 40–48*, is a redactional study which shows that these chapters are a "purposive unity."[20] His thesis is that the core material from the prophet Ezekiel was expanded in the period of the Judean Restoration to include legal materials.

> Ezekiel 40–48 is the religious polity of the Judean Restoration, a present-tense description of the author's self-conception and their conception of God. The final form of the text is built on an authentic vision of Ezekiel, chosen by our editors as the perfect statement of their society's foundation and end: right worship in the right Temple. However, the text assumed its present form in the Persian period, probably during the reign of Darius I.[21]

Tuell's argument is compelling in terms of its locating the final redaction of the text in the Judean restoration period. Through comparative work, he has shown quite convincingly the relationship between the legal material and the Persian period. In my study, I argued that Ezekiel 40–48 is a rhetorical response to the exigence of exile. Tuell has challenged this assumption. Perhaps my assumption needs to be modified to add the context of the Judean Restoration to what I continue to believe was the original exilic context. It is a fruitful possibility to consider.

My chief concern with Tuell's argument is that he has created a dichotomy between two types of material. He argues that the original Ezekiel material is based on an eschatological hope while the Persian era "Law of the Temple" is based on historical and political reality.[22] This is a needless dichotomy which undermines the point of his argument. He bases his work on the work of Clifford Geertz concerning a "semiotic theory of culture," by which "a culture is made up of sets of symbols…which provide the context for the ordered life of a people."[23] Later, Tuell argues that "The bulk of the legislation promulgated in Ezekiel 40–48 is concerned with the proper conduct of the sacrificial cult in the Temple: all else is related to this central organizing principle." He then goes on to state that "Even the

---

[20] Steven Shawn Tuell, *The Law of the Temple in Ezekiel 40–48*, HSM, 49 (Atlanta: Scholars Press, 1992), 13. This assessment is a dramatic reassessment for Tuell who earlier characterized these chapters as a "crazy-quilt" with no "coherent program" (Tuell, "The Temple Vision of Ezekiel 40–48: A Program for Restoration?, *Proceedings Eastern Great Lakes Biblical Society* 2 (1982): 98).

[21] Tuell, 14.

[22] Tuell, 108.

[23] Tuell, 15.

scheme for land division, as will be seen, functions more as a religious doctrine than as a proposal for land reform. But while the program set forth in the Temple Vision focuses on cultic matters, it nonetheless presupposes, and indeed alludes to, a particular political context."[24] The fundamental assertion of a rhetorical perspective is that every text is written by a particular someone, in response to some particular exigence, to accomplish some particular objective in some particular context, based on some particular worldview. There is no conflict between arguing that the program proposed in the Law of the Temple is intended for a particular social and historical context and is based on a particular religious view of the temple. I would also add a human geographical perspective to Tuell's assertion that "proper conduct of the sacrificial cult in the Temple" is the central organizing principle. Proper conduct requires proper control of space.

Without this dichotomy between historical reality and religious worldview, and with the addition of a human geographical perspective, Tuell's work both reinforces and supplements my own thesis. He sees these chapters as a purposive unity intended to create a society based on temple ideology. Tuell's arguments have not yet convinced me that Ezekiel 40–48 "demotes the Levites," for the reasons that are argued below. I am also not satisfied with his treatment of royal imagery which I believe is a significant aspect of the Vision. However, since these are matters which are considered below, I will make no effort to specify them here. Tuell's work is a brilliant analysis which offers much to critical discussion of Ezekiel 40–48.

On the matter of the Zadokites and the Levites in Ezekiel 44, Stephen L. Cook offers an analysis which gathers arguments challenging the Wellhausian use of Ezekiel 44 as evidence of the history of Israelite priesthood. Cook argues that Ezekiel 44 is an interpretation of Numbers 16–18. In the process, he discusses the language of "bearing their guilt" which has been taken as evidence of Levite demotion.[25]

Iain Duguid, in *Ezekiel and the Leaders of Israel*, also argues that the Book of Ezekiel is concerned with restructuring society.[26] Unlike the work of Tuell and myself which focus on 40–48, Duguid considers the whole book of Ezekiel. He concentrates on Ezekiel's attitude toward various leadership groups within Judean society. Duguid addresses the limitations of the ma-

---

[24.] Tuell, 103.

[25.] Stephen L. Cook, "Innerbiblical Interpretation in Ezekiel 44 and the History of the Priesthood, " *JBL* 114 (1995): 193–208.

[26.] Iain Duguid, *Ezekiel and the Leaders of Israel*, VTSup, 56 (Leiden: E. J. Brill, 1994).

jority of Ezekiel studies which fail to consider all leadership classes but focus on only one group, such as the monarchy, or the priests and Levites.
His thesis is that:

> there is a coherent and connected attitude taken toward these
> leadership groups throughout the book: those singled out for the
> most reproach in Ezekiel's critique of the past are marginalized
> in his plan for the future while those who escape blame are as-
> signed positions of honour. Both upward mobility and down-
> ward mobility are evident, as he envisages a radically
> restructured society, designed to avoid repetition of the sins of
> the past.[27]

In separate chapters, Duguid considers Ezekiel's attitude toward
monarchy and *nasi*, priests and Levites, prophets, and lay leadership. He
shows how past behavior of each group determines its role in the future
social structure. On the basis of past cultic abuses and social oppression,
the kings will be replaced by a *nasi*, a lay figure with significant power who
represents the people in cultic matters, but is restricted from priestly privilege. In his consideration of the priests and Levites, Duguid shows how
the Zadokites are being rewarded for past faithfulness by the greatest privileges of access within the temple. In his discussion of the Levites, Duguid
shares the consensus that the Levites are being demoted because of their
past sins. Duguid does not consider the cultic basis of the language of
"bearing their guilt," but regards the phrase as a judgment against the
Levites for past abuses. (For my own discussion of this matter, see below.)
Duguid also considers how the prophets have no place in the future society. Ezekiel is the only true prophet, the new Moses who brings new legislation for the creation of a new world order. Finally, he considers the
"downgrading" of the laity, who have no significant role to play in the new
temple, based on past abuses by the lay leadership and the people.

This is another extraordinary study of the book of Ezekiel in which
Duguid's careful analysis adds substantially to Ezekiel studies. Although
Duguid is not using the language of human geography and territoriality,
he shows throughout how the change in social status involved changed access to space. The question is, How would a human geographical perspective add to Duguid's analysis? In his thesis statement, Duguid refers to
both "upward mobility and downward mobility" in this radically restructured society designed to avoid the sins of the past. What is most significant is that Duguid has used vertical language to describe this social
change while the Book of Ezekiel uses horizontal language. It is not a mat-

---

[27] Duguid, 1.

ter of being *up or down* a social ladder as it is a matter of being *near or far* from sacred space. It is a subtle point, but it significant to grasping the worldview of the book. In our time, we tend to use vertical metaphors to express social status. In the worldview of Ezekiel, the metaphorical language is horizontal, based on the degree of access to sacred space.

If the human geographers are right that we have been operating with an intellectual blind spot about the social importance of space, then it is even more important for us to understand the connections between space, society, and theology in the worldview of the priest Ezekiel. The concern for measurements which seems so tedious and irrelevant to modern readers is consistent with this worldview in which the cultic abuses of the past were perceived as boundary violations of sacred space. The corrective to the sins of the past is to control access to space in the future.

Whatever the inconsistencies we see in the text itself, and however obvious the seams might be between various redactional layers, the world envisioned by the rhetoric of Ezekiel 40–48 has no seams and no inconsistencies. It offers a vision of a world without problems, a cosmic and social order created for the well-being of all. The creator of the vision operates from a worldview which relates temple, holiness, and the presence of God. The key element which ties all of it together into one seamless whole is the control of space which is defined in the dissertation as the concept of *territoriality.* Whether the final redaction was completed in the exile itself, or in the restoration period, Ezekiel 40–48 is a creative response to the experience of exile. It proposes a vision of a new society spatially designed to prevent any recurrence of the boundary violations which led to social chaos and the devastation and scattering of the community by exile.

Introduction

The Book of Ezekiel is the answer to profound questions. Why has this happened to us? Who are we? Do we have a future? Will we go home again? Born out of devastation, horror, and loss, these questions demand answers. They thunder with outrage, they moan with despair, they cry out with grief from a world turned upside down, from a people torn apart, and taken away. No fact is more important for reading the Book of Ezekiel than this: this book is an effort to respond to the devastating experience of exile, to answer these questions and a thousand more.[1] The basic question, the question which must be answered, the question which tears at hearts and minds and souls, is the most difficult question of all. Where is God in all of this? Each question is a question about us and about God. Why did God let this happen to us? Who are we without God? Do we have a future without God? Will God allow us to go home again?

The "us" is the defeated, displaced, and dispirited leadership of Judah in the sixth century b.c.e. The "God" is yhwh, the patron deity of Israel and Judah. The "exile" is the result of King Nebuchadrezzar's imperial policy which forced resettlement of the leadership of conquered peoples to Babylon.[2] This triad of "exile," "God" and "us" combines social identity, theo-

---

[1] Not all Ezekiel scholars agree that the provenance of the Book of Ezekiel was the Babylonian exile. This issue will be considered below.

[2] The spelling "Nebuchadrezzar" rather than "Nebuchadnezzar" is discussed below.

logical ideology, and historical, geographical and political reality, with mythic conceptions of reality. The Book of Ezekiel cannot be limited to theology or social ideology or rhetoric or politics or history or geography or mythology. It is all of these, and more. It is the particular interrelationship of these diverse ways of thinking about reality that creates the Book of Ezekiel as a unique response to the questions of exile, God, and us. However, the Book of Ezekiel is not only response, it also attempts to bring about response. It is more than reaction; it is also persuasion. Its answers attempt to create change by adding another set of questions. What must we do? What does God want us to do? What do we have to change so that this never happens again?

Contemporary readers of the Book of Ezekiel do not—we cannot—have the same questions which demand answers because we are not people of the sixth century b.c.e. exiled to Babylon by Nebuchadrezzar, carrying within ourselves the thoughts and beliefs and world views of the sixth century political and religious elite of Judah. And because these are not our questions, we are seldom persuaded by the answers of this book to make changes in our societies and theologies and ideologies. Our questions are different, and are as varied as we are. But we do ask the same types of questions about our social identities, our theologies and political ideologies, our histories and geographies, and our mythologies. We create our own answers—our own rhetorics—to respond to our own questions, and to persuade others of our truths. Our truths are our truths because they are answers to our particular questions. And because each of us, as individuals and as members of various groups, has many questions, we have many truths.

The Book of Ezekiel tells its own truths about God, about exile, and about society. These truths of the Book of Ezekiel cannot be our truths, but we can, as a matter of choice and intent, attempt to read the Book of Ezekiel as an expression of truths for the one or ones who wrote it. We can try to read this book as an attempt to answer questions which demand answers. Such an effort is an act of profound respect for the truths of another, even when these truths seem so different from our own. And when we are willing to read this book as truths for someone else, we create the possibility that this book might even speak truths to our questions.

The particular portion of the Book of Ezekiel which is the focus of the study is Ezekiel 40–48, the Vision of Transformation.[3] What follows is an effort to read the Vision of Transformation of the Book of Ezekiel as the written answer to profound questions, to read with respect for the truths

---

[3.] I shall discuss my reasons for designating these chapters as *The Vision of Transformation* below.

of whoever produced this complex, difficult, and relentlessly truthful book. My intention is to read this text as a rhetorical response to exile. My single criterion for this reading takes the form of a question. Does my interpretation make sense of this text as an effort to tell the truth and bring about change in the situation of the Babylonian exile? My thesis is that *the Vision of Transformation is territorial rhetoric produced in the context of the Babylonian exile to restructure the society of Israel by asserting* yhwh's *territorial claim as the only King of Israel.*

The Problem

The Vision of Transformation is a narrative account of a vision. Already this genre designation raises significant problems for biblical scholarship which has been defined by the assumptions of the Historical Critical Method. What are the questions which a historian can ask about a vision narrative? Did the vision really occur? When did it occur? When was the narrative written down? Was the narrative written down at one time or is there a history of composition? Is the description of the temple historically reliable? What was the historical relationship between Zadokites and Levites? These are precisely the types of questions which have been raised about this text. Historically-oriented scholarship has focused on the history of composition and the historicity of the elements of the vision.

What is clear about these questions is that they really do not address the text itself. Methods which attempt to determine the history of composition of the text or the historicity of the elements of the text do not attempt to read Ezekiel 40–48 as a coherent, consistent whole which is itself part of the whole Book of Ezekiel, nor do they attempt to explain how these chapters are a rhetorical response to exile.

The fundamental premise of the study is that assumptions about genre determine interpretation. It is a truism that how we read a text is determined by what we think it is. Expressed differently, the perceived genre of the text determines the method used to study the text. Any text can be read by a variety of methods. Almost every method will produce information which will allow the reader to draw conclusions about the text and to use the text for whatever purposes the reader chooses. However, if the goal is to read a text as a coherent and consistent whole text, the responsibility is placed on the reader to use a method or methods which are appropriate to the genre of the text. Many of the interpretative problems with the Vision of Transformation are fundamentally problems of genre.

In his description of the problems involved in the dimensions of the Tabernacle structure in Exodus 26, Richard Friedman discusses the comparison between the measurements of the Tabernacle and the Temple. He then makes this wry observation:

> In my student days it occurred to me that if I would ever be able to read that list of materials and cubits and *care*, then I would be a scholar. And then it turned out years later that these cubits contained a key clue in the investigation into the authors of the Bible.[4]

For many readers, the catalogue of cubits in Ezekiel 40–42 has the same capacity to numb the mind and to raise questions about the mental stability of anyone who would actually *want* to study such material.[5] Yet, just as Friedman found that caring about cubits led him to his key clue about an important issue, caring about the cubits in Ezekiel 40–42 seems to be an equally important prerequisite for figuring out the rhetorical intention of these chapters.

Scholars have in fact devoted meticulous attention to the matter of cubits in Ezekiel 40–42, and on through Chapter 48. Their commentaries are precise in their attention to the dimensions given. The most notable example is Zimmerli's massive Hermeneia commentary.[6] He adds the numbers, draws diagrams, and compares the numbers with the dimensions of the Solomonic temple structure. The work is prodigious and the results impressive in their attention to detail, and my work on these chapters is indebted to his careful scholarship. However, in the case of Ezekiel 40–42, caring about cubits can become the factor which obscures the key clue to the intention of the measurements.

Most of the scholars who care about cubits have operated with an explicit genre assumption that these measurements constitute a *temple blueprint*, or תבנית (*tabnît*). Demonstrating the truism that assumptions about genre determine interpretation, this "blueprint" genre has shaped much

---

[4] Richard Elliott Friedman, *Who Wrote the Bible?* (San Francisco: Harper & Row, 1987), 176. Italics in the original.

[5] For example: "Readers will find themselves embarrassed by these chapters" (Leslie C. Allen, *Ezekiel 20–48*, WBC, 29 [Dallas: Word Books, 1990], 214); "It simply boggles our minds to contemplate the 'preaching' of such dull details" (Ronald M. Hals, *Ezekiel*, FOTL XIX [Grand Rapids: Eerdmans Publishing Company, 1989], 301); "I suspect that many readers of Ezekiel 40–48 are initially overwhelmed or even disappointed" (Ralph W. Klein, *Ezekiel: The Prophet and His Message* [Columbia: University of South Carolina Press, 1988], 169).

[6] Walther Zimmerli, Ezekiel 1: *A Commentary on the Book of the Prophet Ezekiel, Chapters 1–24*, trans. Ronald E. Clements, Hermeneia (Philadelphia: Fortress Press, 1979); *Ezekiel 2: A Commentary on the Book of the Prophet Ezekiel Chapters 25–48*, trans. James D. Martin, Hermeneia (Philadelphia: Fortress Press, 1983).

interpretation of these chapters by the assumption that the prophet is receiving from God a *tabnît* or plan.[7] Scholars have focused on questions related to this assumption. Exactly what did this temple look like? How is this temple different from the First Temple? How is it different from the Second Temple? Is the purpose of the blueprint to ensure correct building of the new temple? Is this an eschatological temple or are these the plans that the post-exilic community is supposed to use? All of these questions are a function of the assumption that the purpose of the measurements is to provide the blueprint of a building and its surrounding structures.[8]

However, if this is supposed to be a blueprint, it is not a very good one. An architectural blueprint is a two-dimensional drawing but it always includes vertical dimensions. This "blueprint" omits this necessary detail. Most scholars have noted, with puzzlement, that most of the dimensions are given in terms of length and width. There are no vertical dimensions for the building itself. The only vertical dimensions are of the wall around the complex 40:5 (קוֹמָה), the tables in 40:42 (נבה), and the wooden altar in 41:22 (נבה).[9] Despite the lack of vertical dimensions, various scholars have produced models and sketches of this temple complex. The variety represented by these efforts demonstrates quite clearly the difficulty of imagining, much less building, a three-dimensional structure with two-dimensional instructions.[10] Other scholars avoid the terminology of "blueprint" by referring to "ground plan" or "temple tour" or such genre designations.[11] However, these genre designations tend to avoid the issue, rather than to deal with it. Rather than answer the question, Why does this description of the temple omit vertical measurements?, their discussions look very much like discussions which refer to a "temple blueprint." The

[7.] For example, see: Corrine L. Patton, *Ezekiel's Blueprint for the Temple of Jerusalem* (Ph. D. diss., Yale University, 1991), 184; Klein, 171.

[8.] See however: "…Ezekiel 40–42 is neither instruction for nor narrative of building, but a vision of an already built complex" (Moshe Greenberg, "The Design and Themes of Ezekiel's Program of Restoration," in *Interpreting the Prophets*, James Luther Mays and Paul J. Achtemeier, eds. [Philadelphia: Fortress Press, 1987], 218); "…too little allowance is made for the purely visionary nature of the building represented here…There is nothing to suggest that it should have a human builder" (Walther Eichrodt, *Ezekiel: A Commentary*, trans. Cosslet Quin, OTL [Philadelphia: Westminster, 1970], 542).

[9.] RSV adds a height dimension for the altar in 43:15 which is not included in the Masoretic text.

[10.] *IDB* (Nashville: Abingdon, 1962), s.v. "Temple, Jerusalem," by W. F. Stinespring.

[11.] For example: Zimmerli, vol. 2, 343; Allen, 228; Joseph Blenkinsopp, *Ezekiel* (Louisville: John Knox Press, 1990), 201.

focus of discussion continues to be the construction and arrangement of the temple.

A related problem is that the description of the temple complex includes few details about furnishings in comparison with the descriptions of the Tabernacle and the Temple in other texts, where the furnishings are described with great care.

> Many furnishings of the Solomonic temple and the desert tabernacle are missing: the ark and its cherubs and the lamp; the only interior furniture mentioned is an ambiguous "altar of wood." Very strange is the absence of a wall around the inner court, to which its three massive gates might stand in relation. No equivalent to the lavers or to the bronze sea appears in the outer court...The implications of these omissions must remain obscure.[12]

Another notable problem for scholars has been the organization of the text, particularly in the middle section of Chapters 45–46.[13] Many scholars have seen a disconnected array of topics with little inherent connection with each other, forming "an amalgam of disparate units."[14] Perhaps the most extreme statement is by Tuell who characterizes the text as a "crazy-quilt" with no "coherent program," and identifies the "crux" of the issue:

> Attractive as it may be to hold for a single interpretive principle explaining all of chapters 40–48, the text itself is too vague, too disparate in nature, too haphazardly presented for such a single-theme approach to be relevant.[15]

Even Greenberg, whose goal is to show that all of 40–48 is the work of one author, has to find an explanation for the apparent disorder of the text.[16] Because of these problems, studies of Ezekiel 40–48 have often been redactional studies of the composition of the text.

In terms of sheer size, Zimmerli's Hermeneia commentary is the most detailed redactional study of the Book of Ezekiel available in English. It is

---

[12.] Greenberg, 225–226.

[13.] "This additional matter is made up of draft proposals for legislation, partly theoretical, partly no doubt intended to be put into force; they are assembled here without much attempt at orderly arrangement; and nothing in them comes from Ezekiel's own hand" (G. A. Cooke, *The Book of Ezekiel*, ICC [Edinburgh: T. & T. Clark, 1937 < 1985 >], 493).

[14.] Patton, 145.

[15.] Steven Tuell, "The Temple Vision of Ezekiel 40–48: A Program for Restoration?," *Proceedings Eastern Great Lakes Biblical Society* 2 (1982): 98.

clear that Zimmerli himself was heavily influenced by Harmut Gese's analysis of Ezekiel 40–48.[17] References to Gese's work appear throughout the pages of Zimmerli's text as Zimmerli uncovers layers, insertions, appendices, additions, and out-of-order sections of text. He frequently expresses his "surprise" at the arrangement of the text, that what "one would expect" does not occur, or what "one would not expect" does. There is a problem in this kind of redactional approach to a text. Crazy-quilts are intentionally produced by stitching together different scraps of cloth, with the intention of producing a quilt. To reverse the process by taking the quilt apart to separate out the scraps would result in a pile of scraps and no more quilt—an engaging pastime, but not much comfort on a cold night. For the text of Ezekiel 40–48, the issue is not that someone pieced together scraps, but that someone wanted a quilt.

Method

In response to this kind of fragmenting redactional analysis of Ezekiel 40–48, this study is a rhetorical analysis of the theme of *territoriality*, a technical term which will be defined below. My premise is that the genre of these chapters is *rhetoric*. The key idea in rhetoric is the intention to produce some effect in the context. For the Vision of Transformation, the context is the Babylonian exile. Whatever the compositional and redactional history of the chapters, and despite the scissors-and-paste quality of the text, the text as we have it was intended to be rhetorically persuasive in the exilic context. This arrangement of text, its selection of some topics, its omission of other topics, its detailed discussion of some details, and its silence about other details, are all part of a rhetorical strategy. My question is always, *What is the rhetorical purpose of writing or redacting it this way?* Throughout this process, Zimmerli has been my constant resource, and has provided substantial help along the way. Frequently, the places where he expresses the most surprise are the places where he has provided the most important insights for my rhetorical analysis. And so, I quote Zim-

---

[16.] "When it came to arranging the two divisions according to the criterion of assigning the static-descriptive material to division 1 and the dynamic-prescriptive to division 2, this unit (a misfit) was broken up in such a way that the passage on the 'holy chambers,' long and overwhelmingly static-descriptive, was put in division 1, while the shorter passage on the kitchens, in which the dynamic-use element was proportionally greater, was put according to its 'chronology' at the end of division 2. Here one can feel something of the strain this heterogeneous material put on its arranger" (Greenberg, 230–231).

[17.] Hartmut Gese, *Der Verfassungsentwurf des Ezechiel (Kap. 40–48)*, Beiträge zur historichen Theologie 25 (Tubingen: J. C. Mohr, 1957).

merli frequently throughout my study, often to disagree with his conclusions, but always with respect for the quality and quantity of his work. Before beginning my rhetorical analysis of Ezekiel 40–48, there are some preliminary matters concerning translation. The Hebrew text of the Book of Ezekiel is notoriously difficult, filled with textual problems and *hapax legommena.* Much of the difficulty involves the architectural language. My goal is not to produce an exegetical commentary which attempts to resolve the multitude of translational, exegetical, and textual problems necessary in order to produce a satisfactory English translation. I have chosen to include only selected texts, rather than the whole of Ezekiel 40–48. Where I have included a text, its translation is that of the Revised Standard Version (RSV). However, I have made a number of changes to the RSV. Any revision of the RSV is indicated by italics. My reason for using RSV as the foil for my territorial analysis is that it has been the standard English language text for American critical scholarship since its publication in 1952.

One of my exegetical and translational decisions is to use the Hebrew Masoretic Text (MT) as it is, without using the versions to make text-critical changes. This decision makes no claim that the MT is a "better" or "more original" text than the versions. It does attempt to read the MT of Ezekiel 40–48 as a coherent and consistent whole text which is intentionally rhetorical, without minimizing the textual difficulties of this version. In contrast, the RSV translation is based on a reconstructed text. The base is the MT of Ezekiel with occasional text-critical reconstructions using other versions. The result is a constructed text which is not really the MT or the Septuagint (LXX) or any other single version. It is a composite text, created by the RSV for its translation. Where RSV has used the versions, I have translated according to the MT.[18]

Other difficulties with the RSV are its inconsistent translations of the same Hebrew word with different English words, and its translations of different Hebrew words with the same English word. For example, in my translation, Hebrew בית is always translated as *house.* RSV has translated בית as *temple* rather than *house* when it refers to the cultic complex. Rather than RSV's translation of Hebrew בתוך, both with and without suffixes, which is variously translated by RSV as *among,* or *in the midst,* I have consistently translated as *in the midst.* RSV has been inconsistent in its translations of אחזה and נחלה as *property, inheritance,* and *possession,* using all

---

[18.] Despite this goal, there are two instances in which I use a version other than the MT. These are 40:49 (discussed in Chapter One) and 43:7 (discussed in Chapter Five).

three terms interchangeably to apply to these two Hebrew terms. I have translated אחזה as *possession* and נחלה as *inheritance*. In addition to these differences which I have noted with italics, I have made several substitutions in RSV which are unmarked. These are terms for which RSV is consistent in its translation and I have chosen to substitute a different term. The terminology for the offerings follows the translations of Jacob Milgrom. The following glossary of terms is a guide to the reader for these consistent substitutions. RSV translation is on the left and my substitution is on the right.

1. יהוה as *the LORD* is transliterated as *YHWH*.
2. כבוד as *glory* is transliterated as *Kabod*.
3. נשיא as *prince* is transliterated as *Nasi*.
4. בן אדם as Son of Man is translated as Mortal.[19]
5. בית as *temple* is translated as *house*.
6. בנין as *building* is transliterated as *Binyan*.
7. אשם as *trespass offering* is translated as *reparation offering*.[20]
8. חטאת as *sin offering* is translated as *purification offering*.[21]
9. שלמים as *peace offering* is translated as *well-being offering*.[22]

I have also chosen to use capital letters to signify proper names for a number of terms which refer to named locations.

One more preliminary matter concerns my terminology of *Narrator* and *Rhetor*. One of the distinctive features of the Book of Ezekiel throughout is its first person narration. Rather than identify this narrator as "Ezekiel" or "the prophet," I use the term *Narrator* in its literary sense as the one who tells the story. The Narrator speaks within the text itself. In contrast, the *Rhetor* is the author/editor who produced the final form of the text.[23] This terminology neither argues for nor denies the possibility that the historical prophet Ezekiel was both Narrator and Rhetor. These are literary categories, used to differentiate between the voice heard within the text and the author of the text.

[19.] This translation follows the New Revised Standard Version.

[20.] Jacob Milgrom, *Leviticus 1–16*, AB (New York: Doubleday, 1991), 339.

[21.] Milgrom, *Leviticus*, 253.

[22.] Milgrom, *Leviticus*, 217.

[23.] This is the context of the "final major composer/editor." This terminology is from Rodney K. Duke, *The Persuasive Appeal of the Chronicler: A Rhetorical Analysis* (Sheffield: Almond Press, 1990), 36. This terminology allows for the possibility that There could be minor changes at a later date.

Overview

Chapter One begins with the concept of territoriality and the rhetorical purpose of the command to "measure the proportion" (43:10) to show that the genre of this material is a territorial claim rather than a blueprint. Chapter Two relates the concept of territoriality to a spatial theology of holiness. Chapter Three concerns territorial access to the three spaces of the House of YHWH, the Portion, and the Land. Chapter Four is a study of the relationship between access and inheritance in the Vision of Transformation. Chapter Five considers the rhetorical context and exigence of the Vision of Transformation, by looking at the beginning and end of the Book of Ezekiel. Chapter Six analyzes the Vision of Transformation as a critique of monarchy. Chapter Seven analyzes the organizational structure of Ezekiel 40–48 according to the topic of territoriality. Chapter Eight identifies Ezekiel 40–48 as political rhetoric in the context of exile, which proposes a new human geography based on a temple society without a human king.

Chapter 1

Territorial Rhetoric

Territoriality

The foundational premise of this study is that assumptions about genre determine interpretation. My genre hypothesis is that Ezekiel 40–48 is *territorial rhetoric*. *Territoriality* is a technical term from the discipline of human geography. Robert Sack defines territoriality as:

> the attempt by an individual or group to affect, influence, or control people, phenomena, and relationships, by delimiting and asserting control over a geographic area.[1]

The three essential facets of territoriality are *classification of area, communication of boundaries*, and *enforcement of access*.[2]

Two basic features of this definition deserve emphasis: territoriality is social and it requires choice. Sack differentiates human territoriality from the instinctive behavior of animals which is called territorial. He also differentiates territoriality from efforts by individuals to claim individual space. His definition of human territoriality refers to social systems, and the deliberate efforts by human beings to control access to space for social

---

[1.] Robert David Sack, *Human Territoriality: Its Theory and History*, Cambridge Studies in Historical Geography (Cambridge: Cambridge University Press, 1986), 19.

[2.] Sack, 21–22.

purposes. Territoriality is place-specific and always involves issues of power.[3]

Territory, as Sack defines it, is not a synonym for space, place, or area. A space can become a place without becoming a territory. A space or place becomes a territory only when there is an attempt to control access to it by using a boundary. A boundary may be a material object, such as a wall, or it may be a natural phenomenon such as a river. A boundary can also be immaterial, established by a gesture, a word, or a sign. By whatever means, a territory requires consistent effort to establish and maintain. This means that a space or place might be a territory at one time and not at another.[4]

The connection between local transformation of place, practices located in place, and power relations is an important theme in the work of Allan Pred. Although Pred does not use the specific word *territoriality*, he explicitly refers to the connection between access to space and power relations.

> Power relations, regardless of their form or source, regardless of whether they involve exploitation, domination, or subjection, cannot be separated from the realm of actual or potential behaviors, from situated actions and practices, from the direct or indirect control of who does or does not do what, *where*, and *when*. Thus, struggles, of whatever scale and focus, are always at some level struggles over the use and meaning of space and time.[5]

Pred differentiates between "power subjects" and "power holders." Power holders are those who control space; power subjects are those whose access to space is controlled by others.[6]

There is considerable overlap between the three facets of Sack's definition of territoriality and Pred's vocabulary of practice and power relations. Both involve the social use of space. There is also a considerable difference in emphasis. Two of the elements of Sack's definition involve the spatial. *Area* refers to physical space. *Boundaries* delineate the area. *Control of access* can refer to physical structures which control access to space, as well as the social processes involved in maintaining the area as a territory. In contrast, *practice* and *power relations* are social categories. Pred is concerned with social processes which bring about changes in any particular place. This means that Sack's definition of territoriality can be sub-

---

[3.] Sack, 1–4.
[4.] Sack, 19.
[5.] Pred, *MHCHG*, with a Foreward by Charles Tilly (Boulder, Colorado: Westview Press, 1990), 12. The italics are Pred's.
[6.] Pred, *MHCHG*, 13.

sumed under Pred's broader view of the social processes involved in local transformation. One means of local transformation is to change access to place by asserting territoriality.

Rhetoric is intentional speech and territoriality is an intentional effort to control access to space. Both involve some form of communication. For rhetoric, the means of communication is always spoken or written language. However, language is not necessary for the communication of territoriality. The effort to assert control of access can be accomplished by means other than language, by building a wall or making a gesture. Territoriality can also be asserted by language, by posting a no trespassing sign or by speech. One way to assert territoriality is to write a text which describes areas, boundaries, and rules of access. Ezekiel 40–48 is such a text. The concept of territoriality allows us to see that the measurements of the temple and the land are fundamentally territorial claims about social space. These chapters focus upon defining areas, boundaries, and the power relationships and place-specific practices which control access to holy space.

Rhetorical Purpose of Tour

The text of Ezekiel 40–48 takes the form of a visionary experience in which the Narrator is taken on a guided tour. The reason for this guided tour is explicitly stated two times in the course of the tour. My rhetorical analysis begins with these two statements.

> And the man said to me,
> "Mortal,
> *see* (רְאֵה) with your eyes,
> and hear with your ears,
> and set (שִׂים) your *heart*
> *to all that I shall cause you to see* (רָאָה),
> for in order that I might *cause you to see it* (רָאָה)
> *you were caused to enter* (בוֹא) here (הֵנָּה);
> *describe* (נָגַד) all that you see (רָאָה) to the House of Israel" (40:4).[7]
> "And you, Mortal,
> describe (נָגַד) to the House of Israel the house
> that they may be ashamed of (כָּלַם) their iniquities (עָוֹן),
> *that they may measure the proportion* (תָּכְנִית).
> and if they are ashamed of (כָּלַם) all that they have done (עָשָׂה),
> *the form* (צוּרָה) of the house,
> its arrangement (תְּכוּנָה),

[7.] The rather awkward and literal translations of the Hiphil verbs as "cause to…" will be discussed below.

its exits (מוצאים)
and its entrances (מובאים),
and its whole form (צורה),
make known (ידע) to them,
all its ordinances (חקה)
and all its *instructions* (תורה);
and write it down (כתב) *for their eyes,*
so that they may observe (שמר) all its forms (צורה)
end perform (עשה) all its statutes (חקה)" (43:10–11).

The first speaker is the guide for the tour, a being with the appearance of bronze (40:3). The second speaker is YHWH. In both cases, the role of the Narrator is to *see,* and to *describe* what he sees on the tour to the House of Israel. It is clear in both speeches that the intended audience of the rhetoric is the House of Israel. In both cases, the emphasis is on what is seen rather than what is heard. Even though the instruction to the Narrator is to *see, hear,* and *set your heart,* the purpose of the visit is to cause the Narrator to see. The primary task of the Narrator is to describe. The verb is the Hiphil of נגד. The root meaning of the verb is to *make conspicuous.* The lexica translate variously as "show," "tell," "declare." In 40:4, RSV has translated as "declare," while in 43:10, it translates as "describe." I have translated both as "describe" to indicate that the primary mode is visual rather than oral.[8]

In 43:11, there is a second verb which defines the Narrator's purpose. The verb is כתב which means *write.* He is to *write it down for their eyes.* The phrase לעניהם is literally, "to" or "for their eyes." This phrase emphasizes the visual mode of the Narrator's rhetorical task. Ellen Davis' study, *Swallowing the Scroll,* argues the thesis that the Book of Ezekiel represents a change from the prophetic mode of prophet-as-speaker to prophet-as-writer.[9] The task of the prophet is to produce a written document as the means of persuasion.

43:10 states the command to the Narrator to "describe the house" to the House of Israel in order to produce two responses. The first is to "be ashamed. " The second is to "measure the proportion" of the house. Since this speech has several exegetical issues which are relevant to my argu-

---

[8.] The various critical commentaries demonstrate a variety of translations. Zimmerli: "proclaim" (40:4); "describe" (vol. 2, 332, 410); Cooke: "shew" (40:4); "tell" (43:10) (430, 465); Allen: "tell" (40:3); "describe" (43:10) (216–238); Eichrodt: "declare" (40:4); "give the information about" (43:10) (532–551).

See also the discussion of the importance of vision in the temple traditions in Jon D. Levenson, *Sinai and Zion* (San Francisco: Harper & Row, 1985), 148–151.

[9.] Ellen Davis, *Swallowing the Scroll: Textuality and the Dynamics of Discourse in Ezekiel's Prophecy,* Bible and Literature Series, no. 21 (Sheffield: Almond Press, 1989), 37–39.

ment, I am going to look more closely at issues of textual criticism here than elsewhere in my study. In order to do this, I include the RSV translation of 43:10, my translation of the MT, and my translation of the Septuagint (LXX). For clarity of discussion, I have indicated clauses by letter. Earlier, I indicated several consistent changes between RSV and my translation. For the purposes of this discussion, my translation uses the RSV terminology of "temple" rather than "house" and "son of man" instead of "Mortal."

A. And you, son of man,
B. describe to the house of Israel the temple
D. and its appearance and plan
C. that they may be ashamed of their iniquities (RSV).

A. You, son of man,
B. describe (הגד) to the House of Israel the temple
C. that they may be ashamed of (ויכלמו) their iniquities (עון),
D. *that they may measure* (ומדדו) *the proportion* (תכנית) (MT).

A. And you, son of man.
B. show (δείκνυμι) the house of Israel the house
C. that they may cease (κοπάζω) from their sins
D. and its appearance (ὅπασις) and arrangement (διάταξις) (LXX).

Comparison of MT with the LXX shows that there are some exegetically significant differences between these texts, particularly concerning C and D. Comparisons of RSV with MT and LXX show that the RSV has used the conjunction in A from LXX, reversed the order of C and D, kept the MT of C and substituted the LXX of D. The result is a text somewhere between MT and LXX.

It is important to acknowledge that these are not random changes on the part of the RSV. The purpose of the RSV is to provide the translation of a critically established text, rather than textual commentary. Where it reads with LXX, it provides a note of the MT reading, but does not include commentary to justify its reading with LXX rather than MT (which would be far beyond the purpose of the translation). Each textual decision RSV has made can be justified by difficulties of grammar and meaning in MT, and the existence of an alternative reading in LXX.

The first matter of translation concerns the relationship between the clauses. The verb הגד in clause B is an imperative form, followed by two verb clauses created by joining a finite verbal form with the conjunction *waw*. The verb in clause C is a prefix (imperfect) form; the verb in clause D is a suffix (perfect) form. Translation of *waw* clauses in Hebrew is rarely a matter of certainty. RSV has translated the *waw* of clause C as the indicator of a purpose clause, "that they may be ashamed." Since there is no verb in

D in LXX (which means that D is a phrase rather than a clause), RSV has used the simple conjunction *and*. All of this is grammatically possible Hebrew, but not the only option. The matter is complicated by the conjunction *waw* and conditional particle אם in 43:11 which Zimmerli calls "remarkable" here. He argues that such a condition would not follow the unconditional proclamation of the temple vision in 43:10. On the basis of LXX, he reads "they" instead of "if" as a textual error of ואם for והם. Therefore, he makes the למדדו the protasis and ואם נכלמו the apodosis, "if they measure, then they will be ashamed." His translation is, "You, son of man, describe to the house of Israel the (temple-)house so that they may be ashamed of their transgressions. And if they measure <its layout> then <they will be> ashamed of all that they have done.[10]

Other efforts to translate these clauses show similar strategies to draw upon the Greek text in order to interpret the relationship between these clauses. What is truly remarkable is that each commentator has made a different set of choices. Cooke's assessment is that "successive editors have confused the text." The phrase, "that they may be ashamed of their iniquities" "does not fit well with the sentence which follows. " He reads D from the LXX rather than the MT for the reason that "the house of Israel would not be told to measure the house just after it had been measured by the Angel; moreover, the grammar is incorrect." He also reads "they" with the LXX instead of "if." His translation is: "Tell the house of Israel (about) the house, that they may be ashamed of their iniquities and its appearances and its pattern or model."[11] Allen also reads "they" instead of "if" since the MT formulation is "logically inferior" to the LXX reading.[12] His rendition is, "You, human one, are to describe the temple to the community of Israel, to make them ashamed of their iniquities. They are to measure its layout, and then they themselves will be ashamed of all they have done."[13] Eichrodt reads clause D with the LXX, and omits portions of the text he regards as secondary insertions. His reading is, "But do you, son of man, give the house of Israel the information about the house [...] and its arrangement and pattern, [...]...[14]

All of this is intended to demonstrate the degree of selectivity involved in turning to the LXX in order to resolve exegetical problems in the MT. If my purpose were a text critical study here, I would endeavor to ac-

---

10. Zimmerli, vol. 2, 409–410.
11. Cooke, 465.
12. Allen, 243.
13. Allen, 238.
14. Eichrodt, 551.

count for the differences in the MT and the LXX. My purpose for including both texts here is to emphasize that these are different readings, and to indicate some of the difficulties involved in using LXX only where MT is difficult. My approach is to attempt to make rhetorical sense of the MT as it is written, without minimizing its syntactic and exegetical difficulties. Therefore, my translation reads the two *waw* clauses as purpose clauses, while recognizing that they could be read differently, and maintains ואם as a conditional particle.

Measuring the Proportion

The second exegetical issue here is the word תכנית (*toknît*). These two speeches have commanded the Narrator to "see," "describe," "make known," and "write." The House of Israel is commanded to "measure its proportion," "observe its forms," and "perform its statutes." What is particularly significant is what is omitted. There is no instruction to *build* the house. This is in contrast to the situation in 1 Chronicles, where David gives the תבנית (*tabnît*) of the temple to his son Solomon. The word תבנית is related to the verb "build" (בנה). David says to Solomon:

Take heed now,
for YHWH has chosen you to build a house for the sanctuary;
be strong, and do it.
Then David gave Solomon his son the plan (תבנית) of the vestibule of the temple,
and of its houses, its treasuries, its upper rooms, and its inner chambers, and of the room for the mercy seat;
and the plan (תבנית) of all that he had in mind for the courts of the house of
YHWH
All this he made clear by the writing from the hand of YHWH concerning it,
all the work to be done according to the plan (תבנית) (1 Chron 28:10–12;19).

Similarly, YHWH gives the תבנית (*tabnît)* of the Tabernacle to Moses:

According to all that I show you concerning the pattern (תבנית) of the tabernacle, and of all its furniture, so you shall make it (Exod 25:9).[15]

In both cases, the purpose of giving the תבנית (tabnît) was to provide instructions for building the Temple or making the Tabernacle.

[15.] RSV has translated תבנית as "pattern" in Exodus 25:9 and as "plan" in 1 Chronicles 28:11, 12, 19.

In contrast, the word תבנית does not occur in Ezekiel 40–48. In 43:10, the word is תכנית (toknît), which differs only by the difference between the consonants ב and כ, and the initial vowel. This word occurs in the Old Testament only in Ezekiel 28:12 and 43:10. In 28:12, it occurs in the oracle against the king of Tyre. There he is described as חותם תכנית. There are as many textual difficulties with the word there as in 43:10. BDB relates the noun to the verb תכן, regulate. measure, estimate, and translates תכנית as measurement, proportion. Holladay translates as (perfect) example. Gesenius translates as measure, structure, arrangement. Zimmerli argues that the essential idea of תכנית is correctness.[16] In 43:11, the similar word תכונתו occurs. Zimmerli emends תכנית in 43:10 to תכנתו on the basis of 43:11. He cites haplography of the final waw to the next word (אם to ואם) or transposition of חו to וח and subsequent metathesis of waw to yod.[17] It is far beyond the task I have set for myself to attempt to sort through the various exegetical suggestions for textual emendation and translation of this word in the commentaries and lexica. My point in all of this is that this frequent emendation of תכנית to תכנתו (as the defectively written form of תכונתו in 43:11) involves a change in verbal root from תכן to כון.

There are three nouns related to the verbal root תכן in Ezekiel 40–48. The sense of the verbal root in the Niphal has to do with what is regulated or standard. In the Piel, it refers to measurement. Two of the nouns which carry these verbal ideas occur in 45:11 which deals with the relationship between units of measurement. The תכן and the מתכנת both refer to weights of the bath and ephah, and are translated by BDB as measurement, proportion. The third noun is תכנית in 43:10. The sense of all of these occurrences is correct proportion of units of measurement to each other. In contrast, the verbal root כון in the Qal has to do with what is firm. In the Hiphil it refers to what is established. The related noun is תכונה which BDB defines as arrangement, preparation, fixed place. In 43:11, the noun occurs with a possessive suffix, which accounts for the consonantal form תכונתו.

According to MT, the House of Israel is commanded to measure the proportion of the house, not its arrangement. However, the majority of Ezekiel scholars have assumed that the purpose of the measurements is to provide a blueprint and so have emended the noun and concentrated on the layout and measurements of the structures—gates, walls, buildings, and altar. This process of emendation has shifted the focus of the MT from measurement of spaces to measurement of structures. Rather than think in terms of instructions for building structures, my goal here is to make a con-

---

16. Zimmerli, vol. 2, 81.
17. Zimmerli, vol. 2, 410.

ceptual shift in focus from structures to spaces. The concern here is not the arrangement and construction of structures, but the spaces defined by the structures. From this perspective, separation of spaces is the real issue. The measurements of the structures are not given to provide a building plan for structures, but to define the spaces which are created by the structures. The distinction is a subtle one, but it is crucial to my argument. The important elements of the layout are its spaces, and the purpose of the structures is to maintain the spaces. For example, what is the purpose of the outer wall except to maintain the space of the complex?[18]

Ezekiel 40–48 concerns the separation of spaces in three areas: the *House of YHWH* or *Holy Place*; the *Portion*; and the *Land of Israel*. The relationship between these three areas is best expressed by visualizing three concentric maps. The first is a map of the whole land. The second map is a detail map of a particular section of the land which is called the Portion. The third map is a more detailed map of a section which is called the House of YHWH or Holy Place. The order of the text begins with the most detailed map, expands it to a larger detail map, and then considers the whole. (The pattern is broken somewhat by 48:30–35 which returns to the City.) The Rhetor begins by defining the spaces of the House of YHWH in 40–42.

The House of YHWH

The building plan genre has determined much interpretation of these chapters, an assumption which has obscured their rhetorical purpose. The issue in Ezekiel 40–42 is not the correct building of structures, but the creation of spaces, and even more importantly, keeping these spaces separate. This is true for each of the structures measured in thorough but incomplete detail. The measurements of the structures are incomplete; however, the spaces are fully defined. This definition of space is the purpose of the measurements. This purpose explains the almost complete lack of vertical measurements of the structures. This point can be demonstrated by looking at the description of the Outer East Gate.

The Outer East Gate is defined by careful measurements. However, it is important to notice that what is actually being measured are the spaces created by the structures, rather than the structures themselves.

> Then he *entered* (בוא) the gateway (שער) facing east,
> going up its steps (מעלות),

---

18. A contemporary analogy concerns the ownership of condominiums. An owner owns the space defined by the condominium walls; the walls which define the space are common property.

and measured the threshold (סף) of the gate (שער),
one reed *broad*
and one threshold (סף)
one reed broad (רחב)[19];
and the side rooms (תא), one reed long (ארך), and one reed broad
(רחב);
and the space between the side rooms (תא), five cubits;
and the threshold (סף) of the gate (שער) by the vestibule (אולם) of the
gate at the
inner end, one reed.
Then he measured the vestibule (אולם) of the gateway (שער), eight cubits;
and its jambs (איל), two cubits;
and the vestibule (אולם) of the gate (שער) was at the inner end.
And there were three side rooms (תא) on either side of the east gate;
the three were of the same size (מדה)
and the jambs (איל) on either side were of the same size (מדה).
Then he measured the breadth (רחב) of the opening of the gateway
(שער), ten cubits;
and the *length* (ארך) of the gateway (שער), thirteen cubits.
There was a *boundary* (גבול) before the side rooms (תא)
one cubit on either side;
and the side rooms (תא) were six cubits on either side.
Then he measured the gate (שער) from the *roof* (גג) of the one side room
(תא) to
the *roof* (גג) of the other,
a breadth (רחב) of five and twenty cubits,
from *opening to opening* (פתח).
And he measured also the vestibule, twenty cubits;
and round about the vestibule of the *gate* was the court.[20]
From the front end of the gate (שער) at the entrance (איתון)
to the end of the vestibule (אולם) of the *inner* gate (שער) was fifty cubits.
And the gateway (שער) had windows round about,
narrowing inwards into their jambs (איל) in the side rooms (תא),
and likewise the *porch* (אילם) had windows round about inside,
and on the jambs (איל) were palm trees (40:6–15).

[19.] 0mitted In RSV

[20.] The MT here reads: "and he made (עשה) the jambs (איל) sixty cubits, and
to the jamb (איל) of the court was the gate all around." This sixty cubit dimension
of the MT reading is clearly inconsistent with the dimensions of the gate which is
twenty-five cubits wide and fifty cubits long. Zimmerli follows Gese by arguing
that elements of 40:15–16 have been included erroneously in 40:14 (Zimmerli, vol.
2, 335). RSV has used the LXX for its translation. See also the discussion in Allen,
220.

This detailed set of measurements is a list of spaces defined by structures. The spaces of the gate are the outer threshold, the six side rooms, the threshold of the vestibule, and the vestibule, the jambs, the openings of the gate and the corridor between the openings, all related in terms of orientation to the House building, each creating a boundary marker. There is an additional boundary marker. The גְבוּל is some sort of barrier wall which separates the spaces of the six side rooms from the central corridor. The important issue is not what this boundary structure looks like, but its function as a marker of a boundary between spaces. The only details of this description which do not define spaces are the details about the windows and the palm tree decorations.

As a blueprint of structures, this set of measurements and descriptions is insufficient to enable anyone to reproduce the structure of this gate. All that could be reproduced exactly is the open space created by the gate openings, the spaces of the side rooms, and the spaces created by the threshold, jambs, vestibule, and porch. (See Figure 1.)

The description of the Outer Court accomplishes the same function. The measurements from structure to structure create an open space one hundred cubits long from gate to gate. The points of reference are the Outer Gate and the Inner Gate, from the innermost point of the Outer Gate to the outermost point of the Inner Gate. This dimension is measured twice: from Outer East Gate to Inner East Gate (40:19); from Outer North Gate to Inner North Gate (40:23).

The Outer Court lies between the Outer Gates and Inner Gates. Its area is precisely defined, created by the structures of the Outer Gates and the Inner Gates, as well as by the pavement which runs parallel to the outer wall from gate to gate. There are thirty Chambers (לִשְׁכָה) around the perimeter of the court, with a pavement (רִצְפָה) between the Chambers and the area of the Outer Court. The only information provided about this pavement is its relationship to the gates.

> And the pavement (רִצְפָה) ran along the side (כָּתֵף) of the gates, corresponding to (לְעֻמַּת) the length (אֹרֶךְ) of the gates; this was the lower pavement (רִצְפָה) (40:18).

The sense of the description is that the gate structures are deeper than the wall and jut into the open space. However, the shape of the Outer Court is a perfect square. In order to keep the outer dimensions of the court perfectly square, the pavement which runs along the outer wall from gate to gate fills in the extra space. This pavement is both boundary marker and buffer zone between the thirty Chambers and the area of the Outer Court. No details are provided about the thirty Chambers, concerning their location, size, or arrangement. In addition to these thirty Chambers,

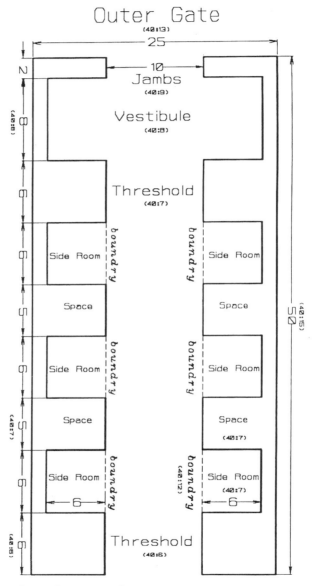

figure 1: Outer Gate

there are also cooking areas in the four corners of the Outer Court (46:21–24).

The boundary of the Inner Court is defined by three gates. These gates have the same structure as the outer gates, with one difference. They are mirror images of the outer gates, with the porch on the side of the Outer Court (40:28, 34, 37).[21] There is no mention of a wall which separates the Outer Court from the Inner Court. Zimmerli assumes that there must have been walls "which one must assume to have flanked the enormous gates, which, in turn, only makes sense as openings in a wall."[22] Allen also remarks about the strangeness of having no mention of a wall around the court.[23]

There are two other details which define space in terms of the inner gates. 40:38–43 describe a Chamber and tables in relation to the vestibule of the inner north gate. 40:44–46 describe two Chambers for the priests in the Inner Court itself. Although these Chambers are located at the sides (כתף) of the north and south gates, no information is given about their specific locations and dimensions. These sections have generated substantial discussion among commentators concerning textual problems and redactional issues, none of which concerns me here. It is clear that this material has a different function than the material which has preceded it, and which will follow it. There are no measurements given for the Chambers, but there is description of tables and instruments, and the measurements of the tables. For Zimmerli, the primary difficulty with the information about the Chambers in the vestibule is that there is no accounting for the difference in height between the Outer and Inner Courts. He wonders about the width of the side (כתף) of the vestibule, which is not adequate for the dimensions of the tables. His assessment of the problem is "planning from afar" which has not taken account of the differences in height.[24] It is precisely the difficulty of figuring out how and where these Chambers were constructed that gives strength to my argument that this is not a construction blueprint.

[21.] The MT has a number of textual difficulties. The Qere readings of 40:31, 34, 37 are plurals. The noun is אילם ("porch") in 40:31 and 34 and איל ("jamb") in 40:37. This is in addition to the spelling of אילם rather than אולם which was observed already in 40:16 which I have indicated by translating אולם as "vestibule" and אילם as "porch." My differentiation is an attempt to represent the difference in Hebrew, although I suspect that the difference is merely a matter of spelling rather than structure. RSV translates as "vestibule" in each instance.

[22.] Zimmerli, vol. 2, 355.

[23.] Allen, 232.

[24.] Zimmerli, vol. 2, 366–367.

After completing the discussion about the gates of the Inner Court, and these Chambers related to the Inner Court, the man makes a final definition of the area called the Inner Court.

And he measured the court,
a hundred cubits long (אֹרֶךְ),
and a hundred cubits broad (רֹחַב), foursquare;
and the altar was in front of (לִפְנֵי) the house (40:47).

The space of the Inner Court is defined as a square area, one hundred cubits on each side. The Altar is located in the Inner Court.

The next significant structure which is defined is the House building itself. The interior spaces of the House are defined in 40:48–41:4. Once again, the purpose of the measurements is to define spaces rather than structures. The House consists of three spaces, the Vestibule (אוּלָם), the Nave (הֵיכָל), and the Inner Room (פְּנִימָה). The dimensions of walls and openings define the spaces. There are no gates in the House. Rather there is a series of openings (פֶּתַח), each narrower than the previous one. The additional boundary structures are the jambs (אַיִל), and the pillars (עַמּוּד) beside the jambs, and a stairway of eight steps (מַעֲלוֹת).

41:1–15 describe the outside of the House building and a structure located behind the House building, identified as the Binyan (which means "structure" or "building"). The textual and architectural difficulties with this material are amply demonstrated by the critical commentaries. Once again, these details are insufficient to serve as a blueprint for construction. What then is the function of this material? The simplest answer is that these details explain how these annex structures can be built in proximity to the House building without intruding on its architectural space. What is being described is post and lintel construction which allows the annex structure to be built upwards and outwards by being attached to the House wall without intruding into it.

Just as Friedman found his clue in the measurement of cubits of the Tabernacle, the difficult set of measurements and description in 41:5–15 provides an essential clue to the meaning of the measurements of Ezekiel 40–42. First, the dimensions for width of the House building are:

The inner room 20 (41:3, 4)
The house wall (קִיר) 6 (41:5)
The side chambers (צֵלָע) 4 (41:5)
The outside wall 5 (41:9)

The last three measurements together total 15 cubits, the width of the wall and annex structure on each side. Therefore, the total width of the structure is 15 + 20 + 15, which is 50 cubits.

The dimensions for the length of the House building are:

The length of the wall 6 (41:5)
The length of the side chambers 4 (41:5)
The length of the outer side chambers 5 (41:9)
The inner room 20 (41:4)
The jamb of the inner room 2 (41:3)
The nave 40 (41:2)
The jamb of the nave 6 (41:1)
The vestibule 12 (40:49)[25]
The jamb of the vestibule 5 (40:48)

The total is 100 cubits. According to these measurements, the dimensions are 100 cubits by 50 cubits, and the ratio is 2:1. It is precisely here where my point about the importance of space and proportion is most evident. In the text, the dimensions do not stop with the structure, but include the measurements of "a space left free" (אֲשֶׁר מֻנָּח) (or "platform") "between the Chambers" (בֵּין הַלְּשָׁכוֹת) which is 20 cubits wide (41:9, 10, 11). There is an additional five cubit measurement (41:11) at the edge of the space left free.[26] When these 25 cubits on each side are added to the 50 cubit width of the structure, the total width is then 100 cubits. The dimension of the space which includes the House then becomes 100 cubits by 100 cubits, which is a perfect square.

Behind the House building, there is a mysterious structure, the *Binyan* (בִּנְיָן) (41:12, 13, 15). The dimensions of this Binyan are:

[25.] In this one instance, I choose to read with the LXX, rather than the MT, which reads " 11 cubits," for the simple reason that the numbers add up to 100 if the vestibule is 12 cubits. Also, the measurements for the vestibule reflect the convention used here and throughout Ezekiel 40–48 which identifies the longer dimension as the "length" (אֹרֶךְ) and the shorter as the "breadth" (רֹחַב). This involves a reorientation from the previous measurement of the Nave, in which the length measurement is along the east/west axis. For the vestibule, what is identified as the length measurement is along the north/south axis. For my calculations, the east/west axis is length and the north/south axis is width for each of the rooms.

[26.] In the MT, the text reads מְקוֹם הַמֻּנָּח, literally "the place of the space left free." RSV does not translate מְקוֹם, but reads the five cubit measurement for הַמֻּנָּח. LXX reads τοῦ φωτὸς which the editors of BHS suggest should be read as גָּדֵר or גְּדֶרֶת ("dividing wall") (as in 42:7, 10, 12). Cody emends the text on the basis of the LXX reading and understands that the five cubit measurement refers to a boundry wall on the edge of the platform (the space left free) which marks the boundary between the area of the House and the area of the outer court. See, Aelred Cody, *Ezekiel: With an Excursus on the Old Testament Priesthood*, OTM (Wilmington, Delaware: Michael Glazier, 1984), 209–210.

wall 5 (41:12)
width 70 (41: 12)
length 90 (41:12)

The dimensions for length are then 5 + 90 + 5 = 100 cubits. The dimensions
for width are 5 + 70 + 5 = 80 cubits. The dimensions of the Binyan are then
100 cubits by 80 cubits with a ratio of 5:4. Once again, the text includes dimensions for a space between the structure and the house building. This is
the גזרה or *restricted area*.[27] The dimensions of this Restricted Area are not
given, but can be easily calculated from 41:13–14.

Then he measured the house,
a hundred cubits long (ארך);
and the *restricted area* (גזרה)
and the Binyan (בנין) with its walls (קיר),
a hundred cubits long (ארך);
and the breadth (רחב) of the east front of the house
and the *restricted area* (גזרה)
a hundred cubits (41:13–14).

What is clear about these dimensions is that the text is defining two
perfect squares. The length (ארך) here is from east to west. The length of
the House is one hundred cubits. Immediately behind it, the Restricted
Area, the Binyan, and its walls, are also defined as one hundred cubits,
which makes the east to west dimension of the Restricted Area 20 cubits.
From north to south, the width (רחב) is one hundred cubits. Total dimension of the Restricted Area is 20 by 100 cubits.[28] By including the spaces in
the dimensions, the ratio of both areas is now 1:1. (See Figure 2.)

In 43:10, which was discussed above, the key instruction for the House
of Israel is "to measure the proportion." The singular indicates that there
is one proportion. To this point, the areas which have been defined are the
Outer Court, the Inner Court, the House area, and the Binyan area. By
shifting focus from the structures to the spaces which are defined by structures, the common proportion is evident. Each measures a perfect square.
The square, with its ratio of 1:1, is the proportion which the House of Israel
is to measure.

The whole complex is a square matrix which can in turn be subdivided
into smaller squares. The accompanying diagram shows that the whole is

---

[27.] On this translation, see Zimmerli, vol. 2, 379.

[28.] Once again demonstrating the convention of the Rhetor to identify the shorter measurement as the width (רחב), and the longer as the length (ארך), the text
identifies the east/west dimension of the restricted area as "breadth." For my calculations, I continue to identify the east/west dimension as length, and the north/
south dimension as width.

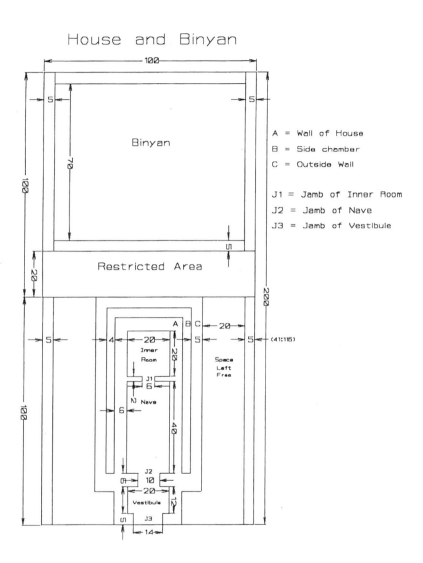

figure 2: House and Binyan

a square five hundred cubits on each side (42:20). (See Figure 3.) The Outer Court is a square which is four hundred cubits on each side, the Inner Court is a square which is one hundred cubits square (40:47). The Altar is located in the Inner Court. The only information given about its location is that it is *before* (לפני) the House. I assume that the Altar is in the exact center of the square which makes the Altar the exact center of the five hundred cubit square House complex, and the focus of worship. The central importance of the Altar is evident in the issues addressed in Ezekiel 40–48, and will be considered further below.

Maier, in his architectural study of the Temple Scroll, notes the same emphasis on the square shape.[29] He also emphasizes that the "remarkable difference" between the Temple Scroll design and the design in Ezekiel is the shift of the center. In Ezekiel, the center is the Altar; in the Temple Scroll, the center is the vestibule of the house.[30]

42:1–12 are another difficult portion of text. Some dimensions are given precisely. The two sets of Chambers on either side of the Binyan are 100 cubits long by 50 cubits wide (42:2, 8) and the Chambers along the wall are 50 cubits long (42:8). There is a "passage inward" (מהלך אל הפנימית) which is 100 cubits long and 10 cubits wide (42:4). In each corner of the Outer Court, there is a place to cook the offerings which is 40 cubits by 30 cubits (46:22). These dimensions by themselves are not sufficient to sketch these structures in relation to each other, and the west wall of the House complex.[31]

Once again, the text is lacking necessary dimensions for a building plan. Here, not only are the vertical measurements missing, but even some of the ground plan measurements are missing. It is not possible to take these dimensions and figure out the arrangement of this complex. Although the Rhetor has strained even my good will in this section, my question continues to be, What is the rhetorical purpose of writing it this way? I leave this question for now with two observations. The square shape, with its proportion of 1: 1, is evident in the central areas of the House com-

---

[29.] Johann Maier, "The Architectural History of the Temple in Jerusalem in Light of the Temple Scroll, " in *Temple Scroll Studies: Papers presented at the International Symposium on the Temple Scroll*. Manchester, December 1987, George J. Brooke, ed. (Sheffield: JSOT Press, 1989), 24.

[30.] Maier, 34.

[31.] For different efforts to draw a ground plan of these structures, see: Aelred Cody uses the work of Karl Elliger for his sketch (Cody, *Ezekiel* 214–215; 266–267); Allen use the sketch of T. A. Busink for the dimensions of the chambers for the laity along the outer court (Allen, 230–231); Cooke's sketch of the layout of these structures shows a different orientation for several of the structures (Cooke, 1937 edition, end).

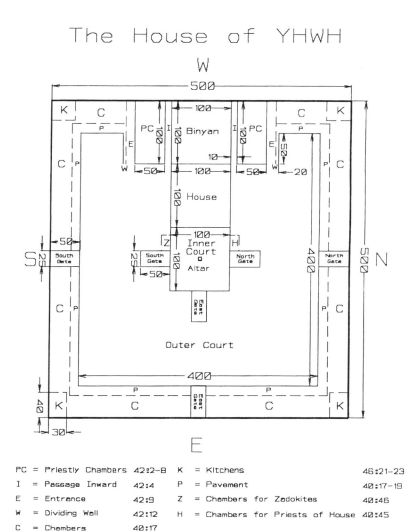

figure 3: The House of YHWH

plex: the House building, the Binyan, the Inner Court, and the Outer Court, and the dimensions of the whole complex. These square areas are completely defined. Conversely, the areas which are not so clearly defined are not square, and they are not located in the central portion of the House complex. The farther away from the center, the less precise the dimensions. For example, there are no dimensions at all for the thirty Chambers along the outside of the Outer Court; no dimension is given for the width of the pavement. The dimensions of the Priestly Chambers of 42:1–12 are included; the dimensions of the Priestly Chambers of 40:44 are not. The four cooking areas in the Outer Court are defined by specific measurements; they are rectangular in shape. The set of Priestly Chambers which are defined by specific measurements are also rectangular in shape.

After finishing the measurements of the interior (פְּנִימִי) of the House, the Narrator is "caused to go out" through the Outer East Gate (42:15). "House" here refers to בַּיִת as the whole temple complex. The tour began at the Outer East Gate with the measurement of the width and height of the outer wall (חוֹמָה). The tour ends with the measurement of the perimeter of this wall. The man measures the four sides or "winds" (רוּחַ) of the wall. The area defined by the wall is a square, five hundred cubits on each side (42:15–20).

The Portion

Chapters 40–42 described a square area which measured five hundred cubits on each side, the House of YHWH. In Chapter 45, this square area is located within another area called the Portion (תְּרוּמָה).[32] Chapter 45 is the area map and Chapters 40–42 are the detail map. This Portion is divided into areas for the priests, the Levites, and the City. Analysis is complicated by a discrepancy in measurements between MT and LXX. In 45:1, 48:9, and 48:13, MT reads the dimension of ten thousand cubits while LXX reads twenty thousand. The problem is that 48:20 defines the area of the Portion as a square twenty-five thousand cubits by twenty-five thousand cubits, comprising the Holy Portion (תרומ הקדש) and the Possession (אחזה) of the City. Since the Possession of the City is defined as twenty-five thousand by five thousand cubits (45:6; 48:16), this means that the portion defined in 45:1 must be twenty-five thousand by twenty thou-

---

[32] תרומה has been variously translated: "Contribution" (Greenberg, "Design," 232); "Whole Portion" (Klein, 184); "Consecrated Area" (Zimmerli, vol. 2, 467); "Reserve" (Levenson, 120); "Oblation" (Cooke, 494); "Reservation" (Allen, 264). All of these translations are possible. My translation is intended to be cognate to the verb רום, to "apportion." The sense is that a part of the Land is to be offered back to YHWH as a type of tithe.

sand cubits. However, in 45:1, MT gives the dimensions as twenty-five thousand by ten thousand cubits. The LXX reads twenty thousand cubits in 45:1 where MT reads ten. In order to make the numbers consistent, the same adjustment is made in 48:9 where MT reads ten and LXX reads twenty. Most scholars read with the LXX. Zimmerli notes that the difference between "ten" and "twenty" in Hebrew is a matter of replacing the final ה with final ים.[33]

There is another explanation for the difference which makes sense of the MT reading of ten thousand. The source of the problem is that the Hebrew root קדש occurs thirteen times in 45:1–7 and thirteen times in 48:8–22, and the noun תרומה occurs four times in 45:1–8 and ten times in 48:8–22. The textual variant seems to be the direct result of the confusion involved in translation of these twenty-six קדש forms and fourteen תרומה forms.

The singular adjective קדש occurs six times without the definite article: 45:1, 1, 3, 4; 48: 12, 14. The plural adjective קדשים occurs twice: 45:3; 48:12. The noun form מקדש occurs seven times: 45:3, 45:4, 4, 4: 48:8, 10, 11, 21. The remaining ten occurrences are of the adjective with the definite article הקדש: 45:2, 6, 7, 7, 48:10, 18, 18, 20, 21, 21. הקדש occurs alone only once, in 45:2. Otherwise it appears in a construct chain, תרומת הקדש. There is one occurrence of the Pual participle המקדש in 48:11.

The noun תרומה occurs in the absolute form four times: 45:1; 48:8, 48:9, 20, 21. The construct תרומת occurs eleven times, ten times in construct with הקדש: 45:6, 7, 7: 48:10, 9, 18, 18, 20, 21, 21; and once in construct with ארץ: 48:12. In addition, there is one occurrence of the similar noun תרומיה: 48:12.

The solution for the problem is the translation of these various combinations. In 45:1, the text reads תרומה ליהוה, "the Portion for YHWH," or "YHWH's Portion." This is the only occurrence of this construction. Significantly, it occurs in 45: 1, which is the source of the text critical problem. The much more frequent construction is the construct chain, תרומת הקדש, "the Holy Portion. " This distinction explains the difference between the twenty thousand cubit width of the Holy Portion and the ten thousand cubit width of YHWH's Portion. The Holy Portion is made up of YHWH's Portion and the Possession of the Levites. When the Holy Portion is added to the Possession of the City, the total is the twenty-five thousand cubit square Portion.

My revision of RSV uses the following definitions: The singular adjective קדש is translated simply as "holy. " קדש in construct with the plural קדשים is translated as "Holy of Holies." מקדש is translated as "Holy

---

33. Zimmerli, vol. 2, 465.

Place." תרומת הקדש is translated as "Holy Portion." הקדש is translated as "Holy Area." תרומה ליהוה is translated as YHWH's Portion, and תרומה is translated as Portion.

> When you allot the land (ארץ) as *an inheritance* (נחלה),
> you shall *apportion* (רום) *YHWH's Portion* (תרומה ליהוה)
> *The holy part of the land* (קדש מן הארץ)
> *its length* (ארך) twenty-five thousand cubits *long* (ארך)
> and *ten* thousand cubits wide (רחב);
> it shall be holy (קדש) throughout its whole extent (סביב בכל גבול).
> Of this a square plot
> of five hundred by five hundred cubits
> shall be for the *Holy Area* (הקדש)
> with fifty cubits for an open space (מגרש) around it.
> and from this measurement (מדה)
> you shall measure off a section twenty-five thousand cubits long (ארך)
> and ten thousand broad (רחב),
> in which shall be the *Holy Place* (מקדש),
> *The Holy of Holies* (קדש קדשים).
> It shall be the holy *part* of the land (קדש מן הארץ)
> It shall be for the priests, *the servants of the Holy Place* (מקדש)
> *who come near* (הקרבים) *to serve* (לשרת) YHWH;
> and it shall be *for them* a place (מקום) for their houses
> and a holy place (מקדש) for the *Holy Place* (מקדש).
> Another section,
> twenty-five thousand cubits long (ארך)
> and ten thousand cubits broad (רחב),
> shall be for the Levites, *the servants of the House* (משרתי הבית),
> as their Possession (אחזה)
> *twenty chambers* (לשכה)[34]
> Alongside the *Holy Portion* (תרומת הקדש)
> you shall assign for the Possession (אחזה) of the City,
> an area five thousand cubits broad (רחב),
> and twenty-five thousand cubits long (ארך);
> it shall belong to the whole House of Israel (45:1–6).

The Possession of the City is divided into the area of the City (העיר) itself, Open Land (מגרש) around the City, and the Remainder (הנותר) (48:15–18). The shape of the whole Possession of the City is a rectangle twenty-five thousand by five thousand cubits. The City itself is a square, four thousand and five hundred cubits on each side. It is surrounded by Open Land which extends out from the City two-hundred and fifty cubits on each side. When the dimensions of the Open Land are added to the di-

---

[34.] RSV reads with LXX: as their possession for cities to live in

mensions of the City, the whole is a square shape, five thousand cubits on each side, which is the same shape and ten times the size of the House of YHWH/Holy Place (42:15–20; 45:2).

In addition to the Portion, there are two areas set apart for the Nasi on the east and west sides of the Portion. This land is the Possession (אחזה) of the Nasi.

> And to the Nasi
> shall belong the land on both sides of the Holy Portion (תרומת הקדש)
> and the *Possession* (אחזה) of the City
> alongside the Holy Portion (תרומ הקדש) and the *Possession* (אחזה) of
> the City
> on the west and on the east,
> corresponding in length to one of the *divisions* (חלקים),
> and extending from the western *boundary* (נבול)
> to the eastern boundary (נבול) of the land (45:7).

The division of the land among the tribes and the tribal boundaries (47:13–48:29) will be considered below. Here, I make only two comments. First, each of these areas is a longitudinal strip of roughly trapezoidal shape (with the east and west boundaries of the divisions defined by the Jordan River and Mediterranean Sea). Second, discussion of the tribal areas moves from north to south.

My discussion so far has been motivated by the statement of rhetorical purpose that the House of Israel is to "measure the proportion" of the House. By a shift in focus from the dimensions of structures to the definition of spaces which the structures define, the proportion became evident. The common proportion of the House of YHWH, the Portion, and the City is the ratio of 1:1, expressed in the square shape. There are no other areas defined by this shape. The Holy Portion, the Possession of the Levites, and the Possession of the City are each rectangular in shape. The Possession of the Nasi and the tribal divisions are roughly trapezoidal in shape. Both the priestly area (YHWH's Portion) and the Possession of the City contain a central square area. The Possession of the Levites and the Possession of the Nasi do not.

One further issue is the north-south order within the Portion of YHWH's Portion for the priests, the Possession of the Levites and the Possession of the City. Scholarship is divided on whether YHWH's Portion is north or south of the Possession of the Levites. Those who argue that YHWH's Portion lies to the north do so on the basis of the order of division of the Land.[35] There are two difficulties with this argument. The first is that it does not recognize that the strategy of the Rhetor is to begin at the center

[35] See Greenberg, 233; Klein, 185.

and move outward, from detail map of the Holy Place, to the detail map of the Portion, and finally to the map of the whole Land. The discussion of the Portion also begins at the center with YHWH's Portion and moves out from there to the Possession of the Levites on one side and the Possession of the City on the other. The second problem with this argument is that it would place the Possession of the Levites in the exact center of the Portion.

If however YHWH's Portion lies between the Possession of the Levites and the Possession of the City, YHWH's Portion lies at the exact center of the Portion. As the accompanying diagram shows, the exact center of the Portion is not the exact midpoint of YHWH's Portion on the north-south axis. In order to locate the Holy Place at the exact center of the Portion, it must be slightly to the north of the midpoint of YHWH's Portion.[36] Admittedly, the text itself does not explicitly locate YHWH's Portion at the exact center of the Portion any more than the text located the Altar at the exact center of the Inner Court. However, this assumption leads to a wonderfully concentric arrangement which overlays the square matrix of the Portion over the square matrix of the House of YHWH or Holy Place. The concentric center of the Land as a whole is also the concentric center of these two square matrices of House and Portion. To be concentric is to share a common center, even if the common center is not the geometric midpoint. According to this, the concentric point of the Land of Israel, the Portion, and the House of YHWH is the square Altar in the Inner Court. (See Figure 4).

Summary of Chapter One

The genre of Ezekiel 40–48 is territorial rhetoric. Territoriality is a technical phrase from human geography which involves deliberate efforts to define area, communicate boundaries and control access. Rhetoric involves intentionally persuasive use of language. The rhetorical purpose of the guided tour is to measure the proportion of the House of YHWH, not to provide a building plan for a temple. The dimensions given define spaces rather than structures, a process which explains the omission of most vertical dimensions of the structures. The three concentric spaces are the House of YHWH, or Holy Place, the Portion, and the Land of Israel. A shift of focus from structures to spaces reveals the importance of the square shape of the House complex, the Outer Court, the Inner Court, the area of the House building, the area of the Binyan, and the Altar. The emphasis on the square shape continues in the description of the Portion, which includes the Holy Portion, made up of YHWH's Portion and the Possession of the Levites, and the Possession of the City. In addition, the

---

[36.] See also Fig. 7, Zimmerli, vol. 2, 535.

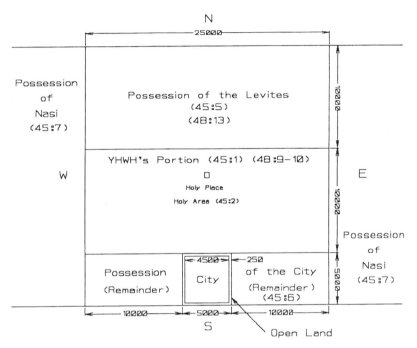

figure 4: The Portion

Nasi has a Possession on both sides of the Portion. The square Altar is at the concentric center of House, Portion, and Land.

Chapter 2

The Shape of the Holy

The Holy

What is the significance of the square Altar at the concentric center of the House, Portion, and Land? The matter of vertical measurements provides the answer to this question. Other than the heights of the Altar and tables, there is only one vertical measurement in these chapters. This is the measurement of the outer wall in 40:5. What is the purpose of including this vertical measurement but omitting the vertical dimensions of the gates, buildings, rooms, and other walls? The answer to this question is found in 42:20 which measures the perimeter of this outer wall.

> He measured it on the four sides.
> It had a wall (חוֹמָה) around it,
> five hundred cubits long (אֹרֶךְ),
> and five hundred broad (רֹחַב),
> to make a separation (בדל) between the holy (קֹדֶשׁ) and the common (חֹל).

This statement is a succinct expression of the religious ideology which motivates this particular layout of places. It shares a set of pervasive assumptions with other Ancient Near East religious ideologies which categorize people, places, and things as *holy* or *common*, *pure* or *impure*. One of the dominant themes of Jacob Milgrom's work on the Priestly cultic system is the insistence that holiness is not an abstract ethical quality but a "thing." Milgrom defines holiness (קָדוֹשׁ) as a dynamic and contagious substance which emanates from gods. The antagonist of holiness is impurity (טמא), the equally dynamic and contagious substance which emanates from demons. Since holiness and impurity are dynamic, they are contagious, and can attach themselves to persons or objects to make them holy or impure.[1] In contrast, the common and the pure are static substances and non-contagious. The presence of holiness ensures life, order, and well-being. Impurity brings death, disorder, and chaos. Milgrom goes on to argue that the only difference between Israelite and non-Israelite ideologies of holiness and impurity is that Israel identified the source of impurity as human beings rather than demons.[2] This concept of holiness and impurity as the consequence of mutually antagonistic, contagious substances is the concept which is perhaps most foreign to many contemporary readers, where "holiness" is usually related to behavior, and the concept of "impurity" seems a quaint relic from less enlightened times. However, this is the concept which underlies much of the religious ideology of the Ancient Near East, and is assumed by the Rhetor.

Another concept which is generally foreign to contemporary readers of the Vision of Transformation but pervasive throughout the Ancient Near East is that gods are *located* in place. Since holiness emanates from gods, and gods are located in place, the well-being of the society depends on two factors. In order to worship a god, it was necessary to know the god's location.[3] Gods were identified with particular locations, particularly with hills or mountains. It was also necessary to ensure that the god remained located in that place. In order to keep the god located in that place, various shrines and temples were built at these locations. At the same time, language about the geography of gods and temples simultaneously refers to the cosmic reality which transcends time and space. The location of a god was understood symbolically. This means that the gods were both transcendent and immanent, and their locations were actual sites with symbolic meaning.[4] The location of a god, the holy place, is the point of intersection between two realities, the actual and the symbolic, the earthly and the heavenly, the social and the cosmic.[5] The role of the cult in the holy place is to mediate between these two realities. The most important point here is that cosmos, society, and cult are interrelated. What happens in one area affects the others.[6]

A temple is a particular type of holy place. It is the dwelling place of a god, and priests are the house-servants. As a mediator between the cosmic

---

[1.] Milgrom, *Leviticus*, 256.
[2.] Milgrom, *Leviticus*, 256.
[3.] R. E. Clements, *God and Temple* (Oxford: Basil Blackwell, 1965), 1.
[4.] Clements, *God and Temple*, 3.

and the social it combines both the actual and the symbolic. It is located in an actual place, and is an actual building, and has particular social functions. It also has symbolic meaning as the earthly *microcosm* of the heavenly *macrocosm*.[7] The House of YHWH is designed to be the place where YHWH dwells in the midst of Israel, ensuring the well-being of the society. It is a holy place *because* YHWH dwells there. By defining the outer limits of YHWH's House, the wall also defines the separation between the holy place and what is common. Whatever the other subdivisions of space within the House area, the whole is holy in relation to what is outside the wall. For this reason, the vertical measurement is included to show this qualitative change.

Zones of Holiness

The distinction between defining territory and providing a blueprint explains why most vertical measurements are omitted in this territorial scheme. However, even some areas of the temple complex lack complete measurements for length and width. It is significant for the theology of holiness that these incompletely defined areas are on the outer edges of the complex.

Jonathan Smith has divided Ezekiel's temple complex into "three zones of relative sacrality." The center zone from east to west contains the two East Gates, the Inner Court, the temple, and the Binyan.[8] This is YHWH's zone. On either side of this central zone, there are spheres of priestly

---

[5.] In his study of Priestly ideology, Gorman argues that: "The world view of the Priestly writers has as its framework three distinct orders of creation—the cosmological, the societal, and the cultic. All three orders were given shape, brought into being, and established by the speech of God. What must be seen, however, is that these various orders are not independent of one another but are intricately connected. The wilderness tabernacle in the center of the wilderness camp is a reflection of the social order which is in turn a reflection of the cosmological order. The cultic order and the social order are part of—reflecting in their own structure and in turn helping to structure — the cosmological order" (Frank H. Gorman, Jr., *The Ideology of Ritual: Space, Time and Status in the Priestly Theology*, JSOTSup, no. 91, [Sheffield: JSOT Press, 1990], 44.)

[6.] See Jon D. Levenson, *Creation and the Persistence of Evil: The Jewish Drama of Divine Omnipotence* (San Francisco: Harper & Row, 1988), for Levenson's argument that "creation" refers to the containment of chaos. The relationship between cosmos and society is two-directional. Inherent in this theology is the ever-present threat of impending chaos, and the role of the cult to prevent the invasion of chaos by the careful maintenance of ritual.

[7.] Clements, *God and Temple*, 3.

[8.] Jonathan Smith, *To Take Place*, 59.

domestic activities, which contain the priestly chambers (40: 44–46; 42:13). On the other side of the priestly zone, there is the zone for the people. This zone contains the pavement (40:18), the chambers (40:17; 42:8), the kitchens (46:22). The areas which are completely defined are in the central zone, which is the most holy zone. In relationship to this most holy central zone, the outer zones on the north and south are less holy. They are also less completely defined. The areas which are completely defined by length and width are in the most holy zone in the center. The areas which are incompletely defined are in the zones for the people, on the outer edges of the complex.

Purgation of Impurity

The House of YHWH is not only the source of holiness, it is also the focal point for impurity. Since impurity is dynamic and contagious, any impurity in society or cosmos is attracted to this holy place. Thus, the House of YHWH is the place of mediation. This is why there are two most holy locations in the spatial layout of the House of YHWH. The relationship between the Holy of Holies and the Altar is at the heart of the ideology of Ezekiel, and is expressed in the architectural layout of the House. The Holy of Holies is the symbolic dwelling place and the altar is the place of purgation. In this geometry of holiness, the architectural center of the complex is not the Holy of Holies but the altar.[9] This focus on the Altar expresses the understanding that societal and cosmic well-being needs more than the presence of YHWH. There is also need for a means of cleansing the so-

<hr>

[9.] In contrast, Zimmerli argues that the "real center of the temple precinct" is not the geometric center, but the Holy of Holies. He argues against the location of the altar in the exact center of the inner court. "…such a location reveals the unconscious influence of the square shape not only of the inner court, but also of the temple area as a whole. Must not this square layout have a center? And will this center not be the altar? Closer consideration, however, makes this assumption questionable…the layout of the temple in Ezekiel 40f is not conceived symmetrically around the center. Already the absence of gates on the west side of the temple area can draw attention to this. It becomes quite clear, however, in the continuation of the leading of the prophet, which has its goal not at the altar, but in the temple building to the west of the altar and there in the most westerly room of that building, the holy of holies. Everything is oriented towards that spot, as will be emphasized in the later complex in 43: 1ff and as is also expressed indirectly in the rules of procedure in the temple. Even the altar is orientated towards that spot, for of it is precisely said not that it stands 'in the center of the court,' but 'in front of the temple.' It does not signify a new center of gravity, but stands submissively in front of the sanctuary whose core is in the holy of holies" (Zimmerli, vol. 2, 355).

ciety and cosmos from the effects of impurity. This is the function of the altar at the concentric center of the Holy Place, the Portion, and the land. The House is a square matrix with the square Inner Court and the square Altar at the absolute center. This is the place of purgation, where the effects of impurity are cleansed. This spatial arrangement is a profound acknowledgement that the true beneficiary of the House is not YHWH but Israel, and through Israel, both heaven and earth, cosmos and society. Israel in exile is suffering the results of impurity which drove YHWH into exile. The solution is to cleanse the impurity of society and cosmos by means of the Altar.

The Landscape of Holiness

In *The City as Text*, the cultural geographer James Duncan analyzes the connection between landscape and the pursuit of social power.[10] In geographical terms, landscape is more than lawns and gardens. Landscape refers to the layout of space, and includes material structures such buildings and walls—as well as the design of lawns and gardens. Duncan argues that constructed landscapes encode social and political information. He studied the relationship between the material remains of the nineteenth century Sri Lankan city of Kandy and Kandyan scriptural traditions. He argues that the last king of Kandy created the landscape of the city as part of his attempt to consolidate and maintain social power. The city of Kandy had a highly literate tradition with a strong connection to Buddhist and Hindu scriptures. The king used elements of these scriptures to construct and redesign the landscape of the city. He modeled himself upon the king of the gods, to become a divine ruler, and designed the landscape of the city to demonstrate that he was a god-king.[11] Thus the city of Kandy was itself a text, which could be read for rhetorical meaning. So, for example, the "wave swell wall" was much more than a wall. It was designed with the shape of waves on the top to represent the churning of the Ocean of Milk at the time of creation, as well as the power of destruction. The rhetorical meaning of the wall is that the king has the same power of destruction over his subjects. Duncan argues that each element of the landscape was designed to convey a similar social and political rhetorical meaning.

[10.] James S. Duncan, *The City As Text: The Politics of Interpretation in the Kandyan Kingdom.* Cambridge Human Geography (Cambridge: Cambridge University Press, 1990).

[11.] Duncan, 5.

The Shape of the Holy

Ezekiel 40–48 also describes a landscape which can be read rhetorical-ly. In the landscape of temple and land in Ezekiel, the square shape is not simply an accident of design. It is rhetorically meaningful and is intended to be the material representation of a theology of holiness. And so, the command to measure the proportion in 43:10 is part of a rhetorical strategy to restructure a society according to a theology of holiness. In Ezekiel 40–48, holiness has a shape. Both the Holy of Holies and the Altar are square. The same central zone of holiness also has the square spaces of the Inner Court, the House, and the Binyan. In contrast, neither the zone for the priests, nor the zone for the people has a square area. (The only square area to which the people have access is the Outer Court; however, part of the Outer Court lies within the holy inner zone belonging to YHWH.) The di-mensions which are included are sufficient to define the spaces of YHWH's zone. In contrast, the area measurements in the zone of the priests and the zone of the people are incomplete. The measurements of area of one set of priestly chambers are given but not the other. However, except for the dimensions of the cooking areas in the four corners of the Outer Court, there are no dimensions given for the places for the people. The shape of the cooking areas is the rectangle, the shape of the common, rather than the holy.

This same distinction between the square and the rectangular, the holy and the common, is evident in the description of the central portion and the tribal divisions of the land itself. In all of this, the use of the square shape plays a significant role in the theology of holiness of Ezekiel. In the rhetoric of Ezekiel, the square shape can be read as a sign of the holy. Mai-er, in his architectural study of the Temple Scroll, notes the same emphasis on the square shape.[12] He also emphasizes that the "remarkable differ-ence" between the Temple Scroll design and the design in Ezekiel is the shift of the center. In Ezekiel, the center is the Altar; in the Temple Scroll, the center is the vestibule of the house.[13]

Territoriality

Ezekiel 40–48 defines a system of territoriality which reflects this view of holiness and impurity, a system designed to prevent and purge the in-

---

[12] Johann Maier, "The Architectural History of the Temple in Jerusalem in Light of the Temple Scroll, " in *Temple Scroll Studies: Papers presented at the Interna-tional Symposium on the Temple Scroll,* Manchester, December 1987, George J. Brooke, ed. (Sheffield: JSOT Press, 1989), 24.

[13] Maier, 34.

vasion of impurity into the holy. The exigence of the Book of Ezekiel is the experience of exile. Israel in exile is suffering the results of impurity which drove YHWH into exile. The solution is to cleanse the impurity of society and cosmos by means of the Altar. The rhetoric makes clear that the disputed issues motivating this layout of space are not matters of access to the House building itself, but access to the Altar.

The definition of territoriality involves both the spatial and the social. It refers to spaces and places, and the power-relationships and place-specific practices which are involved in controlling access to those spaces and places. The next section focuses on the spatial aspects of territoriality in Ezekiel 40–48 by looking at the topic of *place*. What are the areas, the boundaries, and the material means of controlling access? The next chapter focuses on the social aspects of territoriality by looking at the topics of power relations and place-specific practices in terms of access by social role.

Territoriality of the House of YHWH

The first place is the House of YHWH. The pattern of defining the territory involves the three factors of location, elevation, and orientation. The vocabulary of location is "outside" and "inside," "outer" and "inner," in relation to the central point of the House complex, which is the Altar in the Inner Court. In terms of location, the man begins at the outside and moves toward the center, and then back to the outside. After defining the outer boundary of the territory, the man begins by defining the areas involved in the whole complex of the House of YHWH. The House complex has three areas: the outer area, the inner area, and the House building itself. Each of these areas is further subdivided. The outer area comprises the Outer Court and various Chambers around the outside of the Court. The inner area comprises the Inner Court and Chambers related to the Inner Court. The House building is divided into three sections: the Vestibule, the Nave, and the Holy of Holies. Each of these areas is marked by structures which mark boundaries. After the man defines each area, he then considers the means of controlling access. Each area has some type of opening in the boundary which controls access between the areas. The vocabulary of elevation is "lower" and "upper." Each area is marked by elevation, with stairways leading from one area to the next. The vocabulary of orientation relates to the points of the compass. The House complex is oriented toward the east. It has gates only in the east, north, and south. There are no west gates. The route of the tour is Outer East Gate, Outer North Gate, Outer South Gate, then Inner South Gate, Inner East Gate, Inner North Gate.

Each of the items measured and described in this tour can be identified in terms of its territorial function. The areas are the gates, the courts, various types of chambers, the House building, the Altar. The boundaries are walls, gates, doorposts and jambs, and stairways. The means of access are gates, stairs, passageways, and various openings. Walls are boundary structures. The most important territorial measurement is the outer boundary of the area. Therefore, the man begins by measuring the outer wall (חומה). The word חומה occurs in Ezekiel 40–48 only in 40:5 and 42:20, which mark the beginning and the ending point of the tour which stakes the territorial claim. The wall on the outside is the largest and thickest. חומה is used elsewhere in the Book of Ezekiel and the rest of the Old Testament to refer to city walls. It is never used elsewhere to refer to temple walls. This means that the word which is usually used to describe the enclosing wall around cities is here used to refer to the wall which encloses a temple. Rather than a temple within a city, this temple complex takes over the functions of the city. The initial description of the temple complex is "a *form* (מבנה) like a city (עיר)" (40:2). This temple complex with the "form like a city" has a city wall and city gates. There is no mention of a wall between the Outer and Inner Court.[14] Contrary to those who argue that there must be a wall between the Outer and Inner Courts, such a wall is not required in order to define the boundary. In this case, the difference in area is marked by elevation.[15] The Inner Court is eight steps higher than the Outer Court (40:31, 34, 37). Nor would a wall be required in order to control access. The combination of stairway and gate structure, which is the physical means of access to the court, is sufficient to control unauthorized access. There is also a benefit to marking the boundary by elevation rather a wall. Without a wall, worshipers can see the rituals conducted at the Altar in the Inner Court, and the priests in the Inner Court can see what is occurring in the Outer Court below.[16] Other walls are the walls (קיר) of the House and the Binyan (41:2, 3, 5, 6, 9, 17,

---

[14.] I have already noted that Greenberg, Zimmerli, and Allen comment on the "omission" of a wall around the inner court: Greenberg, "Design," 225–226; Zimmerli, vol. 2, 355; Allen, 232.

[15.] "The royal place is, at one and the same time, both the most inclusive category—'the place where I will dwell for all time *in the midst of Israel'* (Ezekiel 43:7)—and the most sharply distinguished and delineated. These distinctions are reenforced by their verticality. Despite the blueprint character of the first map, we should picture the hierarchy of places not as concentric circles on a flat plane but instead as altitude markers on a relief map. Each unit is built on a terrace, spatially higher than that which is profane in relation to it" (Jonathan K. Smith, *To Take Place: Toward Theory in Ritual* (Chicago: University of Chicago Press, 1987), 57.

20, 22, 25; the smaller barrier walls (גדר) and (גדרת) (42:7, 10, 12); and the barrier walls (גבול) of the gates (40:12).

The gates are one of the most distinctive elements of the temple vision, remarkable both for the amount of attention devoted to their description, and for their massive size and arrangement. The emphasis on the gates is evidence of territoriality. In a territorial system, gates, doors, and openings are the means of access through the boundaries. If the primary motivation of the design of the temple complex is to ensure maintenance of boundaries, then gates are the most important structural features of the design. Control of access requires defensible gates. This fact accounts for the massive size of these gates. At fifty by twenty-five cubits, they are half the length of the Inner Court. Not only are these gates massive in proportion to the rest of the temple complex, they are also without precedent as temple gates. However, similar gate structures have been excavated at the Solomonic era cities of Hazor, Megiddo, and Gezer.[17]

Just as the discussion of the gates takes up a significant percentage of the text, their territorial function is also significant. Gates are the only items in the text which can function according to all three facets of territoriality. They are themselves areas, subdivided into areas called side rooms, jambs, and thresholds. Access to each of these areas of the gates is a matter of social role. The gates not only are boundary structures, they also have inner boundaries which control access within the gates. The side rooms are places for the guards, with a barrier wall as a boundary which separates the guards from anyone who would enter the gate. The basic purpose of a gate is to control access into an area. Any effort to assert territorial control is only as effective as the means to control access. The gates are massive structures because they are the first line of defense against unauthorized entry. Within the territory of the Inner Court, the House, and the Chambers for the priests, there are no more gates. Instead there are openings (פתח) (41:2, 2, 3, 3, 3, 11, 11, 11, 17, 20; 42:4, 11, 12; 47:1) and doors (דלת) (41:23, 24, 24, 24, 24, 24, 25) which mark boundaries, but do not have guards stationed within them.[18]

[16.] "The inner court must be open to visual surveillance from the outer court to insure that the cultic activities proceed as regulated; however, entry into this space must be carefully controlled to protect the power of the cultic personnel" (John Wright, "A Tale of Three Cities: Urban Gates, Squares, and Power in Iron Age II, NeoBabylonian, and Achaemenid Israel," Paper presented to the *Sociology of the Second Temple Group,* Society of Biblical Literature Annual Meeting, New Orleans [November 17, 1990]: 17).

[17.] Zimmerli, vol. 2, 352–353.

Territoriality of Portion, Possessions, and Land

The definition of territoriality clarifies the material on the Portion and the Possession of the Nasi. It can explain what is included, and can also explain the seeming redundancy of the text which first defines the dimensions of the Portion and Possession of the Nasi in 45:1–7 and then again in 48:8–22. The apparent redundancy results from the fact that these two chapters have different purposes in this territorial claim. Chapter 45 defines the areas according to their dimensions. The specific numbers were considered above and do not need to be discussed here. Chapter 48 defines boundaries and access. Although 45:1–7 give the dimensions of the areas, these verses did not define the boundaries of these areas. In order to define the boundaries, the Portion and Possession of the Nasi must be located in relationship to the rest of the Land. This is exactly what the text does by first defining the boundaries (גבול) of the whole Land in 47: 13–20.

A territorial claim requires the establishment of boundaries. This is the topic of 47:15–20 which uses the word גבול eight times to define the outer boundary of the territory of Israel.[19] Unlike the territorial definition of the House and the Portion, the area of Israel is not defined by cubit measurements. This is completely consistent with pre-exilic practice. The cubit was a unit of measurement used for items which could be measured by the forearm. Long distances were indicated by other means.[20] Here, place names and physical geography define the boundaries. The boundaries indicated by features of physical geography are the Mediterranean, or Great Sea, on the west; the Jordan River on the east; and the "Brook of Egypt" on the south. The other boundary designations are place names and therefore more difficult to identify.

After defining the area of the whole Land by defining its boundaries, the Land is further subdivided into thirteen longitudinal strips. Twelve are for the tribes (שבטים) and the thirteenth is for the Portion and the Nasi's Possession (48:1–29).

[18.] The word פתח also occurs in relation to the gates, variously translated by RSV: 40:11 ("opening"); 40:13, 13 ("door to door"); 40:38 ("door"); 40:40 ("entrance"); 46:3 ("entrance").

[19.] 47:15, 16, 16, 16; 17, 17; 18, 20. RSV uses "boundary" or "border." Although גבול has a range of translational possibilities including "border," "boundary," or "territory," a consistent translation as "boundary" throughout 47:13–48:29 conveys the importance of boundaries in territorial claims.

[20.] See: R. B. Y. Scott, "Weights and Measures of the Bible," in *BAR*, vol. 3, ed. Edward F. Campbell, Jr. and David Noel Freedman (Garden City, New York: Doubleday & Company, 1970), 346–350.

It is in this context of the definition of boundaries that the Rhetor returns to the material about the Portion and the Possession of the Nasi. Although this section repeats the dimensions of 45:1–7, the purpose here is to orient each area in relationship to the areas around it by defining areas in terms of their boundaries. The northern boundary of the Portion is the territory of Judah and the southern boundary is the territory of Benjamin (48:8, 22). The Holy Place is located "in the midst" (בתוך) of YHWH's Portion (הרונה אשר תרימו ליהוה) (48:8).[21] The "Special Portion" (תרומיה) for the priests adjoins the *boundary* (גבול) of the Levites (48:12), while the area of the Levites is alongside the *boundary* (גבול) of the priests (48:13).

There is additional information about the Possession of the City. This area is subdivided into the area of the City itself (48:16), the Open Space (מגרש) around the City (48:17), and the Remainder (הנותר) (48:15, 18), with the dimensions for each. These areas are related to each other. The City is "in the midst" (בתוך) of the Remainder. The Open Space is a boundary between the City and the Remainder. The whole Possession of the City is related to the boundaries of the Holy Portion (48:18).

The Possession of the Nasi is related to the boundaries of the Holy Portion and the Possession of the City, as well as the boundaries of Judah and Benjamin. (48:21–22). YHWH's Portion and the Possession of the Levites and the Possession of the City are "in the midst" (בתוך) of the Possession of the Nasi and "between" the boundary of Judah and the boundary of Benjamin (48:22). In all of this, the intention to establish territories by defining boundaries is evident.

The third facet of territoriality is means of access. The end of the Book of Ezekiel defines the means of access into the City as twelve gates, three on each side of the city (48:30–34). There is no mention of a wall, but there is mention that the circumference of the City is eighteen thousand cubits. This is the outer boundary which defines the area of the City.

Summary of Chapter Two

The square Altar at the concentric center of the House, Portion, and Land is rhetorically significant in this landscape and is meant to be read as part of a theology of holiness which ensures the well-being of the reshaped society by cleansing the society and cosmos of impurity. The shape of the holy is the square while the shape of the common is the rectangle. The House is divided into zones of holiness, with complete area measurements for the central holy areas and incomplete measurements for the zones for

---

[21.] This construction is literally, "The Portion which is apportioned for YHWH."

the priests and people. The whole layout of space in House, Portion, and Land is territorial, demonstrating concern for measuring areas and defining boundaries.

Chapter 3

Access

YHWH as Power Holder

A territorial system has power holders and power subjects. The power holders are the ones who make the rules which define areas, establish boundaries, and control access. The power subjects are the ones who follow the rules of the power holders. In the territorial system of Ezekiel 40–48, there is one power holder, YHWH, the King of Israel. Even though there is little explicit royal language, these chapters are the territorial claim of YHWH as King. Within this territorial system, there are social roles with more or less territorial access, but all are power subjects within YHWH's territory. The claim of the Rhetor is that everything which occurs in the vision is under the control and timing of YHWH.

By the power of the hand of YHWH, the Narrator takes a visionary journey into the Land of Israel. All that follows is identified as the result of the "visions of God."

> In the twenty-fifth year of our exile,
> at the beginning of the year,
> on the tenth day of the month,
> in the fourteenth year after the city was conquered,
> on that very day, the hand of YHWH was upon me,
> and *he caused me to enter* (בוא) *there* (שׁמה) in the visions of God
> into the land of Israel,
> and set me down upon a very high mountain,
> on which was a *form* (מבנה) like a city *on the south.*

When he caused me to enter (בוא) *there* (שמה)
Behold, there was a man,
whose appearance was like *the appearance*[1] of bronze,
with a line of flax and a measuring reed in his hand;
and he was standing in the gateway (שער) (40:1–3).

This beginning makes clear that YHWH is claiming a territory. The
guided tour through the temple complex begins at the Outer East Gate
where the Narrator sees a bronze-like man who has a measuring reed and
a cord in his hand (40:4). These details convey all that the reader needs to
know about this man. The first is that this "man" is no man; he is an angelic
being, a messenger from God, sent to provide a revelation to the Narrator.
The reed and cord are measuring instruments indicating that the man's
primary revelatory role is to "stake a claim" to a place by measuring it. In
order to make a territorial claim, the claimed area must be defined. The essential function of this messenger is to mark out a territory, by defining its
areas, and communicating its boundaries and its means of access. The revelation which he communicates is both words and actions; it is a "show
and tell" with more emphasis on "show" than on "tell."[2] Although the
man does speak, his primary means of revelation is through measurement.[3] The angelic being is an agent from God whose responsibility is to
define the territory itself. However, YHWH is the one who defines the territorial rules by defining which social groups have territorial responsibilities within the territory.

In 43:2–4, the Kabod YHWH enters the House by the Outer East Gate
to take possession. In 43:5, the Narrator is once again "caused to enter"
into the Inner Court by means of the "spirit."[4] In this location, the Narrator
hears "one speaking" from the House (43:6). The very first statement of the
speech is the territorial claim of a king.

Mortal,
This is the place (מקום) of my throne
and the place (מקום) of the soles of my feet,
where I will dwell *there* (שם)[5]
in the midst (בתוך) of the *sons* (בנים)[6] of Israel for ever (43:7a).

[1.] RSV: omitted

[2.] Revelation through action as well as words is evident in Ezekiel 4–5 in the
sign actions the prophet is commanded to perform.

[3.] The man speaks only in 40:4; 40:45–46; 41:4; 41:22; 42:13–14.

[4.] Translation of Hebrew רוח is notoriously difficult. Possibilities here include:
" wind, " "breath, " " spirit, " "the Spirit. "

[5.] Omitted in RSV

The speech is the assertion of a territorial claim to be the power holder of a place. The importance of place is evident. After the address, "Mortal," the speech begins with defining the location. Each clause has a signifier of location: *the* place, *there*, *in the midst*. The place which is there in the midst is the Holy of Holies of the House. The royal language is explicit here. This the place of YHWH's throne, the place where YHWH will be King forever.

The date of the vision is specified by three distinct elements: "the twenty-fifth year of our exile"; "at the beginning of the year on the tenth day of the month"; "the fourteenth year after the city was conquered." Zimmerli has understood the importance of the number twenty-five as a symbolic indication of the year of Jubilee. The twenty-fifth year is the half-way point to the year of release. He notes the importance of twenty-five in various measurements as an indication of the Jubilee.[7] The third date indication refers to the fall of Jerusalem, which makes this date 573 B.C.E.

The significance of the "tenth day of the month" is the date which is most difficult.[8] Eichrodt can find no convincing reason for this terminolo-

---

[6.] RSV: "people of Israel." Translation of this phrase is difficult since it brings to the surface two sometimes conflicting goals. The first is to read the text as it is, as a coherent, consistent whole which is intentionally rhetorical. One component of such reading is to pay attention to repetitions and use of language. The other goal is shaped by contemporary efforts to avoid "exclusive" translations. The difficulty is recognizing when masculine grammatical gender is intended to be gender specific and when it is intended to be gender inclusive, and conveying that in translation in a language such as English which makes few gender distinctions. The Hebrew בני ישראל is grammatically masculine, "the sons of Israel," but here clearly refers to the whole people. However, there is a very good Hebrew word for "people," the Hebrew עם which is used elsewhere in these chapters. To use "people of Israel" here as RSV has done obscures that fact. In Chapter 44, the masculine plural construct בני occurs five times. There, the masculine is clearly intended at least four of the five times. To omit "sons" in translation obscures the repetition of important vocabulary in the text. Since my primary goal is to read the Vision of Transformation as it is, I have chosen to translate בני as "sons" each time it occurs, even where such translation makes the text more "exclusive" than it is.

In addition, the language of "father/son" is an ancient means of defining the relationship between YHWH and Israel (Christopher J. H. Wright, *God's People in God's Land: Family, Land and Property in the Old Testament* (Grand Rapids: William B. Eerdman's Publishing Company, 1990), 15–22).

[7.] "But if the date in 40:1 is understood as the day in the middle of the period of captivity leading up to the great liberation, then the whole system of the temple measurements, whose inner structure is built on the numerals twenty-five, fifty and their multiples, acquires a hidden depth of significance with regard to the occurrence of the great liberation in the 'year of fifty years'" (Zimmerli, vol. 2, 347).

gy, and concludes that the reference must be to the month which was the first month of the year.[9] Blenkinsopp suggests that the tenth day of the first month, according to the Babylonian calendar, would correspond to preparation for Passover."[10] Greenberg suggests the possibility that the date is connected with Yom Kippur.[11] I suggest another possibility.

In Babylonia, the New Year ceremony was the *akitu*. During this annual ceremony, the king renewed his kingship, and "the gods decreed the destinies of mankind."[12] Baruch Halpern describes the variety involved in various New Year ceremonies throughout Mesopotamia. His description of the Babylonian ceremony which enthroned Marduk provides a parallel to the events described in Ezekiel 40–48. In Babylon, the ceremony lasted for several days, involving the arrival of several deities for an assembly, and included a triumphal procession during which the king "took the hand of Marduk" and led him into the *akitu* temple. The significant item in this description is that Marduk takes up residence in the *akitu* temple on the tenth day of the month.[13] On the next day of the ceremony, the gods gather to fix the cosmic order for the coming year.[14] As part of this whole ceremony, the temple is purified.[15]

In a recent study which compares the Book of Ezekiel with the Akkadian "Poem of Erra," Daniel Bodi identifies a common theme of Ancient Near East religious ideology as "the absence of divinity from its shrine."[16] The poem describes the disastrous consequences when Marduk leaves his

---

[8.] "What is strange, however, is the more precise information 'at the beginning of the year on the tenth of the month'...It remains obscure why the beginning of the year should be on the tenth of the month and not the first" (Zimmerli, 345–346).

[9.] Eichrodt, 540–541

[10.] Blenkinsopp, 200.

[11.] Greenberg, "Design," 223.

[12.] Baruch Halpern, *The Constitution of the Monarchy in Israel*, HSM (Chico: Scholars Press, 1981), 52.

[13.] "Sometime thereafter, the king took Marduk's hand, and led him in procession out the Ishtar Gate and across the Euphrates to the...*akitu* temple...On the tenth day, this leads to a banquet, 'when the king of the gods, Marduk, and the gods of heaven and earth take up dwelling in...the house...'" (Halpern, 54).

[14.] "On 11 Nisan, the gods again gathered in the Chamber of Destinies. This was the day of judgment, the day on which cosmic order was fixed for the coming year..." (Halpern, 55).

[15.] "That the temple is purified and exorcised during the festival (rather than before it) indicates that the sanctuary is in a ritual sense being renewed and, perhaps, refounded" (Halpern, 59).

[16.] Daniel Bodi, *The Book of Ezekiel and the Poem of Erra*, Orbis Biblicus et Orientalis (Freiburg: Universitätsverlag, 1991), 215.

shrine. Only when Marduk leaves can Erra, the god of confusion, destroy Babylon and cause the Babylonians to go into exile for seventy years.[17] As long as Marduk dwells in the midst of Babylon, the city is safe.[18] Bodi's comments are particularly relevant for my study of Ezekiel 40–48.

> The theme of 'the Absence of the Divinity from its Shrine' is of central importance for the plot of the Poem of Erra and is crucial for the correct understanding of the Poem. Only when Marduk absents himself from his shrine in Babylon can Erra carry out his destruction. It should be recognized that Marduk leaves his shrine in the first place because of a cultic offense on the part of the Babylonians. They have neglected his statue, implying improper worship. The dissolution of the social and political order is perceived as a consequence of Marduk's absence. Erra symbolizes the forces of destruction and chaos which are unleashed once the restraining power of Marduk's presence is lacking.[19]

Bodi then makes this comparison with the Book of Ezekiel.

> The feature which the Book of Ezekiel shares with the Poem of Erra and with a number of Akkadian texts is that fact that the divinity leaves its shrine because of moral, social, cultural and political offense. Ezek 8 describes the cultic abominations and irregularities committed in the Jerusalem temple. In Ezekiel 9:9 further moral and social crimes are cited as reasons for YHWH's merciless destruction of the population, 'The guilt of the house of Israel and Judah is exceedingly great; the land is full of blood, and the city full of injustice' (cf. also 11:2, 6).[20]

These two themes of "the absence of the divinity from his shrine," and the *akitu* ceremony, provide the structure for the Vision of Transformation. Ezekiel 40–48 is a narrative of the return of YHWH from exile to his shrine, to renew his Kingship and take possession of his House on the tenth day of the New Year ceremony. However, unlike the Babylonian *akitu* ceremony, there is no human king to take the god by the hand and lead him into the house. This god comes alone. This vision is the territorial claim of YHWH as the power holder of the territory, and the renewal of YHWH's claim to kingship.[21]

[17.] Bodi, 205.
[18.] Bodi, 191.
[19.] Bodi, 212–213.
[20.] Bodi, 215.

Power Subjects

Within this territorial scheme, all human beings are power subjects. Since there are three Places, there are three sets of rules of access for the power subjects. In 40:3, the Narrator sees "a man whose appearance was like bronze" standing in the gate. The first role the man plays here is to serve as the gate-keeper of the territory. Whenever the Narrator passes through a gate, he is crossing a boundary. The Narrator is not just following the man. He passes through boundaries only where he is allowed by the gate-keeper/guide.

An indicator of the importance of territorial access is the use of Hiphil verbs of motion to describe the course of the Narrator's tour (הֵשִׂיב, הֵבִיא, הוֹצִיא, הוֹלִיךְ, הֵעֱבִיר, הֵסֵב).[22] The most common meaning of the Hiphil is the causative of the corresponding Qal. However, with intransitive Qal verbs of motion, the Hiphil is usually translated as the simple transitive.[23] For example, Lambdin's possibilities for the Hiphil of בוא are "to bring (take, lead, send) in, to, into." These possibilities indicate two issues. First, the verb בוא is a common verb in Hebrew with a range of meanings. Second, there is a range of options for translating the Hiphil. The Hiphil of בוא occurs thirteen times during the tour. RSV consistently conveys the Hiphil sense as "brought." RSV is less consistent in its understanding of the meaning of בוא, and translates variously as "to," "into," or "through."[24]

Although these translations are lexically and grammatically correct, RSV has missed the territorial significance of the Hiphil of בוא in these chapters. The fundamental issue in territoriality is access. Areas are defined and boundaries communicated in order to control access. In such a

---

[21.] An extremely interesting parallel between the Poem of Erra and the Book of Ezekiel is that neither involves a human king. "In the majority of cases the kings act as the gatherer of the dispersed. Apparently, the motif is part of the royal ideology. In the Book of Ezekiel it is Yahweh who decides and promises to gather the dispersed. Likewise in the Poem of Erra, it is the god Erra who decides and decrees the restoration of the dispersed Babylonians. Here, in our opinion appears a significant link between the Book of Ezekiel and the Poem of Erra" (Bodi, 292–293).

[22.] הֵבִיא 40:2, 3, 4, 17, 28, 32, 48; 41:1; 43:5; 44:4; 46:19. הוֹצִיא 42:1, 15; 46:21; 47:2. הוֹלִיךְ 40:24; 43:1; 47:6. הֵשִׂיב 44:1; 47:1, 6. הֵעֱבִיר 46:21; 47:3, 4, 4. הֵסֵב 47:2.

[23.] See Thomas O. Lambdin, *Introduction to Biblical Hebrew* (New York: Charles Scribner's Sons, 1971), 212.

[24.] "brought me...into" (40:2); "brought me" (40:3); "you were brought" (40:4); "brought me into" (40:17); "brought me to" (40:28); brought me to" (40:32); "brought me to" (40:35); "brought me to" (40:48); "brought me to" (41:1); "brought me to" (42:1); "brought me into" (43:5); "brought me" (44:4); "brought me through" (46: 19).

system, the most important issue concerns authority to cross the boundaries of the territory in order to enter an area. In the Vision of Transformation, the verb which deals with the authority to cross a boundary is the Hiphil form of the verb בוא. This is why nouns and verbs related to the Hebrew root בוא are among the most frequent and important in these chapters. Although the verb בוא has a wide range of meanings, its primary meaning involves the sense of *entering*. However, it is not just a matter of entering; the Hiphil of בוא involves authority to cross a boundary. My translation of the Hiphil of בוא as "cause to enter" looks like the work of a Hebrew beginner. However, this hyperliteral English translation is a deliberate effort to emphasize the territorial importance of this verb. The awkward "he caused me" makes explicit that the whole visionary tour is under the control of someone other than the Narrator. Whenever the Hiphil of בוא is used of the Narrator, he enters an area by crossing a boundary: Israel (40:2, 3, 4); the Outer Court (40:17); the Inner Court (40:28, 32; 43:5; 44:5); the Inner North Gate (40:35); the Vestibule and Nave of the House building (40:48; 41:1); the Priestly Chambers (42:1); the Priestly Cooking Area (46:19). Use of the Hiphil emphasizes the territorial claim involved. Each of these areas is part of YHWH's territory. Access is granted only by YHWH, through YHWH's agent, the bronze-like man. When the Narrator crosses a boundary to enter an area, the verb is בוא. When he crosses a boundary to leave an area, the verb is יצא, again in the Hiphil. He is "caused to go out" from the House building (42:1), the Outer East Gate (42:15), the Cooking Area for the priests (46:21), and the North Gate (47:2).[25]

The other Hiphil verbs of motion (סבב, עבר, שוב, הלך) do not involve crossing boundaries. However, as the Narrator moves from place to place, his route is still under the control of the man. "He caused me" also conveys the sense of these Hiphil verbs. There is little need here to discuss the various translation possibilities of these verbs in the Vision of Transformation. Each conveys a type of motion within an area. The Narrator is "caused to walk" (הוליך) to the South Gate (40:24), the East Gate (43:1), and along the bank of the river (47:6).[26] He is "caused to return" (השיב) to the Outer East Gate (44:1), the opening of the House building (47:1), and along the bank of the river (47:6).[27] He is "caused to pass over" (עבר) to

---

[25.] RSV translates as "led me out" (42:1); "led me out" (42:15), "brought me forth" (46:21); "brought me out" (47:2).

[26.] RSV translates as: "he led me toward" (40:24); "he brought me to" (43:1); "he led me back" (47:6).

[27.] RSV translates: "he brought me back" (44:1); "he brought me back" (47: 1); omits the verb in 47:6.

the four corners of the Outer Court (46:21), and the water (47:3, 4, 4).[28] He is "caused to go around" (הסב) from the Outer South Gate to the Outer East Gate (47:2).[29] The Narrator is allowed to enter every part of the complex except for the Inner Room. In that instance, he waits in the Nave while the man measures the room (41:3–4).[30]

Access of the Priests

Those who have the greatest access within this system are the Zadokite priests. Their access is summarized in 44:15–16.

> …[31]
> *they are the ones who* (המה) shall come near to me (קרב אל)
> to *serve* (שרת) me; and they shall *stand before me* (עמד לפני)
> *to bring near* (הקריב) to me the fat and the blood,
> says YHWH God
> *they are the ones who* (המה) shall enter (בוא) my *holy place* (מקדש),
> and *they are the ones who* (המה) shall *come near to* (קרב אל) my table,
> to *serve* (שרת) me,
> and they shall *guard my guard post* (שמרו את משמרתי) 44:15b-16).

This instruction defines the tasks of the priests according to access rights. The threefold repetition of the pronoun "they" (המה) emphasizes the exclusiveness of this task. The independent personal pronoun is often left untranslated. However, since the finite verb form in Hebrew includes person, number, and gender (if relevant), there must be some significance when the pronoun is used. One of the reasons is emphasis.[32] This seems to be the function for such "unnecessary" pronouns throughout the Vision of Transformation. Where המה is used in this emphatic sense, I have translated as: "they are the ones who…"

Each of the verbs has a technical, territorial meaning in this system. Each function refers to a specific location. In 44:15, the location is the Altar. 44:16 refers to two locations, the Nave of the House and the gates of the Inner Court. קרב אל is translated here as "come near to." The basic meaning of the verb is to "come near." Its cognate adjective is קרוב which means "near." The verb קרב occurs three times here, twice as a Qal with

---

RSV: "led me to" (45:21); "led me through" (47:3, 4, 4).

29. RSV: "led me round" (47:2).

30. Access to the inner room is restricted to Aaron on Yom Kippur in Leviticus 16. In later tradition, only the High Priest had access to this area, and only on the occasion of Yom Kippur.

31. 44:15a will be considered below.

32. Bruce K. Waltke and M. O Connor, *An Introduction to Biblical Hebrew Syntax* (Winona Lake, Indiana: Eisenbrauns, 1990), 293.

the preposition אֶל, and once in the Hiphil without אֶל. The Qal is the active form which means "to come near." The Hiphil is the causative form which means "to bring near."

In the Priestly narratives of the Pentateuch, the laity are allowed to offer their own sacrifices by bringing them to the opening of the Tent of Meeting. However, the actual offering of the sacrifice on the altar is the responsibility of the priests. An example which can serve to represent many others occurs at the beginning of Leviticus.

> When any man of you *brings near* (הקריב) an offering to YHWH,
> you shall *bring near* (הקריב) your offering of cattle from the herd or from the flock.
> If his offering is a burnt offering the herd,
> he shall *bring near* (הקריב) a male without blemish;
> he shall *bring* it *near* (הקריב) to the door (פתח) of the tent of meeting,
> that he may be accepted before YHWH (לפני יהוה).
> he shall lay his hand on the head of the burnt offering,
> and it shall be accepted for him to make atonement (כפר) for him.
> Then he shall kill the bull before YHWH (לפני יהוה);
> and Aaron's sons the priests shall *bring near* (הקריב) the blood,
> and throw the blood round about against the altar that is at the door (פתח) of the tent of meeting.
> And he shall flay the burnt offering and cut it into pieces;
> and the sons of Aaron the priest shall put fire on the altar,
> and lay wood in order upon the fire;
> and Aaron's sons the priests shall lay the pieces, the head, and the fat,
> in order upon the wood that is on the fire upon the altar;
> but its entrails and its legs he shall wash with water.
> And the priest shall burn the whole on the altar,
> as a burnt offering,
> an offering by fire,
> a pleasing odor to YHWH (Levit 1:2b-9).

In this instruction in Leviticus, the location of sacrifice is the opening ("door") of the tent of meeting. This is the location of the altar, identified as "before YHWH." The laity have full access rights to this location, and the right to bring their offerings and do the preparation, including slaughter. However, they are not permitted to offer the sacrifice on the altar. This is the role of the priests, specified as the sons of Aaron.

The Hiphil verb הקריב "bring near" occurs five times in these lines. This is the same verb which occurs in Ezekiel 44:15 for bringing near "the fat and the blood." Jacob Milgrom translates the Qal of קרב אל, as "to have access to" or "be admitted to."[33] He argues that the issue is not prox-

---

[33.] Milgrom, *Leviticus*, 33.

imity to the altar but the right to officiate upon it. However, for the instructions in the Book of Ezekiel, there is little point in arguing this distinction since the territorial arrangement of the Altar in the Vision of Transformation excludes the laity from the Inner Court where the Altar is located. This is a significant change from the wilderness camp of the Priestly narratives where the laity are allowed to approach the altar.

The verb שרת means "to serve." Milgrom states that the verb has multiple meanings in Biblical texts.

> Thus priests "officiate" (in which case the direct object is rarely used) whereas Levites "guard" the Tabernacle and "assist" the laity and the priesthood (the direct object always being used.) In any case, the usual translation "minister" (e.g., Eerdmans, 122f.) is inadequate.[34]

The verb with preposition עמד לפני means "to stand before," which Milgrom notes is the "language of subordination."[35] The location is the Altar, where the priests stand in subordination to YHWH, as YHWH's servants.

44:16 refers to the מקדש or Holy Place. The "table" is the wooden altar in the Nave described in 41:22.

> an altar (מזבח) of wood,
> three cubits high (גבה),
> two cubits long (ארך),[36]
> its corners
> its *length* (ארך),
> and its walls (קיר)
> were of wood.
> He said to me,
> "This is the table which is before YHWH (לפני יהוה)" (41:22).

The function of the table is not specified. In the description of Solomon's temple, there is an incense altar and a table for the Bread of the Presence, both of gold (1 Kings 7:48). In contrast, the item described in Ezekiel 41 is called both an altar and a table, and is made of wood. The significant territorial issue is that this table is located in the Nave where only the priests have access.

My translation of 44:16b is unique and requires explanation. BDB defines the verb שמר as "guard," "keep," "preserve," and the noun משמרת

[34.] Jacob Milgrom, *Studies in Levitical Terminology I: The Encroacher and the Levite: Term Aboda* (Berkeley: University of California Press, 1970), 67.

[35.] Milgrom, *Studies*, 52.

[36.] RSV adds: and two cubits broad

as "guard," "watch," "charge." However, the prefix *mem* often indicates a locative. In several other biblical texts, שָׁמַר מִשְׁמֶרֶת refers to guarding at particular locations.[37] In 2 Kings, Jehoiada arranges with the Carite guards to protect Joash.

> And he commanded them,
> "This is the thing that you shall do:
> one third of you,
> those who come off duty on the sabbath
> and guard (שֹׁמְרֵי מִשְׁמֶרֶת) the king's house
> (another third being at the gate Sur)
> and a third at the gate behind the guards,
> shall guard (שְׁמַרְתֶּם אֶת מִשְׁמֶרֶת) the palace
> and the two divisions of you,
> which come on duty in force on the sabbath
> and guard (שָׁמְרוּ אֶת מִשְׁמֶרֶת) the house of YHWH
> shall surround the king,
> each with his weapons in his hand;
> and whoever approaches the ranks is to be slain.
> Be with the king when he goes out
> and when he comes in (2 Kings 11:4–7).

This text describes armed guards of the king's palace and the temple who are posted at various locations. In 1 Chronicles, the listing of the Levite gatekeepers includes this statement.

> So they and their sons were in charge of the gates of the house of YHWH, that is, the house of the tent, as guards (לְמִשְׁמָרוֹת) (1 Chron 9:23).

In 2 Chronicles, the priests are located at guard posts. "The priests stood at their posts (וְהַכֹּהֲנִים עַל מִשְׁמְרוֹתָם עֹמְדִים) (2 Chron 7:6).
40:45–46 describe two Chambers in the Inner Court for the priests.

> And he said to me,
> "This chamber which faces south is
> for the priests who *guard the guard place of* (שֹׁמְרֵי מִשְׁמֶרֶת) the house,
> and the chamber which faces north is
> for the priests who *guard the guard place of* (שֹׁמְרֵי מִשְׁמֶרֶת) the altar;
> *they are the ones who* (הֵמָּה)[38] are the sons of Zadok
> who alone among the sons of Levi
> may come near to (קָרֵב אֶל) YHWH serve (שָׁרַת) him (40:45–46).

[37.] Milgrom argues that the original meaning of מִשְׁמֶרֶת is "watch post" (Milgrom, *Studies*, 9).

[38.] RSV: these

This language refers to two groups of priests. The same differentiation between priestly responsibilities is used in Numbers 18:5:

> and you shall שמרתם את משמרת of the *holy place*
> and the משמרת duties of the altar...[39]

Many commentators have assumed that the two groups here are the Levites and the Zadokites. In 44:10–14, the Levites are identified as guards of
the House. In 44:13, the language is explicit that the Levites are not to be
priests. Therefore, Zimmerli assumes that 40:45–46 reflect an earlier stage
in Israel's history when Levites were priests. The situation in 44:13 is therefore "diminution of the rights" of the Levites.[40] This whole matter of the
so-called "demotion" of the Levites will be considered below.

Milgrom argues that the problem here is that "house" (בית) has both
"broad and narrow use" in Ezekiel 40–48 either as the "Temple Area" or as
the "Temple building." Here in 40:45–46, בית refers to the temple building;
in 44:14, בית refers to the whole temple area. In 40:45–46, both groups
must be priests, since only priests have access to the Inner Court.[41]

If this text is not about Zadokites and Levites, it indicates the existence
of two priestly groups, one which guards the Altar and one which guards
the house. This raises the possibility that the power issue involved is the
assertion of power by the Zadokites over other priests. The new practice is
a differentiation among the priests which did not exist before. The Zadokites have access to the Altar; the rest of the priests guard the Inner Court
and the House building.

The question for translation is whether both can be translated in a locative sense as "guard the guard post." My speculation is that the Chambers themselves are the guard posts. There is no other function given for
these two Chambers in the Inner Court. They are not the Priestly Chambers described 42:13–14, where the priests eat the offerings and change
their vestments. It is difficult to imagine what other function such structures in that location could have except to serve as places to guard the holiness of the Altar and House building. Therefore, I translate both
occurrences as "guard the guard place."

42:13–14 describe some Chambers for the priests.

> Then he said to me,
> "The north chambers and the south chambers
> opposite the *restricted area* (גזרה)
> *they are the ones which* (הנה)[42] are the holy chambers

[39.] RSV: attend to the duties of the sanctuary and the duties of the altar
[40.] Zimmerli, vol. 2, 458.
[41.] Milgrom, *Studies*, 14.

where the priests who approach (קרב ל) YHWH
shall eat *there* (שׁם) the most holy offerings;
there (שׁם) they shall put (נוח) the most holy offerings—
the cereal offering,
the purification offering,
and the reparation offering,
for the place (מקום) is holy.
When the priests enter (בוא),
they shall not go out (יצא) from the *Holy Area* (הקדשׁ) into the outer court
without laying (נוח) there (שׁם)
the garments in which they *serve* (שׁרת),
for *they are the ones which* (הנה) are holy;
they shall put on other garments
before they go near (קרב אל) that which is for the people" (42:13–14).

This speech concerns access to two rooms set apart within the holy area for the priests. Access to these rooms is restricted to those who have access to YHWH. The territorial claim is that this area is necessary to contain the contagious holiness of the priests, their clothing, and the most holy offerings.

Two important words in the Vision of Transformation are the adverb "there" (שׁם) and the third person plural independent personal pronoun ("they") (הנה/המה). In translation from Hebrew to English, שׁם is not always translated, especially when used in conjunction with the אשׁר in which שׁם is used resumptively.[43] This is the situation in the phrase, "where (אשׁר) the priests who have access to YHWH shall eat *there* (שׁם)." My translation is intended to emphasize the locative adverb. The adverb is used three times in these lines. Each indicates a particular relationship between location, function, and social role. The priests will eat *there*; the most holy offerings are to be put *there*; the priestly garments are to be put *there*. The third person feminine plural pronoun הנה is used emphatically twice, to emphasize the holiness of the rooms and the garments.

In addition to these territorial rights and responsibilities, the priests are entrusted with some additional responsibilities.

They shall teach my people the difference
between the holy (קדשׁ) and the common (חל),
and show them how to distinguish
between the *impure* (טמא) and the *pure* (טמא)
In a controversy *they are the ones who* (המה) shall *stand* (עמד) *to judge* (שׁפט),

---

[42.] Omitted in RSV
[43.] See Waltke and O Connor, 334.

and they shall judge it (שפט) according to my judgments (שפט).
and my instructions (תורה)
and my *ordinances* (חקה)
in all my appointed feasts (מועד)
and they shall keep (שמר) my sabbaths holy (קדש) (44:23–24).

The basic function of the priests is to teach distinctions. Gorman's summary of this priestly responsibility locates this teaching of distinctions in relation to holy place, society, and cosmos, and the themes of space, time, and status.

> The separation of conceptual categories focuses on three areas in the Priestly ritual material—space, time, and status—and Priestly ritual functions within the context of clearly defined and demarcated categories of space, time, and status. Each of these conceptual categories is given concrete expression through a foundational image of separation: space in the separation of the holy of holies from all other areas; time in the separation of the Sabbath from all other days; status in the separation of the priests from all other persons. Each of these is said to be 'set apart' and categorically distinct by the Priestly traditionists. Thus, the central conceptual element of the Priestly world view that is present in the cosmological, existential, and praxeological elements of that world view, and is operative within the framework of the cosmological, societal, and cultic orders, is the idea that order is established through the careful observation of categorical divisions, through the recognition and maintenance of boundaries.[44]

This ideology of separation between categories which Gorman describes for the Priestly material is the same ideology of separation which is evident in the Book of Ezekiel.

The ideology of separation is also evident in the description of the place where the priests cook the most holy offerings. The Narrator is "caused to enter" into another area reserved for the priests

> Then he *caused me to enter* (בוא) through the entrance (מבוא),
> which was at the side (כתף) of the gate,
> to the north row of the holy (קדש) chambers (לשכה) for the priests
> and there (שם) I saw a place (מקום) at the extreme western end of them.
> This is the place where the priests shall boil *there* (שם)
> the reparation offering
> and the purification offering,
> and where they shall bake the cereal offering,

---

44. Gorman, 44–45.

in order not to bring them out (יצא) into the outer court
and so communicate holiness (לקדש) to the people (46:19–20).

Access of the Levites

In the territorial hierarchy of the Holy Place, the Levites are secondary clergy. Most scholars understand that the material in Chapter 44 "demotes" the Levites from being priests to this subordinate status, an assumption that I shall address below. Here, my discussion is focused on the Levites' territorial access. These instructions grant them access to some areas and deny them access to others. 44:11 and 44:14 specify their particular territorial roles.

> They shall be in my *holy place* (מקדש)
> *serving* (משרתים) *as armed guards* (פקדות) at the gates of the house (בית),
> and serving (משרתים) in the house (בית);
> *they are the ones who* (המה) shall slay the burnt offering (עולה)
> and the sacrifice (זבח) for the people,
> *they are the ones who* (המה) shall *stand* (עמד) *before them* (לפני),
> to serve (שרת) them.
> …
> Yet I will appoint them
> as *guards of the guard places* (שמרי משמרת) of the house (בית),
> to do all its *work* (עבדה)
> and all which is to be done (עשה) in it (44:11;14).

Just as the instructions for the priests were expressed in technical territorial language, these instructions for the Levites use technical language which locates their specific territorial access rights and responsibilities. In order to consider access rights, some preliminary matters of definition and syntax must be clarified. First, one of the sources of confusion concerning social roles in these chapters is the fluid use of language. בית ("House") in some instances refers to the whole temple complex; in other instances, it refers only to the House building itself.[45] מקדש ("Holy Place") has a similar range of meaning. In some instances, מקדש refers to the whole complex; in others it refers to the inner precincts.[46] Both מקדש and בית in these lines refer to the whole House complex rather than the House building.

[45.] בית (40:5, 7, 9, 45, 47, 48; 41:5, 5, 6, 6, 7, 7, 8, 9, 9, 10, 12, 13; 41:14, 15, 16, 17, 19, 26; 42:15; 43: 4, 5, 6, 10, 11, 12, 12, 21: 44:4, 4, 5, 5, 11, 11, 14, 14, 17: 45:5, 19, 20, 46:24, 47:1, 1, 1, 1, 1: 48:21).

[46.] מקדש (43:21; 44:1, 5, 7, 8, 9, 11, 15, 16; 45: 3, 4, 4, 4, 5; 47:12; 48: 8, 10, 21). Milgrom argues that מקדש never refers to the building in either Ezekiel or P (Milgrom, *Studies*, 23–24).

The root שׁרת occurs here once as a finite verb and twice as a participle. The construction מְשָׁרְתִים פְּקֻדוֹת deserves comment. It is composed of a Piel participle (מְשָׁרְתִים) and a feminine plural noun (פְּקֻדוֹת).[47] פְּקֻדוֹת occurs elsewhere in the Book of Ezekiel only in 9:1 to describe the armed men who go through the city to kill everyone without the mark on their foreheads. There, RSV translates as "executioners." In my earlier discussion of שָׁמַר מִשְׁמֶרֶת, I cited the episode in 2 Kings 11 concerning Jehoiada and the Carite guards.[48] In the same episode, the priest sets פְּקֻדוֹת in the house, which RSV translates as "watchmen" (2 Kings 11:18). The clear implication is that these are armed guards.[49] Most translators separate פְּקֻדוֹת from מְשָׁרְתִים. RSV treats the participle as a predicate nominative to read: "They shall be ministers (מְשָׁרְתִים) in my sanctuary. " פְּקֻדוֹת is then translated in a separate clause: "Having oversight (פְּקֻדוֹת) at the gates of the temple." However, the MT accentual system treats מְשָׁרְתִים פְּקֻדוֹת as a unit by use of the conjunctive accent, the מוּנַח. The disjunctive accent פַּשְׁטָה separates פְּקֻדוֹת from מְשָׁרְתִים.[50] In addition, RSV translates the first participle as a substantive and the second as a predicate. In my translation, both participles are treated as predicates. In my discussion of 44:16b, I discussed the translation of מִשְׁמֶרֶת as guard place. Here, the noun occurs in a construct chain with the participle of שָׁמַר, translated here as a substantive.

The verb עמד with the preposition לִפְנֵי means "stand before." RSV has translated as "attend" which does not convey the locative sense. The text does not specify exactly what form this service takes. However, the Levites serve the people by slaughtering their offerings and then cooking these offerings for them. "Service" would then refer to the whole process involved in doing these cultic tasks for the people.

The last technical term is the word עֲבֹדָה, which occurs in the Vision of Transformation only here.[51] In his study of P, Milgrom argues that it refers to the physical work required of the Levites to set up, take down, and

---

[47.] For the use of feminine gender nouns as collectives, see Waltke and O'Connor, 105. For the use of the feminine plural פְּקֻדוֹת as an example of Late Biblical Hebrew, see Mark F. Rooker, *Biblical Hebrew in Transition: The Language of the Book of Ezekiel*, JSOTSup, no. 90 (Sheffield: JSOT Press, 1990), 77.

[48.] I note in passing that the Carites are foreign guards. See *IDB*, s. v. "Cherethites and Pelethites," by J. C. Greenfield.

[49.] See Milgrom, *Studies*, 84.

[50.] I refer to the accents here cautiously and with awareness that use of the accentual system as an indication of syntax is an endeavor full of difficulty. See William Wickes, *Two Treatises on the Accentuation of the Old Testament* (New York: KTAV Publishing House, 1970), 3. However, in this instance, phrasing according to the accents enhances the understanding of the text.

move the tabernacle.[52] Such transport service is not necessary in a stationary cultic complex, but it is easy to imagine that the ongoing functioning of the House would require substantial amounts of physical labor. Since the focus of the Rhetor is on territorial issues, such details are left unspecified.

According to this understanding of the technical language and syntax of 44:11 and 14, the Levites are those who are "*in* my Holy Place" (במקדשי). The emphasis is on their location in the House, referring to the whole complex. They have two roles: to be guards and to "serve." The guarding function is primary and occurs "in the gates" and in the "guard places of the House complex." The second function is to "serve." The beneficiaries of this service are the people. The Levites stand before the people to serve them. It is significant that these instructions use the personal pronoun המה for emphasis twice. The Levites slaughter the animal offerings and the Levites cook the portions offerings for the people. These functions are located in particular areas of the House complex. Both areas were discussed earlier. The slaughtering occurs in the Inner North Gate (40:38–43) and the cooking in the corners of the Outer Court (46:21–24).

The territorial access of the Levites is also restricted.

> But they shall not *draw near* (נגש אל) me
> to serve me as priest (לכהן),
> nor *draw near* (נגש) any of my *holy* things/*holy areas* (קדשי)
> and the things that are *most holy/Holy of Holies* (קדש קדשים) (44:13a).

The fluidity and multivalence of the language of the Vision of Transformation are also evident here, and are indicated by giving two options for translation. The phrase קדשים קדש, with or without the definite article and with or without the possessive suffix occurs six times in the Vision of Transformation.[53] In these other occurrences, context makes clear what is intended by the phrase. However, the phrase in 44:13a can not be so easily defined. Perhaps that is the point. Any place or thing which is defined as

---

[51.] The cognate noun העבד ("worker") and verb יעבדוהו ("shall work it") occur in 48:19.

[52.] "...Levitic עבדה never veers from its root meaning of 'physical labor,' and that within that range it can refer to (1) physical labor, in general; (2) the job of moving the Tabernacle, in particular; and (3) a portion of this job, either (a) to dismantle and reassemble the Tabernacle or (b) to transport it" (Milgrom, *Studies*, 61).

[53.] קדש הקדשים refers to the inner room of the House of YHWH (41:4); הקדשים קדש occurs twice in 42:13 to refer to the offerings which the priests eat; קדשים קדש in 43:12 refers to the whole territory on the top of the mountain; קדשים קדש in 45:3 refers to YHWH's Portion in the Portion of the land; קדש קדשים in 48:12 refers to the Special Portion of the Portion for the priests.

"most holy" is off-limits to the Levites, whether it is access to the Altar or the offerings.[54] The Levites are not allowed to serve as priests. The contrast between the territorial access of the priests and the Levites is explicit. The priests stand before YHWH; the Levites stand before the people. The priests guard the guard places of the House building and the Altar; the Levites guard the gates. The priests have access to the Inner Court; the Levites guard the gates of the Inner Court and slaughter and prepare the offerings in the Inner North Gate, but they do not cross the boundary of the gate to enter the Inner Court. The priests come near the Altar; the Levites do not approach. The priests eat the most holy offerings; there is no mention of offerings for the Levites.

The "Demotion" of the Levites

There are three categories of access rights to the House of YHWH. The priests have access to the Inner Court, House building, and Priestly Chambers. The Levites have access to the gates of the Inner Court, but are not permitted to enter the Inner Court. The laity have access only to the Outer Court. (The territorial access of the Nasi will be considered below.) I turn now to the question, Does Ezekiel 44 demote the Levites from priestly to non-priestly status? The assumption that it does can be traced to Wellhausen's Documentary Hypothesis, a brilliant synthesis covering a wide range of texts and topics.[55] Wellhausen's exegesis of Ezekiel 44 was an important piece of evidence for two related assertions. The first concerns the historical development of the Levitical priesthood. Wellhausen argued that the Levites were originally priests of the tribe of Levi. However, the Zadokites were not originally Levites. They not only usurped the priesthood from the Levites, but they also claimed Levitical origin. The second argument concerns the order of composition of the Pentateuchal sources. Wellhausen's exegesis of Ezekiel argues that D was pre-exilic and P exilic, with the Book of Ezekiel written between D and P.[56]

This brief summary of Wellhausen's arguments leads to some preliminary comments. The first is that there is a great deal riding on the exegesis

---

[54.] The same fluidity of meaning is evident in other Priestly writing. See Menahem Haran, *Temples and Temple-Service in Ancient Israel: An Inquiry into the Character of Cult Phenomena and the Historical Setting of the Priestly School* (Oxford: Clarendon Press, 1978), 172.

[55.] Julius Wellhausen, *Prolegomena to the History of Ancient Israel*, trans. J. S. Black and A. Menzies, Preface by W. Robertson Smith (New York: Meridian Library, 1957).

[56.] Wellhausen, 121–151.

of Ezekiel 44. The relationships between the Pentateuchal sources and the history of the priesthood in Israel are enormously complex, controverted, difficult issues, issues about which scholars have had, and continue to have, strong opinions. The second comment concerns method. Wellhausen's exegesis of Ezekiel 44 depends on his exegesis of numerous other texts from other Biblical books, particularly Deuteronomy 18:6–8 and 2 Kings 23:8–9. An adequate evaluation of his exegesis of Ezekiel 44 would also require an evaluation of his exegesis of these other texts.

The influence of Wellhausen's Documentary Hypothesis continues to be felt in biblical scholarship, and is particularly evident in exegesis of Ezekiel 40–48. Although much of Wellhausen's synthesis has been disputed and denied, the notion of Zadokite demotion of the Levites continues as the majority opinion in critical scholarship.[57] There have also been a few dissenting voices.[58]

My goal is to read Ezekiel 44 as an intentionally rhetorical text, without attempting to resolve either of these long-standing issues concerning the priesthood and the development of the Pentateuch. What are the exegetical issues which have resulted in this long-standing consensus concerning Levitical demotion? Above, I considered only 44:11, 13a, 14. I now turn to the rest of the material concerning the Levites by beginning with the RSV translation of these texts.

> But the Levites who went far (רחק) from me,
> going astray (תעה) from me after their idols
> when Israel went astray (תעה),
> shall bear (נשׂא) their punishment (עון).
> …
> Because they ministered (שרת) to them before their idols
> and became a stumbling block of iniquity (מכשול עון) to the House of Israel,
> therefore I have sworn (נשׂא יד) concerning them (עליהם),

[57.] For a representative sample, see: Aelred Cody, *A History of the Old Testament Priesthood* (Rome: Pontifical Biblical Institute, 1969), 166–168; Haran, 99–111; Nigel Allan, "The Identity of the Jerusalem Priesthood During the Exile," *HeyJ* 23 (1982): 259–69; Jonathan Smith, *To Take Place*, 62–63; Cooke, 480–481; Eichrodt, 564–566; Klein, 178; Blenkinsopp, 219; Zimmerli, vol. 2, 456–463; Greenberg, "Design," 227.

[58.] Rodney K. Duke, "Punishment or Restoration? Another Look at the Levites of Ezekiel 44.6–16," *JSOT* 40 (1988): 61–81; J. Gordon McConville, "Priests and Levites in Israel: A Crux in the Interpretation of Israel's History," *TynBul* 34 (1983):3-31; Raymond Abba, "Priests and Levites in Ezekiel," *VT* 28 (1978): 1–9; Rodney K. Duke, "The Portion of the Levite: Another Reading of Deuteronomy 18:6–8," *JBL* 106 (1987): 193–201; Milgrom, *Studies*, 14; J. G. McConville, *Law and Theology in Deuteronomy*, JSOTSup, no. 33 (Sheffield: JSOT Press, 1984),124–153.

says the YHWH God,
that they shall bear (נשׂא) their punishment (עון).
...
but they shall bear (נשׂא) their shame (כלם),
because of the abominations which they have committed (עשׂה)
(44:10;12;13b) (RSV).

Read this way, this is a strong indictment of the Levites. The *Levites* went astray after *their* idols. They were the stumbling block to the House of Israel. *They* shall bear *their* punishment because of the abominations which *they* have committed. YHWH has sworn concerning *them*.

However, this indictment of the Levites does justice neither to the MT text nor the Levites. Working under the influence of the Wellhausen paradigm, the RSV has stacked the deck against the Levites by several exegetical decisions concerning two difficulties with the text. The first is that the MT text is hardly a model of clarity with its third person pronouns and suffixes. "*They* served *them* before *their* idols." "*They* shall bear *their* punishment." "I have sworn concerning *them*." Do all of the third person forms here refer to the Levites? Do some of them refer to the Levites and some to other referents? If so, what are the referents? Wellhausen's exegesis assumes that all refer to the Levites: the idols; the punishment; and the shame. The Levites are being demoted to a subordinate status since the Levites went astray after the Levites' idols. The second reason for misunderstanding this text is that this text uses technical language for the Levites' cultic role which Wellhausen, and the scholars who have followed Wellhausen's analysis, have read as the language of punishment against the Levites.

Is the language of punishment appropriate in this context? Once again, the genre issue is primary. Zimmerli's form critical treatment of 44:6–31 is an instructive example of the relationship between genre assumption and interpretation. He begins his form critical analysis by noting the "rather complex structure" of the unit. He assumes that the genre of the unit is the two-part prophetic oracle of judgment composed of a "motivating reproach" followed by a "declaration of judgment.[59] The unit begins in 44:6 with the expected messenger formula כה אמר אדני יהוה ("thus says YHWH God"). The motivating reproach or "invective" is signalled by the phrase רב לכם ("enough for you"). Zimmerli sees the expected introduction of the declaration of judgment by reading לכן ("therefore") instead of לכם ("for you") at the end of 44:8. However, "instead of the expected statement of judgment or punishment," 44:9 is "a legal regulation which gives no hint of any punishment which must befall

---

[59] Zimmerli,vol.1, 235.

the house of Israel who were addressed in the invective." However, the element of punishment "suddenly appears" in 44:10–14 with a double statement of the motivation for reproach. According to this analysis, 44:10a is the motivation for reproach which describes the Levites' sin and 44:10b, 11 announce the punishment. The second motivation for reproach begins with the יען ("because") clause in 44:12a. 44:12b–14 are another declaration of punishment against the Levites. Zimmerli argues that this section demonstrates a "unique" and "uncontrolled use" of the יען formula. One more deviation from the customary judgment oracle formula is that the declaration of punishment against the Levites is followed by the "declaration of reward" for the Zadokites in 44:15–16. On the basis of this genre analysis, Zimmerli analyzes 44:6–16 as a "homologous section" which was "composed as a unit," but which is substantially different from a "genuine, prophetic declaration of punishment." A genuine declaration of punishment announces a historical act of punishment, but here, "the threat of punishment is in the form of a cultic prescription which is to be observed in the future."[60]

There are two fundamental problems with Zimmerli's analysis, one acknowledged by Zimmerli himself, and one which he does not recognize. The first is that this material does not fit the criteria of a judgment oracle. In two places, he expresses surprise that what follows the motivation for reproach is not the announcement of a historical act of punishment, but a "legal regulation" or a "cultic prescription." He also notes with surprise, but does not explain, that this unit which begins with the motivation for reproach against the House of Israel results in the purported punishment of the Levites.

Despite Zimmerli's efforts to pound the square peg of the text into the round hole of the form here, the basic problem is not the failure of the text to follow the form of a judgment oracle, but his genre assumption. The messenger formula "thus says YHWH God" (כה אמר אדני יהוה) in the Vision of Transformation does not necessarily introduce a judgment. It is used in 43:18; 44:6 and 44:9; 46:1 and 46:16; 47:13 to introduce a command or regulation, rather than a punishment. There is more flexibility in the use of the formula than Zimmerli allows.[61]

In rhetorical, rather than form critical categories, the difference between declaring punishment for past action and prescribing a regulation for the future is the difference between *legal* and *political* rhetoric.[62] Legal rhetoric is focused on the past. It concerns charges of wrongdoing, directed at persons or groups. The goal of legal rhetoric is to vindicate or convict

---

[60.] Zimmerli, vol. 2, 452–453.
[61.] See Duke, "Punishment," 67.

individuals, or groups, not society as a whole. In contrast, political rhetoric is focused on the future. Political rhetoric is used in accordance with the basic meaning of the word *politics* which refers to the regulation and control of society. Contemporary discourse has tended to narrow the concept of politics to the actions of self-interested individuals or groups. In its basic sense, however, political rhetoric refers to persuasion about the society as a whole.[63] According to Zimmerli's own analysis, he has described political rather than legal rhetoric. The access rights and restrictions described in Chapter 44 describe the regulations for the future society, not future punishment for past wrongdoing.

What then of the specific language of punishment in 44:10–14? Understanding this language is the second fundamental problem with Zimmerli's genre analysis, a problem which he does not recognize. The phrase עון נשא is composed of two words, each with a range of possible translations. עון means "iniquity," "guilt," or "punishment." The verb נשא means "lift," "bear," "carry," "take." If the variable of the verb is kept constant, the potential for translation is: "bear iniquity"; "bear guilt"; "bear punishment." These three phrases have different connotations in English. The difficulty for translation is to understand the connotation intended at a particular point by the Hebrew. Discussions of Ezekiel 44 tend to use the language of punishment, consistent with the consensus understanding that this is legal language which demotes the Levites. Zimmerli relates the phrase to an Assyrian legal formula which means "to bring offense upon oneself, to make oneself punishable."[64] What he does not do is relate the phrase to the technical cultic language about Levite guards in the P material of the Old Testament.

This language in P is the response to the Korah episode in Numbers 16–18 in which a Levite guard encroached on a priestly function by offering incense. The response to this trespass made the people afraid to approach the holy place. The solution was to make the priests and Levites responsible for all future encroachments. This responsibility to prevent territorial violation is expressed in the phrase, עון נשא.

> So YHWH said to Aaron,
> "You and your sons and your fathers' house with you
> shall bear iniquity (עון נשא) in connection with the sanctuary;

---

[62] There is considerable variety in the terminology used in various rhetoric textbooks to describe these two genres. Legal rhetoric is also called *forensic* or *judicial*. *Political* rhetoric is also called *deliberative, hortative,* or *advisory.*

[63] Edward P. J. Corbett, *Classical Rhetoric for the Modern Student.* 3d ed (New York: Oxford University Press, 1965 <1990>), 28.

[64] Zimmerli, vol. 1, 305.

and you and your sons with you shall bear iniquity (עָוֹן נָשָׂא) in connection with your priesthood.

...

But the Levites shall do the service of the tent of meeting,
and they shall bear their iniquity (עָוֹן נָשָׂא);
it shall be a perpetual statute throughout your generations;
and among the people of Israel
they shall have no inheritance (Num 18:1;23).

Here, RSV has translated the phrase as "bear iniquity" in each of its three occurrences. In his discussion of this material, Milgrom uses the language of "guilt" and "punishment." The Levite guards are given authority to kill anyone who attempts to violate the territorial role restrictions of the holy place.[65] The reason for this solution was to protect the well-being of the community because such intrusion into the holy place threatens the well-being of the whole community. This gives to the Levite guards a military function to kill any enemy who threatens the life of the community. This solution removes the threat to the community by making the Levites responsible. Only the Levites will be punished for trespass, not the whole people, וְהֵם יִשְׂאוּ עֲוֹנָם ("they (the Levites) will bear their guilt"). The question remains about the referent of the possessive in *their* guilt. Milgrom identifies the traditional exegesis as "the Levites shall bear their own guilt." He rejects this exegesis on the basis of the Levites' unique role in Israel. Instead, he argues for the exegesis that "the Levites shall bear Israel's guilt." The Levites function as a "lightening rod to attract God's wrath upon themselves" for Israel's guilt of trespass.[66]

In the Vision of Transformation, the same priestly language is used to describe the guarding function of the Levites. Violation of territoriality is the responsibility of the Levites because it is their responsibility to prevent such violation for the well-being of the whole House of Israel. This explains why the address to the House of Israel involves the assertion of the Levites' territorial role. 44:10–14 is not legal rhetoric which punishes the Levites for their own past actions, but political rhetoric which is concerned about the future well-being of the society. (It is surely significant that the role of the Narrator is also to נָשָׂא עָוֹן for Israel (4:5). I know of no commentator who takes this as evidence that the Narrator is being punished for his own guilt.)

There is a second phrase in Ezekiel 44:13 which has not received as much attention. The Levites are also to נָשָׂא כְלִמָּה, "to bear shame. " The apparent tendency in exegesis of this text is to treat "shame" as a synonym

---

[65.] See Numbers 18:7b; Milgrom, *Studies*, 21.
[66.] Milgrom, *Studies*, 31.

for "guilt." However, Margaret Odell argues that the meaning of "shame" in the Old Testament "has little to do with an internal experience of unworthiness," but is instead "associated with a loss of status."[67] Experiences of shame involve assigning blame for whatever caused this loss of status. The significant issue she identifies is that shame is often the result of the actions of others.

> Thus, although one can come to shame as a result of her own failed risk (cf. Num 12:14), some biblical passages suggest that people can experience shame as a result of what others do or fail to do. The types of situation in which one might come to shame as a result of others' actions involve pledging loyalty to another in exchange for recognition, protection or security (Judg 18:7; 1 Sam 25:7, 15). In these latter situations, the person who experiences shame is the one whose loyalty proves to have been ill founded.[68]

According to this understanding, the phrase נשא כלם, "to bear shame," also does not refer to the Levites' responsibility, but to their cultic role as the ones who experience the effects of Israel's territorial violation. This meaning is consistent with the phrase נשא עון in P which made the Levites responsible for the territorial trespass of others.[69]

Another reason for reading these lines as judgment against the Levites is the expression in 44:12: נשאתי ידי עליהם which RSV has translated "I have sworn against them." More literally, it means, "I have lifted my hand against them." It is the same verb as in the technical phrase נשא עון. Since the construction נשא יד על occurs nowhere else in the Old Testament, the exact meaning is not clear.[70] However, the form of the verb is a perfect without a preceding *waw*, which implies a completed action in the past. In contrast, the tense of the verb with the *waw* in the construction נשא עון refers to the future. If the phrase נשאתי ידל עליהם refers to an act of judgmeet, it is an action which has occurred in the past, not the promise of an action in the future. This is another piece of evidence that the rhetorical genre is political rather than legal. In the context of the Book of Ezekiel, the act of judgment which YHWH took against Israel was the exile, an act which has already occurred.[71] In the context of the Book of Ezekiel, these

---

[67] Margaret S. Odell, "The Inversion of Shame and Forgiveness in Ezekiel 16:59–63," *JSOT* 56 (1992): 103.

[68] Odell, 104.

[69] It is also consistent with the meaning Zimmerli identifies for the Assyrian legal formula, "to bring offense upon oneself, to make oneself punishable."

[70] See the discussion in Duke, "Punishment," 69.

instructions come as a promise of a transformed future after the period of judgment is over. To read these instructions as legal rhetoric, promising additional judgment against the Levites, is inappropriate in the context of 40–48.

This expression too has the same ambiguity of third person forms which has complicated interpretation of this chapter. Who is the "them" of the phrase, "I have lifted my hand against them"? This raises yet another question. Who, or what, is "the stumbling block"? According to RSV's translation, the Levites are the stumbling block. However, the MT word order is more ambiguous.

> because they ministered (שרת) to them before (לפני) their idols
> and *they were* (והיו) to the House of Israel
> a stumbling block of *guilt* (מכשול עון),
> therefore I have *lifted up my hand against them* (נשאתי ידי עליהם),
> says YHWH God,
> that they shall bear (נשא) their *guilt* (עון) (44:12).

The question here is the referent of the verb והיו. RSV makes the Levites the subject of both clauses and thereby identifies the Levites as the stumbling block. Although the consensus of scholarship is that the Levites are the stumbling block, the verb והיו occurs immediately after the noun "idols." This MT word order suggests the possibility that the idols are the subject of והיו ("and they were") rather than the Levites. In addition, the word מכשול ("stumbling block") is used in construct with עון ("guilt") (or "iniquity" or "punishment") six times in the Book of Ezekiel.[72] In each other occurrence, the "stumbling block of guilt" clearly refers to idols. According to this possibility, the Levites "served them [the House of Israel] before their [the House of Israel's] idols and they [the idols] were to the House of Israel a stumbling block of guilt" (or "iniquity" or "punishment").

RSV has made some other exegetical choices which have focused blame on the Levites. In 44:10, RSV has translated the verb רחקו as an active verb rather than a stative. The verb רחק has a stative meaning, related to the adjective רחוק which means *far* or *distant*. Rather than translate the verb with a stative meaning, *be far*, the RSV has made the verb active by translating, *went far*, which makes the location of the Levites the result of Levite choice. The RSV has also reversed the order of two phrases so that the burden of guilt is placed on the Levites. The RSV has translated 44:10 as: "But the Levites who went far from me, going astray from me after their

---

71. See Duke, "Punishment," 71.
72. 7:19; 14:3, 4, 7; 18:30; 44:12.

idols when Israel went astray, shall bear their punishment." This incriminating translation has the Levites actively going far away and going astray after their idols. As a result, the Levites will be punished. However, the Hebrew word order places the responsibility on Israel rather than the Levites.

> But the Levites who *were* far (רחק) from me,
> when Israel went astray (תעה),
> going astray (תעה) from me after their idols
> shall bear (נשא) their *guilt* (עון) (44:10).

In the MT order, Israel went astray after Israel's idols. It was Israel which did the going astray. Admittedly, the text still reads "their idols" but the Hebrew word order indicates that these idols belonged to Israel as a whole, rather than to the Levites.

In addition to these misinterpretations of the MT text, the Wellhausian notion that the text is about the demotion of the Levites has had another result. By making the Levites the focus, Wellhausen, and those who have followed his interpretation, have obscured the actual rhetorical intention of the text. The intended audience of the speech is not the Levites but the House of Israel. There are several syntactic signals which indicate that the rhetorical purpose of the text is contrast rather than judgment. The contrast is between the past territorial practices of Israel and the new territorial practices commanded by YHWH in the transformed Holy Place. The first is the translation of the verbs. My translation of the perfect verbs uses the English simple past tense, referring to past practice, rather than RSV's English present perfect and present tenses which imply current practice: "when you brought near" rather than "when you offer"; "they broke" rather than "you have broken";[73] "you did not guard" rather than "you have not kept charge"; "you set" rather than "you have set."

Another clue to the translation of 44:10 is the conjunction כי אם. RSV has translated as the simple adversative, "but." However, כי אם after a negative clause indicates restriction and is better translated as "rather."[74] The intention of the text is to set up a contrast. Rather than past practice which placed foreign guards in the Holy Place, the House of Israel will have Levites as guards in the Holy Place. This intention to make a contrast also explains the purpose of לכם at the end of 44:8, which RSV reads as לכן ("therefore") in accordance with the LXX, and in accordance with the assumption that the issue is judgment against the Levites rather than contrast with the past practice of the House of Israel which used foreign

---

[73.] RSV reads "you" with the Greek rather than MT "they."
[74.] Waltke and O'Connor, 671. See also Duke, "Punishment," 65.

guards. According to the MT, the House of Israel used the foreign guards "for you," a task which Israel was supposed to do for itself by using "sons of Israel" rather than "sons of foreigners."

There is also a contrast within the instructions for the Levites between the particular access rights of the Levites and their particular access restrictions. The switch between access and non-access is signalled by the use of the disjunctive *waw,* at the beginning of 44:13 and 44:14. RSV, with its presumption of Levite demotion, treats all of this material as statements of restriction, and thus leaves the first disjunctive *waw* untranslated in 44:13. 44:10–12 concern Levite access; 44:13 concerns Levite restriction; 44:14 restates Levite access. For consistency, I have translated each disjunctive *waw* as "but."

> access:
> *Rather,* the Levites who were far from me,
> when Israel went astray
> going astray from me after their idols
> shall bear their guilt.
> They shall be in my Holy Place
> serving as armed guards at the gates of the house,
> and serving in the house;
> *they are the ones who* shall slay the burnt offering
> and the sacrifice for the people,
> and *they are the ones who* shall stand before them,
> to serve them.
> because they served them before their idols
> and they were to the House of Israel
> a stumbling block of iniquity,
> therefore I have lifted up my hand against them,
> says YHWH God,
> and they shall bear their guilt (44:10–12).

> restriction:
> *But* they shall not approach me,
> to serve me as priest,
> nor approach any of my holy things/holy areas
> and the things that are most holy/Holy of Holies
> And they shall bear their shame and their abominations
> which they have done (44:13).

> access:
> *But* I will appoint them
> as guards of the guard places of the house,
> to do all its work
> and all which is to be done in it (44:14).

Another contrast is the emphatic use of the pronoun "they" (המה) two times in 44:11. If it were just a matter of listing their responsibilities, the two verbs ישחטו ("they shall slay") and יעמדו ("they shall stand") would have been sufficient. The use of the personal pronoun preceding the verb emphasizes that these are exclusive tasks for the Levites. The implicit contrast is with the past practice of Israel in which the slaughtering and cooking of sacrifices were done by the laity. It is these last two functions which are marked by the emphatic pronoun, not the guarding function. If Milgrom is correct that the Levites were never priests but were originally guards of the Tabernacle and camp, then the Vision of Transformation is not demoting the Levites but returning them to their original function. There is no need to argue that P is prior to the Book of Ezekiel in order to recognize that they both share a common vocabulary of priestly technical language.

However, there *is* an innovation and this innovation does involve "demotion. " In the Vision of Transformation's territorial system the laity no longer have access to the area of the Altar, and are excluded from the entire Inner Court. They are not permitted to slaughter the animals for sacrifice. The Levites take over the responsibility of slaughtering and cooking the sacrificial animals. The emphatic pronouns before these two functions indicate the contrast with past practice. If the word "demotion" is going to be used in regard to this text, then it is appropriate to apply it to the laity whose access rights are being restricted. (A case could be made that the Levites are being "promoted" rather than "demoted" here.)

The same intention to contrast territorial access according to social role continues in the material on the Zadokites. 44:15 begins with another disjunctive *waw* to contrast the access of the Levites with the access of the Zadokites. The emphatic use of the personal pronoun המה defines their territorial access and tasks in contrast to the Levites and laity. This speech is for the benefit of the House of Israel. The ultimate responsibility for prior territorial violations is placed on the House of Israel, not on individuals or members of a social role. I return to the matter of genre. Legal rhetoric seeks to convict or exonerate. Studies of Ezekiel 44 which have concentrated on the guilt of the Levites have managed to create a strong case to convict. My goal is not to exonerate the Levites. Such a defense would be difficult to accomplish. It is clear that the Rhetor holds the Levites guilty of particular past behaviors. Even though foreign guards were serving the guarding function, the Levites were also involved in the cultic system "when Israel went astray." "They served Israel before their idols." Similarly, the Rhetor claims that the Zadokites are innocent of wrongdoing, since they did not go astray when Israel did.

In contrast to legal rhetoric, political rhetoric is concerned with the future organization of society. The Rhetor asserts the past guilt of the House of Israel and the Levites, and the innocence of the Zadokites, but this is not the point of the rhetoric. The rhetorical purpose of this chapter is to give the rules for access to the Holy Place of the future. The distinction is a fine one, but it moves the discussion from the presumption of Levite demotion to the territorial regulation of the society.

After this piecemeal discussion of 44:6–16, it is now time to provide a complete text.

> and say to the rebellious [house][75],
> to the House of Israel,
> thus says YHWH God:
> O House of Israel,
> let there be an end to all your abominations,
> when you caused foreigners to enter,
> uncircumcised in heart
> and uncircumcised in flesh
> to be in my Holy Place,
> to make my house common,
> when you brought near to me my food,
> the fat and the blood.
> they broke my covenant,
> in addition to all your abominations.
> But you did not guard the guard places of my holy things
> and you set guards of my guard places
> in my Holy Place for you.
> "thus says YHWH God:
> no foreigner,
> uncircumcised in heart and uncircumcised in flesh,
> shall enter my Holy Place
> of all the foreigners who are in the midst of the sons of Israel,
> Rather, the Levites who were far from me,
> when Israel went astray
> going astray from me after their idols
> shall bear their guilt.
> They shall be in my Holy Place
> serving as armed guards at the gates of the house,
> and serving in the house;
> they are the ones who shall slay the burnt offering
> and the sacrifice for the people,
> and they are the ones who shall stand before them,
> to serve them.

[75.] RSV adds "house" which is not in MT

because they served them before their idols
and they were to the House of Israel
a stumbling block of iniquity,
therefore I have lifted up my hand against them,
says YHWH God,
and they shall bear their guilt.
But they shall not approach me,
to serve me as priest,
nor approach any of my holy things/holy areas
and the things that are most holy/Holy of Holies
And they shall bear their shame and their abominations
which they have done.
But I will appoint them
as guards of the guard places of the house,
to do all its work
and all which is to be done in it.
But the Levitical priests, the sons of Zadok,
who guarded the guard places of my Holy Place
when the sons of Israel went astray from me,
they are the ones who shall come near to me
to serve me;
and they shall stand before me
to bring near to me the fat and the blood,
says YHWH God
they are the ones who shall enter my Holy Place,
and they are the ones who shall come near to my table,
to serve me,
and they shall guard my guard post (44:6–16).

Summary of Chapter Three

Ezekiel 40–48 is the territorial claim of YHWH to be the only King of Israel. YHWH is the only power holder; all others are power subjects in YHWH's territory. The date of the vision as the tenth day of the month at the beginning of the year corresponds to a significant date in the Babylonian New Year ceremony, the *akitu*. The vision of the Kabod YHWH coming to take possession of the House of YHWH is YHWH's claim as power holder of the territory and the renewal of YHWH's claim to kingship.

All others are power subjects, beginning with the Narrator who is allowed to cross territorial boundaries. As power subjects, the priests have maximum access to the territory of YHWH's House. The Levites have lesser access, and the laity have the least access to the House. Contrary to the dominant assumptions of scholarship, the Levites are not demoted to a secondary status by this territorial claim. Instead, the laity of Israel is restricted from access to the Inner Court and the Altar.

Chapter 4

Access and Inheritance

Inheritance

The genre of territorial rhetoric, which uses the terminology of area, boundaries, and access, clarifies the material about the House of YHWH. The same genre also clarifies the material in the Vision of Transformation about the division of the Land. However, there needs to be a redefinition of the concept of access. Access to the House involves the crossing of boundaries in order to enter various areas within the House complex. Access to the Land refers to land ownership.

The essence of the definition of territoriality is that it involves the control of space for social purposes. Access to space is a power issue. Those who control access to space are the power holders; those whose access is controlled are the power subjects. In the Vision of Transformation's territorial system, whether one is a power holder or a power subject is predetermined and cannot be changed. The criterion of access is family origin, and the means for becoming a power subject or power holder is by *inheritance* (נחלה). The topic of inheritance is one of the most significant themes of the Vision of Transformation. It is the thread which sews together the topics of place, power, and practice. Inheritance defines inalienable rights to power by defining inalienable rights to space.

The concept of inheritance in the Vision of Transformation has two fundamental and interrelated components. The first is based on the religious ideology of divine ownership of land. The Vision of Transformation expresses an ideology of land ownership which is consistent with the pervasive Ancient Near East notion about the relationship between gods, land, and human beings. No human being *owned* land, since all of the land within an area belonged to the local god. The gods owned the land, but allowed human beings to have access to the land as a place to live and raise crops and livestock. The term for this access without ownership is *inheritance*.[1] The second use of the term "inheritance" refers to the transmission of property rights through families. In Israel, this inheritance was *patrimonial*, the transmission of property rights from father to son.[2] The Vision of Transformation expresses an ideology of human land ownership which gives (or denies) access to land based on membership within one of the "tribes" of Israel.[3]

These two connotations of inheritance are evident in 47:13–14.

> Thus says YHWH God:
> "These are the boundaries (גבול)
> by which you shall divide (נחל) the land for inheritance (נחלה)
> among the twelve tribes of Israel.
> Joseph shall have two portions (חבל).
> and you shall divide (נחל) it equally;
> I swore to give it to your fathers
> and this land shall fall to you as your inheritance (נחלה) (47:13–14).

Just as the speech in 43:7 was the territorial claim of a king to take possession of the House, this speech is the territorial claim to ownership of the Land. YHWH owns the Land and divides it among the tribes as an inheritance. The Land is given as a gift, and land division is made by YHWH. This means that there is only one power holder in the Land. All human beings are power subjects, whose access to the Land is determined by

---

[1.] Clements, *God and Temple*, 53.

[2.] "Apart from inheritance within the family, there was no legal method devised whereby (an Israelite) might come into permanent possession of landed property and there was therefore no proper way in which to dispose of property except to apportion it to his legal heirs" (Christopher Wright, 56–57).

The situation of Zelophehad's daughters deals with transmission of inheritance rights to daughters when there is no male heir (Numbers 26:33; 27:1, 7; 36:2, 6, 10–11; Joshua 17:3; 1 Chronicles 7:15). The need for the daughters to appeal to Moses in order to retain inheritance rights to their father's property is the exception which proves that the norm was transmission of property from father to son.

[3.] On the Israel's theology of land inheritance, see: Clements, *God and Temple*, especially 52–53; Christopher Wright, 3–70; Eryl W. Davies, "Land: Its Rights and Privileges," In *The World of Ancient Israel: Sociological, Anthropological and Political Perspectives*, ed. R. E. Clements (Cambridge: Cambridge University Press, 1989), 349–369.

YHWH. However, just as the power subjects of the House had more or less access depending upon social role, access to the Land is also a function of social role. Social role is itself a matter of tribal identity. The House of Israel is divided into twelve tribes. Of these twelve tribes, eleven have greater territorial access to the Land and one has greater territorial access to the House. The other side of the formulation is that the eleven have less territorial access to the House and the one has less territorial access to the Land. The tribe with greater access to the House is the tribe of Levi, which includes both the Zadokite priests and the Levites. The Levitical tribe does not inherit land. However, the land division in 47:13 refers to twelve tribes rather than eleven, by giving two portions to the Joseph tribe as Manasseh and Ephraim.

The topic of Chapter 48 is access to the areas of the Land, Portion, and Possession of the Nasi. 48:1 begins with the statement, "These are the names of the tribes." 48:1–8 and 48:23–30 define access to each of the tribal divisions defined by the boundaries. The arrangement from north to south is Dan (48:1), Asher (48:2), Naphtali (48:3), the two Joseph tribes of Manasseh (48:5) and Ephraim (48:6), Reuben (48:7) Judah (48:8), the Portion, Benjamin (48:23), Simeon (48:24), Issachar (48:25), Zebulun (48:26), and Gad (48:28), making seven tribes to the north of the Portion and five to the south. 48:30–34 define the access of the tribes to the City which lies within the Portion. Each tribe has its own gate. The arrangement is Reuben, Judah, and Levi on the north; Joseph, Benjamin, and Dan on the east; Simeon, Issachar, Zebulun on the south; and Gad, Asher, and Naphtali on the west. The difference in these lists is that Levi has a gate but does not inherit a tribal division of the Land. In order to maintain the number twelve, the Joseph tribe which has one gate for access to the City is separated into the two tribes of Ephraim and Manasseh for access to the Land.

These two lists have received considerable attention in scholarship, since they have both similarities and differences from other biblical lists which orient the tribes.[4] Some obvious distinctions concerning the Land allocation have been noted in the commentaries.[5] In the Land allotment,

---

[4.] For the division of the Land in the Book of Joshua, see Joshua 13–19. Compare the gates of the City with the arrangement of the tribes around the Tabernacle in the wilderness camp in Numbers 2. In Numbers, Asher, Dan, and Naphtali are on the north, Zebulun, Judah, and Issachar on the east, Gad, Reuben, and Simeon on the south, and Manasseh, Ephraim, and Benjamin on the west. The tribe of Levi is arranged around the Tabernacle as Gershonites on the west, Kohathites on the south, Merarites on the north, and Aaronites on the east (Numbers 3:21–39). For the boundaries of the Land in P, see Numbers 34:1–12.

[5.] See particularly the discussions in: Zimmerli, vol. 2, 540–542, 546; Levenson, *Theology of the Program of Restoration*, 116–122.

the sons of the concubines Zilpah and Bilhah are farthest away from the Portion. Dan and Naphtali, the sons of Bilhah, and Asher, the son of Zilpah are in the north; Gad, the older son of Zilpah is in the south.[6] For the arrangement of the City gates, the six Leah tribes are arranged on the north and south, with Reuben, Judah, and Levi on the north and Simeon, Issachar, and Zebulun on the south. Three of the sons of concubines, Gad, Asher, and Naphtali, are on the west. Joseph and Benjamin, the two sons of Rachel, and Dan, the son of Bilhah, are on the east.

Another obvious concern is to locate all of the tribes west of the Jordan River. This means that the trans-Jordan tribes of Reuben, Gad, and half of Manasseh are relocated from to east to the west side of the Jordan.

Scholars have generally noted that the Land allotment does not coincide with any historical period in Israel's history, either before or after the exile. They have also generally noted the geographical impossibility of these distinctions. As has happened throughout scholarly discussions of Ezekiel 40–48, various explanations have been offered to account for the differences. Levenson's comment expresses one approach.

> The order of the allotments to the tribes is not in conformity with that of any period in Israelite history, nor is there evidence that it was even attempted upon the restoration. There never was a *status quo* for which this program could have been the rationaliza-

---

[6.] Levenson also indicates the importance of birth order in the arrangement. Although I find his discussion extremely unclear on this point, he is apparently assuming that proximity to the Portion is determined by priority of birth. However, he does not explain this "principle." (See the discussion in Levenson, 116–121.) According to the narrative in Genesis, the order is: (1) Reuben (29:32), (2) Simeon (29:33), (3) Levi (29:34), (4) Judah (29:35), (5) Dan (30:6), (6) Naphtali (30:8), (7) Gad (30:19), (8) Asher (30:12–13), (9) Issachar (30:18), (10) Zebulun (30:20), (11) Joseph (30:23), and (12) Benjamin (35:17–18). It is difficult to see any kind of consistent relationship between priority of birth and proximity. The two sons of Rachel are the elder Joseph, here divided into Manasseh and Ephraim, and the younger, Benjamin. However, Benjamin is immediately to the south of the Portion while the two Joseph tribes have two other tribes between them and the Portion on the north. The order of the Leah tribes is Reuben (1), Simeon (2), Levi (3), Judah (4), Issachar (5), and Zebulun (6). Since the allotment of Levi is within the Portion, only the other five tribes need to be considered here. If the eldest were the closest, then Reuben would be closest to the Portion, but is north of Judah who is the fourth in birth order. However, there is some support for the principle since Issachar, who is fifth is closer than Zebulun which is sixth. Even with the sons of the concubines, Dan, the elder son of Bilhah, is farther north than the younger son, Naphtali. In terms of birth order of all of the sons, Judah, the fourth, and Benjamin, the twelfth are closest.

tion. Instead, it is purely ideal, and its idealism, incidentally, argues strongly that it is the product of the Exile, where the practicalities of living-patterns, especially as limited by geography, could be easily forgotten by a nostalgic priest.[7]

I completely agree with Levenson that this work is an idealistic product of the Exile. My quarrel with him is his assumption that differences from the other biblical accounts can be explained by conjuring up the notion of a nostalgic priest, who simply forgot the geography of Israel. That is not idealism; it is simply bad geography. It is much more helpful to ask what the exiled Rhetor wants to accomplish in the rhetoric of the Vision of Transformation with this idealistic land division.[8] This is a question which will be addressed below.

Here, the issue is access to the Land by the tribes. One of the distinctive features of this Land division is the simultaneous concern for equality and differentiation of status. The tribal divisions are as equal as the geography of the Land permits. Each tribe has access to one division. At the same time, the differentiation between the sons of Jacob's wives and the sons of his concubines indicates that this is not an equality which levels all social differences.

In addition, the Vision of Transformation provides an inheritance to aliens.

> So you shall divide (חלק) this land among you
> according to the tribes of Israel.
> You shall allot it as an inheritance (נחלה) for yourselves
> and for the aliens who reside *in your midst* (בתוך)
> and have begotten *sons in your midst* (בתוך).
> They shall be to you as native-born sons (בני) of Israel;
> with you they shall be allotted (נפל) an inheritance (נחלה)
> *in the midst of* (בתוך) the tribes of Israel.
> In whatever tribe the alien resides
> there (שם) you shall assign him his inheritance (נחלה),
> says YHWH God (47:21–23).

[7.] Levenson, 116.

[8.] In his study of the *Temple Scroll,* Schiffman makes a comment which is equally relevant for this material in Ezekiel. "Much energy has been expended in attempting to explain how and why the order of the sons of Jacob and their placement differ from that in the various biblical lists. We remain unconvinced of the explanations but still cannot offer a better alternative (Lawrence H. Schiffman, "Architecture and Law: The Temple and Its Courtyards in the *Temple Scroll*," in *From Ancient Israel to Modern Judaism: Intellect in Quest of Understanding.* Essays in Honor of Marvin Fox, vol. 1, Jacob Neusner, Ernest S. Frerichs, and Nahum M. Sarna, eds. (Atlanta: Scholars Press, 1989), 276–277.

The division of the land ends with the summary statement:

> This is the land which you shall allot (נפל)
> as an inheritance (נחלה) among the tribes of Israel.
> and these are their several *divisions* (חלקים),
> says YHWH God (48:29).

In addition to access to land through patrimonial inheritance (נחלה), the Vision of Transformation provides for access to land as *possession* (אחזה). The difference between inheritance and possession is the difference between *patrimony* and *prebend*. Patrimonies are properties transmitted through families. Prebends are land grants given by a sovereign.[9] There are three areas given as possessions in the Vision of Transformation: The Possession of the City, the Possession of the Levites, and the Possession of the Nasi.

The Possession of the City

The City is a Possession within the Portion. The territorial significance of this location is that the City is not within the division of any tribe, but is accessible to each of the tribes by means of its own gate. In addition to access to the City itself, the tribes have access to the rest of the land of the Possession of the City, defined as the Remainder (הנותר) (48:15). The tribes have access to this area for dwelling places (מושב). In addition, the *workers of the city* have access to the Open Land (מגרש) as a place to grow their food.

> And its produce (תבואה)[10]
> shall be food (לחם) for the workers of the city (עבדי העיר).
> and the workers of the city (עבדי העיר),
> from all the tribes (שבטים) of Israel,
> shall *work* (עבד) it (48:18b-19).

[9.] Although I know of no other scholar who makes this distinction here, such a distinction makes sense of the text itself, and is also consistent with practices in agrarian societies. The closest comment expressing this distinction is by Allen: "Essentially the priests and Levites were 'grace and favor' (to use a British royal idiom) tenants of religious property, while the laity occupied their own tribal areas and had rights of disposal..." (Allen, 265). Allen does not account for the Nasi in this remark. See also: Bernhard Lang, *Monotheism and the Prophetic Minority: An Essay in Biblical History and Sociology* (Sheffield: Almond Press, 1983), 116; "Frequently rulers granted members of the governing class vast landed estates or the incomes from them" (Gerhard E. Lenski, *Power and Privilege: A Theory of Social Stratification* [New York: McGraw-Hill, 1966; Chapel Hill: University of North Carolina Press, 1984], 220). Zimmerli, however, defines אחזה as "arable land" (Zimmerli, vol. 2, 533, 536).

[10.] Literally, "what enters from it"

shall *work* (עבד) it (48:18b-19).

The Possession of the Levites

The Possession of the Levites was described earlier as a section of land within the Portion, twenty-five thousand cubits long and ten thousand cubits wide (45:5; 48:13). 45:5 includes a difficult phrase in the MT, עשׂרים, לשׁכת which means literally, "twenty chambers, " a phrase Zimmerli calls "meaningless" and Cooke calls "impossible."[11] The LXX reads here πόλεις τοῦ κατοικεῖν, "cities to dwell in." This is the reading followed by RSV. When this phrase is translated into Hebrew, it is ערים לשׁבת.[12]

In addition to the difficulty of making sense of the MT, scholars quickly emend the MT on the basis of grants to the Levites in Numbers and Joshua. In Numbers 35:2–8, the Levites are granted forty-eight cities throughout Israel as ערים לשׁבת ("cities to dwell in"), which include מגרשׁ ("open land") for their livestock. Joshua 14:4 uses the same language of "cities to dwell in" and "open land" for livestock. Joshua 21:41 also refers to forty-eight cities for the Levites and the "open land. " In the Vision of Transformation, the Levites are gathered into one place within the Portion rather than scattered in the Levitical cities throughout Israel. It seems logical that instead of cities throughout Israel, the Levites would live in "cities" within their own Possession. However, the Vision of Transformation's instructions do not mention any open land for the Levites. In this case I have no adequate explanation for the MT reading, but question the appropriateness of the LXX. I wonder how many "cities" could fit into the twenty-five thousand by ten thousand cubit Possession of the Levites. The references to "the City" in these chapters implies that there is only one city. I question whether this text which refers only to the one City would refer to "cities" for the Levites. The word לשׁכת refers to chambers for different purposes. Perhaps these "chambers" are some type of dwelling places within the Possession of the Levites. For now, I leave this specific issue unresolved.

The text does include an important prohibition concerning this Levitical land.

> They shall not sell any of it
> *and they shall not* exchange
> and they shall not alienate (עבר)
> *the first* (ראשׁית) of the land,
> for it is holy (קדשׁ) to YHWH (48:14).

[11.] Zimmerli, vol. 2, 466; Cooke, 496.
[12.] See Allen, 246; Zimmerli, vol. 2, 446.

This command prohibits alienation of this land. Alienation is the process which removes land from the family which has access to it.[13] This land does not belong to the Levites and so they are not allowed to exchange or sell it. It must remain within the Portion, available to the Levites. In territorial terms, the Levites are power subjects who have access to this Possession as a place to live, but they do not have the power to dispose of this land.

The particular reason given for this prohibition is that this area is holy, which means that it has been offered to YHWH as a Portion of the Land. It is called רֵאשִׁית (the "first") of the Land. What has been offered to YHWH as a tithe cannot be treated as common, by selling or exchanging it. 48:14 hints at the ideology of the tithe behind it. Although the Vision of Transformation does not discuss the concept of the tithe for the Levites, Deuteronomy and Numbers associate the tithe with the Levites. This Levitical tithe is considered holy.[14]

The Possession of the Nasi

The Nasi has access to the Land as a Possession.

> And to the Nasi shall belong the land
> on both sides of the *Holy Portion* (תרומ הקדשׁ)
> and the *possession* (אחזה) of the city, alongside the *Holy Portion*
> (תרומת הקדשׁ)
> and the *possession* (אחזה) of the city,
> on the west and on the east,
> corresponding in length to one of the *divisions* (חלקים),
> and extending from the western to eastern boundary (גבול) of the land.
> It is to be his *Possession* (אחזה) in Israel (45:7–8a).

The distinction between a possession and inherited land is made clear in the instructions concerning the Nasi's Possession.

> Thus says YHWH God:
> If the Nasi makes a gift to any of his sons
> out of his inheritance (נחלה),
> it shall belong to his sons,
> it is their *possession* (אחזה) by inheritance (נחלה),
> But if he makes a gift out of his inheritance (נחלה)
> to one of his servants,
> it shall be his to the year of liberty
> then it shall revert to the Nasi;

[13.] See Christopher Wright, 55–65.

[14.] See the discussion in J. G. McConville, *Law and Theology in Deuteronomy*, JSOTSup, no. 33 (Sheffield: JSOT Press, 1984), 68–87.

only his sons may keep a gift from his inheritance (נחלה)
The Nasi shall not take any of the inheritance (נחלה) of the people
thrusting them out of their *possession* (אחזה);
he shall *cause his sons to inherit* (נחל) out of his own *possession* (אחזה)
so that none of my people shall be *scattered from* (פוץ) his *possession*
(אחזה)(46: 16–18).

The issue here is the inalienability of inherited land. The Nasi is permitted
to give land gifts only if the land is part of his own inheritance. What is not
made clear here is the relationship between the Possession of the Nasi
which is on either side of the Portion and the Nasi's own inherited tribal
land. There is nothing in these chapters which identifies the tribal affilia-
tion of the Nasi.[15] The word inheritance was not used to describe the Possession of the Nasi earlier, and the word Possession is not used here. No
land which is transferred by the process of inheritance may be given as a
possession. The distinction between a gift of land given to a son and one
given to a servant is that the land gift to the son can be inherited, but the
land gift to the servant cannot be inherited. This instruction comes with
the implicit critique of past practices in Israel, an issue which will be considered more fully below. The Nasi's access to the Land shows that he is
both restricted and privileged. He is a power subject in YHWH's Land,
with his Possession separate from the Portion, and also separate from the
tribal lands.

The Possession and Inheritance of the Priests

The priests are the only group in Israel which has no access to the Land
either by inheritance or possession. Their possession and inheritance are
defined as access to the House and to the offerings. To this point, I have focused on access to place. The material about offerings is an equally significant element of the territorial rhetoric of the Vision of Transformation. In
the next section, I consider the role of the offerings in this territorial claim.
Here, the issue is the relationship between access to place and the offerings.

and on the day that he enters (בוא) the *holy area* (קדש),
into the inner court,
to *serve* (שרת) in the *holy area* (קדש),
he shall *bring near* (קרב) his *purification offering* (חטאת),
says YHWH God.
and it shall be to them for an inheritance (נחלה);
I am their inheritance (נחלה):
and you shall give them no possession (אחזה) in Israel;

---

15. The relationship between the Nasi and David will be considered below.

I am their possession (אחזה).
The cereal offering (מנחה),
and the purification offering (חטאת),
and the reparation offering (אשם);
they (המה) *shall eat* (אכל)
and every devoted thing in Israel shall be theirs.
and the first of all the first fruits of all kinds,
and every *portion* (תרומה) of all kinds
from all your *portions* (תרומה),
shall belong to priests;
you shall also give to the priests
the first of your coarse meal
that a blessing may rest on your house (44:27–30).

RSV reads 44:28 as, "They shall have no inheritance" on the basis of the Vulgate reading. However, the sense of the MT text is clear enough that access to the Inner Court is both inheritance and possession. Included in this access to place is the right to the cereal, purification, and reparation offerings, and the first fruits. The phrases, "I am their inheritance" and "I am their possession," grant to the priests right of access to place and to offerings.

They also have access to land as a place to live.

It shall be the holy (קדש) *part* of the land
it shall be for the priests,
who *serve* (שרת) *the Holy Place* (מקדש)
who *come near* (קרב) YHWH
to serve (שרת) YHWH
and it shall be a place for their houses
and a holy place (מקדש) for the Holy Place (מקדש) (45:4).

Some have taken this instruction as a contradiction of the statement in 44:28 that the Priests have no Possession.[16] They do have access to the Holy

---

16. "The manipulation of the text of 44:28…had shown that a later age found a certain difficulty with the fact that in chapter 48 the priests are also allocated a portion of land, while 44:28 had stated beyond all ambiguity that the priests in Israel were to receive no possession. It is this very question that 45:1–8 tries to answer in its gentle re-emphasis of the allocation plan for the 'consecrated area'"…It cannot, however, be overlooked that only the priests are now subject to the old, sacred Levitical regulation of non-ownership of land" (Zimmerli, vol. 2, 467, 469); Blenkinsopp, 223.

Allen provides an important perspective: "This allocation of land creates some tension with the lack of land mentioned in 44:28, but it was a tension that already existed with the older system of levitical cities … which this plan replaces" (Allen, 265).

Portion of the Portion as a place to live, but the text is very clear that this is YHWH's Portion, not theirs. Here, the identification of YHWH's Portion with the place for the priests emphasizes that the priests do not have their own land.

The material on access to place in the Vision of Transformation can be summarized as a balance of power between access to the House and access to the Land. What is most striking about the territorial power issues of the House, Portion, and Land is the balance of power between the Levitical and non-Levitical tribes. The inheritance and possession of the priests is access to the House. However, this access is balanced by lack of access to the Land, as either inheritance or possession. The Levites have lesser access to the House, but they do have a Possession of the Land. The Nasi has restricted access to the House, and a Possession. The non-Levitical tribes have restricted access to the House but they have inheritance of the Land. It is a carefully devised system which ensures that YHWH is the sole power holder, and all others are territorial power subjects.

The Offerings

Much of the material in the Vision of Transformation concerns various offerings, especially the עולה, the זבח, the חטאת, the אשם, the מנחה, and the שלמים. Each of these offerings has been the subject of intense critical discussion concerning etymology, historical development, function, and appropriate translation. My concern is with the territorial significance of these offerings in the Vision of Transformation. All of these offerings are place-specific practices, which reflect particular power relations, as part of a territorial claim to control of access to place. For issues of etymology, function, and translation, I follow the work of Jacob Milgrom. Through his lifelong study of the priestly ritual system, he has developed a coherent, systematic, and brilliant understanding of these particular offerings. His solutions to critical issues have been landmarks in the field; they have also generated substantial critical dissent. In what follows, Milgrom's understanding of the role of the offerings in the priestly ritual system is the foundation of my territorial analysis of the offerings in the Vision of Transformation. His work provides information about the territorial issues characteristic of each of these offerings. I begin by looking at etymology, function, translation, and territorial issues concerning each of these six offerings.

The עולה is the *burnt offering*, derived from the verb עלה which means "go up." The burnt offering is never eaten by a human being, but is completely burned up. It was the earliest type of offering in Israel, and served many functions, including expiation for sin.[17]

The זֶבַח means simply *sacrifice*. The difference between it and the burnt offering is that the offerer eats the meat.[18] Therefore, what is offered is the blood of the animal. Its function in P is to serve as a well-being or thanksgiving offering.[19]

A particular type of זֶבַח is the שְׁלָמִים, which is translated as *well-being offering*, a translation Milgrom calls an "educated guess." The name comes from the motivation for the sacrifice. Milgrom identifies three categories of motivation: freewill, vow, and thanksgiving. What is common to all of these is rejoicing. Since the meat is eaten by the offerer, the well-being offering involves the blood of the animal.[20]

The basic meaning of מִנחָה is "gift" or "tribute." In P, the מִנחָה is the *cereal offering*. It has a wide range of functions and serves as a substitute for those who cannot afford an animal or bird for a burnt offering. It is either offered by itself with oil or frankincense, or as the necessary accompaniment to the burnt offering and the well-being offering. Originally, the cereal offering was entirely burned on the altar. Milgrom argues that one of P's innovations was that only a token of the cereal offering was burned on the altar. The rest was eaten by the priests.[21]

What each of these offerings has in common is that each was practiced in Israel before worship was localized into the tabernacle or temple. According to Milgrom, the חַטָּאת and the אָשָׁם were later historical developments, devised to meet the needs of worship located at the tabernacle or temple.[22] The חַטָּאת is translated by Milgrom as *purification offering*.[23] With this translation, Milgrom set himself against the traditional translation as "sin offering." The issue is whether the function of the חַטָּאת is expiation or purification. Milgrom argues that the translation of חַטָּאת as "sin offering" is completely inaccurate in terms of biblical context, morphology, and etymology.[24] The noun is derived from the Piel verb which means to "cleanse, expurgate, decontaminate." The function of the offering is purification rather than expiation. The purification offering does not purge the one who offers the sacrifice. Its function is to purge the holy place and the objects of the holy place. The means of purification is the blood of the of-

---

[17.] Milgrom, *Leviticus*, 172–177.

[18.] Milgrom, *Leviticus*, 204.

[19.] Milgrom, *Leviticus*, 197.

[20.] Milgrom, *Leviticus*, 217–225.

[21.] Milgrom, *Leviticus*, 195–202.

[22.] Milgrom, *Leviticus*, 176.

[23.] A recent study on the חַטָּאת is the dissertation by N. Kiuchi, *The Purification Offering in the Priestly Literature: Its Meaning and Function,* JSOTSup, no. 56 (Sheffield: JSOT Press, 1987).

[24.] See Milgrom, *Leviticus*, 253–264.

fering, which is daubed on places and objects, but never on a person. Behind this located practice is a theology of the dynamic nature of impurity and collective responsibility. Impurity in the society invades the holy place, and is attracted to the holy objects. Human behavior in the society pollutes the holy place. If the holy place becomes sufficiently polluted, YHWH will leave the holy place. There are two types of purification offering, depending on the location of the procedure. One type is offered at the altar, in order to purge the outer altar, and is eaten by the priests. The other type is completely burned in another location, and is therefore not eaten. This type purges the temple building including the Holy of Holies.[25]

The אשם is the *reparation offering*. Milgrom argues against the translation as "guilt offering." אשם does not refer to the state of guilt but to the feeling of guilt as a consequence. The offering is required when there has been damage to YHWH's property. It is a means of restitution or reparation for the damage. The reparation offering is eaten by the priests.[26]

The second function of the offerings is to cleanse from impurity. The particular offering which accomplishes this purpose is the purification offering (חטאת). The material on the purification offering in the Vision of Transformation can be divided into two categories: start-up procedures and maintenance procedures. 43:18–27 describe the one-time process required for getting the Altar ready for its work of purification. 44–46 describe the on-going practices of the House of YHWH.

Three times in 43:18–27, the text specifies that the purpose of this seven day process is to get the Altar ready (43:20, 22, 26). The specific vocabulary for this process is the חטאת offering, and four verbs: חטא, כפר, טהר, and מלא. RSV translates חטאת as "sin offering." It translates חטא as "cleanse"; כפר as "make atonement for"; טהר as "purify"; and מלא as "consecrate." This choice of vocabulary combines the language of expiation ("make atonement for" and "sin offering") with the language of purification ("cleanse" and "purify"). Milgrom's insistence that the חטאת is concerned with purification rather than expiation clarifies the rhetorical issues involved in this text.

The definition of the territory called the House of YHWH is based on the concept of holiness and impurity as mutually antagonistic, dynamic substances. It is also based on the understanding that the holy attracts to itself the effects of impurity in the society. The fact that the Altar lies at the exact center of the House indicates its importance as the means for removing the effects of impurity from the society. What is particularly significant about the ritual practices of the Vision of Transformation is that there is

---

[25.] Milgrom, *Leviticus*, 253–284.
[26.] Milgrom, *Leviticus*, 339–345.

nothing concerning the practices within the House building. The focus is on the practices concerning the Altar, indicating that access to the Altar was the rhetorical issue, rather than access to the House.

The meaning of the verb כפר in also significant in this territorial system. It is usually translated as "atone" or "expiate." However, Milgrom argues that its basic meaning is "rub." In the context of חטאת, כפר always means "purge." This is evident from its parallel use with חטא and טהר. The sense is that the blood is daubed on the altar, which rubs off impurity.[27] In order to be cognate with the translation of חטאת as purification offering, I translate the verb חטא as "purify," and the verb טהר as "cleanse."

> And he said to me,
> "Mortal,
> Thus says YHWH God:
> these are the ordinances (חקה) for the altar:
> on the day when it is erected (עשה)
> for offering (עלה) burnt offerings (עולה) upon it
> and for throwing blood against it,
> you shall give to the Levitical priests,
> *they* (המה) *who are* of the family of Zadok
> who *come near* (קרב) to me to *serve* me (שרת),
> says YHWH God,
> a bull for a purification offering (חטאת).
> and you shall take some of its blood,
> and put it on the four horns of the altar,
> and on the four corners of the ledge,
> and upon the rim (גבול) round about;
> thus you shall *purify* (חטא) the altar
> and *purge* (כפר) it.
> you shall also take the bull of the purification offering (חטאת),
> and it shall be burnt in the appointed place (מפקד) belonging to the House,
> outside the *holy place* (מקדש).
> And on the second day
> you shall *bring near* (קרב) a he-goat without blemish for a purification offering
> (חטאת);
> and the altar shall be *purified* (חטא),
> as it was *purified* (חטא) with the bull.
> When you have finished *purifying* (חטא) it,
> you shall *bring near* (קרב) a bull without blemish
> and a ram from the flock without blemish.
> You shall *bring* them *near* (קרב) before (לפני) YHWH,

Milgrom, *Leviticus*, 1079–1084.

and the priests shall sprinkle salt upon them
and offer them up (עלה) as a burnt offering (עולה) to YHWH.
For seven days
you shall provide (עשה) daily
a goat for a purification offering (חטאת);
also a bull and a ram from the flock,
without blemish, shall be provided (עשה).
Seven days shall they *purge* (כפר) the altar
and *cleanse* (טהר) it,
and so consecrate it (מלא יד).
and when they have completed these days,
then from the eighth day onward
the priests shall offer (עשה) upon the altar
your burnt offerings (עולה)
and your well-being offerings שלמים;
and I will accept you,
says YHWH God" (43:18–27).

The purification process cleanses, purges, and purifies the Altar. The rights of access are given to the Levitical priests. After this cleansing process, the House is ready for use.

Several interrelated territorial issues are evident in the material about offerings. The first is that the offerings involve place-related power relations. The offerings are the inheritance and possession of the Levitical tribe.[28] The priests receive neither an inheritance nor a possession of the Land of Israel. YHWH is their inheritance and possession. In practical terms, this means that the priests are entitled to eat some of the offerings made "to YHWH." The list in 44:29–30 identifies the cereal offering, the purification offering, the reparation offering, every devoted thing, and the "firsts of other types of offerings. Of this list, only the cereal offering, the purification offering, and the reparation offering are mentioned elsewhere in the Vision of Transformation. This territorial system is careful to create separate places for every aspect of dealing with these three offerings for the priests. They are slaughtered, cooked, and eaten separately from other offerings made in the House of YHWH. The purification offering and the reparation offering are slaughtered on the four tables inside the vestibule of the Inner North Gate (40:39). The *burnt offerings* (עולה) are also slaughtered in the vestibule of the Inner North Gate along with the reparation and purification offerings for the priests (40:39). The cooking areas for the offerings are also separate. 46:19–20 describe a place (מקום) at the end of the Priestly Chambers for boiling the reparation and purification offerings

---

[28.] The Vision of Transformation is silent about the particular offerings for the Levites, but concentrates on the offerings for the priests.

and baking the cereal offering. 42:13 specifies that the priests eat the cereal, purification, reparation offerings in the two Priestly Chambers on the north and south of the Restricted Area.

In contrast, the *sacrifices* (זבח) which the people themselves eat are slaughtered, cooked, and eaten in other locations. These sacrifices are slaughtered on the four tables outside the vestibule of the Inner North Gate (40:41–42). 46:21–24 describe cooking areas in each of the four corners of the Outer Court for boiling the "sacrifices (זבח) of the people." Other than the specification that the Nasi is permitted to "eat bread" in the vestibule of the Outer East Gate (44:3), there is no specific reference to the locations where the laity may eat their offerings. However, the thirty Chambers around the Outer Court seem to be the likely places provided for eating these sacrifices (40:17).

The justification for this separation is made explicit in the instructions about cooking the offerings.

> And he said to me,
> "This is the place (מקום)
> where the priests shall boil *there* (שם)
> the reparation offering (אשם)
> and the purification offering (חטאת),
> and where they shall bake the cereal offering (מנחה),
> in order not to bring them out into the outer court
> and so communicate holiness to the people" (46:20.)

The concern is not just that impurity might invade the holy, but that holiness might invade the common. In this, the priestly concern for the separation of the holy from the common is evident.

There is nothing in the Vision of Transformation which defines which offerings are for the benefit of the Levites. However, there is a significant territorial issue relating to the Levites. 44:11 gives to the Levites the responsibility for slaughtering the burnt offering and the sacrifice for the people. Although the Levites are not mentioned by name in 46:24 as the ones who cook the sacrifices for the people, the language which is used is similar to the language of 44:11 where the Levites were identified the ones who "serve in the House" (משרתים את הבית). Here, the "servants of the House" (משרתי הבית) cook the sacrifices. It is a safe assumption that these cooks are the Levites. The people are removed from any of the responsibility of preparing the sacrifices. The Levites do the slaughtering and cooking. The priests offer them on the Altar, and the Nasi presents them in their behalf. There is no instruction in this system for the presentation of offerings by individuals. Instead, the Nasi is the one who offers on behalf of the people.

The specific responsibility of the Nasi is to provide the offerings for the people (45:16–17, 22–25; 46:2–7, 11–15). The territorial significance of these instructions is that the people do not present their own offerings.[29] The instructions indicate not only the type and quantity of these offerings, but also when and where they are to be offered. What is particularly evident is that the people are restricted in their access.

Summary of Chapter Four

Two interrelated themes are inheritance and territorial access. There are two types of inheritance. The first is cosmic inheritance, which refers to the gift of the Land to Israel from YHWH. The second is social inheritance, which refers to the transmission of land from father to son. In the Vision of Transformation, access to the Land, the Portion, and the House is determined by social role. The role of cosmic inheritance is evident in the material concerning the Portion and the offerings. They are a type of tithe returned to YHWH. Social inheritance refers to access to land ownership. Eleven tribes have access to Land by ownership but restricted access to the House of YHWH. The Levitical tribe has access to the House of YHWH but restricted access to Land. The Nasi receives a portion of Land as a grant from YHWH.

[29.] This is not a complete ritual system, and so it is unjustified to assume that there was no provision for individual offerings. The issue is the relationship between the community of Israel and the House of YHWH, and the Nasi's role as the intermediary.

Chapter 5

Beginning and End

Stasis

David Ball, in *Backwards and Forwards*, gives principles for reading drama. One principle is that drama begins and ends with stasis.

> Stasis is motionless; a condition of balance among various forces; a standing still; an *unchanging* stability; a state in which all forces balance each other, resulting in no movement.

The dramatic action of the play begins when there is some sort of an intrusion which interrupts the stasis.

> Intrusion is a pushing, thrusting, or forcing in.

The goal of the play is to reestablish stasis.

> *Stasis comes about at the close of the play when the major forces of the play either get what they want or are forced to stop trying.*

The essence of drama is a conflict between want and obstacles to achieving that want. Every word of the drama is intended to overcome some obstacle to what the speaker wants. The play ends when a new stasis achieved. The "end" of the play is the "end" of the drama: the conclusion of the play accomplishes the purpose of the playwright. Therefore, Ball suggests that the most effective means for understanding a play is to look at the beginning and the end, to identify the intrusion into stasis, and the new stasis at the end of the play.[1] This is a fruitful suggestion for analysis of any intentionally persuasive text. The author creates a narrative world in order to accomplish some purpose in the author's own context. The end of the text reveals the accomplished purpose of the writer. I assume that the outcome of the Book of Ezekiel has accomplished the purpose of the Rhetor. Obstacles have been overcome and conflict resolved. Identifying the intrusion into stasis at the beginning of the Book of Ezekiel, and analyzing the ending as the resolution of the conflict created by this intrusion, are potent means of determining the Rhetor's intention for writing the book.

The Beginning

The Book of Ezekiel begins with this information.

> In the thirtieth year,
> in the fourth month,
> on the fifth day of the month,
> as I was *in the midst of* (בתוך) the exiles (הגולה) by the river Chebar,
> the heavens were opened,
> and I saw visions of God.
> On the fifth day of the month
> (It was the fifth year of the exile (גלות) of King Jehoiachin),
> the word of YHWH came to Ezekiel, the priest, the son of Buzi,
> in the land of the Chaldeans by the river Chebar,
> and the hand of YHWH was upon him there (שם) (1: 1–3).

The situation of stasis is the Babylonian exile. The intrusion is a precisely dated divine revelation to the Narrator who is identified as the priest Ezekiel, son of Buzi. Critical discussion of these lines has identified several distinct problems. Some of these problems are related to the two dates. The first date, "the thirtieth year," lacks a referent. The question which cries out for an answer is, The thirtieth year of what? However, the text does not answer the question. Scholars have offered several possibilities: it refers to the thirtieth year of the Narrator, when he was ordained a priest;[2] it marks the thirtieth year since the scroll was discovered in the temple, which marked the beginning of the Josianic reform;[3] it is deliberately cryptic, to

---

[1.] David Ball, *Backwards and Forwards: A Technical Manual for Reading* Plays, with a Foreword by Michael Langham (Carbondale, Illinois: Southern Illinois University Press, 1983), 19–21. Italics in the original.

[2.] See: William H. Brownlee, *Ezekiel 1–19*, WBC, 28 (Waco, Texas: Word Books, 1986), 3–4; Bruce Vawter and Leslie Hoppe, *Ezekiel,* International Theological Commentary (Grand Rapids: Wm. B. Eerdmans Publishing Company, 1991), 24–25.

mark in-group language;[4] it is an editorial gloss.[5] Each of these suggestions is possible. However, the problem remains that the text itself does not provide an explicit answer. The second date is the "fifth year of the exile of King Jehoiachin. " The problem with this date is not lack of a referent, but the dating system. The dating system of Biblical materials reflects both Babylonian and Egyptian conventions for calculating the regnal years of kings, and the calendar month of the new year. Freedy and Redford describe these dating systems in their analysis of the dates in the Book of Ezekiel.[6] In the Babylonian system, the first month of the new year was Nisan (March/April). The king's first regnal year was regarded as the first full Nisan-Nisan period following his accession. This is a post-dated system which disregarded any portion of the preceding year during which the king ruled before Nisan.[7] In contrast, the Egyptian system used a pre-dated system. The first month of the Egyptian calendar was January, and the regnal years were calculated according to the new year's day preceding the accession to throne.[8] One of the enduring problems in biblical scholarship has been to understand the dating system used during the later years of the Judean monarchy. Did the system begin the new year in Nisan (March/April) or Tishri (September/October) and was it a pre-dated or post-dated system? Freedy and Redford present the various solutions presented for this problem. They argue that the Book of Ezekiel used a postdated Nisan system for its chronology. Rather than the accession of a king, the fixed point is the first full year of Jehoiachin's captivity.[9] They argue further that 2 Kings and the corresponding material in Jeremiah used a pre-dated Nisan system. On the basis of these assumptions, Freedy and Redford coordinate the Babylonian and biblical materials. My purpose here is not to evaluate their solution, but to use the dates they provide for my analysis. According to their solution, the fifth year of the exile of King Jehoiachin coincides with a determinative event in the history of Judah. Before identifying this event, I identify one other problem in Ezekiel scholarship concerning 1:1–3.

A problem which has generated substantial discussion concerns location. The text locates the Narrator in the Babylonian exile. This is clear

---

[3.] See Moshe Greenberg, *Ezekiel 1–20*, AB (Garden City, New York: Doubleday & Company, 1983), 39–49.

[4.] Davis, 78.

[5.] Zimmerli, vol. 1, 112–115.

[6.] K. S. Freedy and D. B. Redford, "The Dates in Ezekiel in Relation to Biblical, Babylonian and Egyptian Sources," *JAOS* 90 (1970): 462–485.

[7.] Freedy and Redford, 462.

[8.] Freedy and Redford, 464.

[9.] Freedy and Redford, 463.

from the references to the "river" Chebar, the Land of the Chaldeans, and
the specific word הגולה, which can mean either "the exile," or "the exiles."[10] However, much of the focus of the book is on Jerusalem and Israel.
Therefore, some scholars have argued that the prophet Ezekiel actually
lived and worked in Palestine, or that he spent part of his time in Palestine
and part in Babylon. The exilic location claimed by the text is actually the
product of redaction. The most recent commentary to make this claim is by
Brownlee, who argues that the הגולה of 1:1 is actually a redactional cor-
ruption of an original הגלנלה or הגולנילה "to Gilgal, Ezekiel's home-
town." According to Brownlee, "Ezekiel was either solely or initially a
Palestinian prophet, but later editing has confused the issue. " He goes on
to argue that Ezekiel worked with the Jewish exiles in Egypt, which was
the location where he received the vision of chapters 40–48.[11] The net result
of Brownlee's reconstructions is that the authentic Ezekiel was just about
everywhere except Babylon. In this, Brownlee represents an earlier era of
scholarship which was reluctant to accept a Babylonian provenance for the
authentic Ezekiel.[12] In more recent years, scholars have been more willing
to give credence to a Babylonian setting for the prophet. The episode
which still seems most troubling for a Babylonian provenance is the account in 11:1–13 of the death of Pelatiah in Jerusalem. One solution is to argue that the prophet spent most of his time in Babylon, but visited
Jerusalem one or more times.[13]

On this question, as with other issues concerning the composition of
this text, my goal is to read the Book of Ezekiel as it is. What is clear is that
this text locates the prophet in Babylon. Far from invalidating a Babylonian provenance for the book, the emphasis on Jerusalem is consistent
with the concerns of an exilic community, a point I shall consider more fully below. On this whole issue, Eichrodt's words on the various attempts to
place the prophet in Palestine rather than Babylon are worth considering.

> This unsatisfactory fluctuation in the theories is no mere matter
> of chance; it is the necessary result of all the difficulties encoun-
> tered by any attempt to work out such a fundamental theory on
> the basis of a text which states the exact opposite...For it is obvi-
> ous as to be a certainty that Ezekiel was first and foremost a

---

[10.] The feminine here can be an abstract or collective noun. See Waltke and
O'Connor, 104–105.

[11.] Brownlee, xxv, xxix.

[12.] For a survey of the early critical literature on this question, see Zimmerli,
vol. 1, 3–8.

[13.] See Blenkinsopp, 9

prophet for the exile, and that his influence upon the homeland was entirely secondary.[14]

Rather than to ask about the redaction of the text, I ask about its rhetoric. What is the rhetorical purpose of this information? How does this intrusion of divine revelation into the stasis of exile function rhetorically? The topic of territoriality which clarifies the rhetorical purpose of 40–48 also clarifies the rhetorical context and exigence of the Book of Ezekiel. Territoriality is an effort to assert control over a place. The historical, geographical, and political context of the Book of Ezekiel can most accurately be defined as the result of conflicting territorial claims. The context of the Book of Ezekiel is the territorial power vacuum created by the collapse of the Assyrian empire. Assyria had been the territorial power holder in the Ancient Near East for more than a century. The collapse of Assyria created a situation in which various groups and rulers asserted territorial claims over areas which had been under the control of Assyria. The Chaldeans (or Neo-Babylonians) under Nabopolassar and his son Nebuchadrezzar attempted to claim the territory of the fallen Assyrian empire.[15] At the same time, a series of pharaohs in Egypt also responded to the Assyrian collapse by attempting to reassert Egyptian hegemony over the area of Palestine.

One of the beneficiaries of this Assyrian collapse was King Josiah. The whole of Josiah's reform program can be analyzed as a territorial claim to control space. He claimed control over the Assyrian provinces of Samerina and Magiddu (1 Kings 23:15, 19: 2 Chron 34:6). It was an effort to reassert the territorial boundaries of the kingdom of David. As part of this territorial claim, he instituted a reform movement which consolidated worship at the Jerusalem temple. This constituted a territorial claim that Jerusalem was the only legitimate place for worship. Josiah's territorial claim was defeated by the territorial claims of Pharaoh Necho. The death of Josiah was the death of his territorial claim to assert the power of Judah as an independent territorial power holder.

The politics of the Book of Ezekiel must be set in the context of sixth century Ancient Near East international politics, which were dominated by Babylon and Egypt. The twenty-three year period between the death of Josiah in 609 and the fall of Jerusalem in 586 was a turbulent time of shift-

---

[14.] Eichrodt, 8–9.

[15.] Use of name Nebuchadrezzar rather than the more common form Nebuchadnezzar follows the suggestion of Wiseman, since it is a closer transliteration of the Babylonian royal name. The Old Testament uses Chaldean (כשדים) for the rulers of Babylon from Nebuchadrezzar onwards in accordance with the normal contemporary references to the dynasty by outsiders. (D. J. Wiseman, *Nebuchadrezzar and Babylon* [Oxford: Oxford University Press, 1985], 3, 7).

ing political realities.[16] The history of the period from 609–586 is a complicated one, involving four kings of Judah: Jehoahaz (609), Jehoiakim (609), Jehoiachin (597–?) and Zedekiah (597–586); two kings of Babylon: Nabopolassar (626–605), and Nebuchadrezzar (605–539; and three pharaohs of Egypt: Necho II (610–594); Psammetichus II (594–588); and Apries (588–569).

The last years of the kingdom of Judah are years of shifting allegiance, between Egypt and Babylon. Judah was one of several small vassal states, caught in the middle of the conflicting territorial claims of imperial powers. For most of this time, Babylon was the dominant power, under the imperialistic leadership of the strong and ambitious King Nebuchadrezzar. Babylon, as the dominant Ancient Near East power was a short-lived entity, its era of dominance coinciding with the reign of Nebuchadrezzar. It was a time when Babylon was engaged in a program of building and restoration. Its policy was to take captives into exile, both to do the work of building, but also to be trained for Babylonian service.[17] Nebuchadrezzar had a deliberate policy of re-educating foreigners for use in their own homelands or in the Babylonian internal administration, a policy which helps to explain some of the Babylonian literary influence in the Book of Ezekiel.[18] Egypt was also in a state of flux. For a short period of time, the Egyptian Pharaoh Psammetichus II reigned as king. He was as ambitious as Nebuchadrezzar, and his imperialistic maneuvers had profound effects on the situation in Palestine.[19]

In the game of territorial tug-of-war, Judah was the rope, pulled first one way and then the other. The status of Judah as a territorial power sub-

---

[16.] My goal is to consider the territorial issues involved in these twenty-three years, without rehearsing the various problems and solutions for chronology and calendar year. For the dates of these various rulers, I follow the chronology of Freedy and Redford, who discuss the various critical issues involved. For an alternative reconstruction, see A. Malamat, "The Last Kings of Judah and the Fall of Jerusalem: An Historical—Chronological Study," *IEJ* 18 (1968): 137–156.

[17.] "While Nebuchadrezzar was rebuilding the great city of Babylon and adorning it with the tribute extracted from the territories he now dominated, his concern was that the city should regain its place as the culture center of the ANE. One way of achieving this was by training selected foreigners in the whole range of Babylonian science which was itself an expression of the local philosophy and wisdom. At the highest level members of the royal families from nations who had been overrun, or were still hostile, were treated with special attention. They received rations from the king's palace in Babylon itself" (Wiseman, 81).

[18.] Wiseman, 84

[19.] See Moshe Greenberg, "Ezekiel 17 and the Policy of Psammetichus," *JBL* 76 (1957): 304–309.

ject was defined and ritualized by vassal oaths sworn by the kings of Judah to their Babylonian and Egyptian overlords. After the death of Josiah, even the occupant of the Judean throne was determined by Egypt or Babylon. Josiah was killed in an effort to stop the territorial advance of the Egyptian king Necho. In his place, the "people of the land" chose Jehoahaz, presumably for his anti-Babylonian tendencies. His brief reign lasted three months, until he was deposed by the Egyptians and replaced by Jehoiakim. During his reign, Jehoiakim was first a vassal of Egypt and then a vassal of Nebuchadrezzar.

The intrusion which interrupts the stasis of exile is dated according to two reference points. The first reference point is the fifth day of the fourth month of the thirtieth year. The second is the fifth day of the month of the fifth year of the exile of King Jehoiachin. The second reference does not explicitly state the number of the month, however I assume that it is the fourth month on the basis of 1:1. This means that the date of the intrusion into the stasis of exile is doubly-dated, first by reference to the "thirtieth year" and second, by reference to the exile of Jehoiachin. However scholars resolve the various problems of dating, what is clear is that the second date is as precise as the first date is mysterious. The question is then, What happened in the fifth year of the exile King Jehoiachin which was significant in the territorial rhetoric of the Book of Ezekiel? According to Freedy and Redford, the fifth year of the exile of Jehoiachin is 593 B.C.E. The significant event was that Zedekiah held a meeting in Jerusalem which gathered representatives from various Palestinian vassal states. The purpose was to discuss common action against Nebuchadrezzar. This revolt against Nebuchadrezzar set in motion the reprisals which destroyed the temple and the city of Jerusalem. The instigator was Psammetichus, who ascended to the throne of Egypt in 594. Greenberg was the first scholar to identify the importance of Psammetichus during these years. Psammetichus was ambitious, and eager to reassert territorial control over the area of Palestine. His reign was short, but his effect on Palestinian politics was of exceptional importance.

The context of the Book of Ezekiel is the Babylonian exile, but the exigence is this act of revolt which violates Zedekiah's oath of covenant with Nebuchadrezzar. When Jehoiachin was taken into captivity, Zedekiah was installed in his place. However, Zedekiah was not regarded as the king, but as a type of regent for the real king Jehoiachin. He had sworn a fealty oath to Nebuchadrezzar as vassal. At the heart of the Book of Ezekiel is the question of Zedekiah's loyalty to his Babylonian overlord, Nebuchadrezzar. On the basis of Hittite vassal treaties, Tsevat argues that an oath of fealty to a suzerain involved an vow of loyalty to one's own god.[20] Lang's study, *Kein Aufstand in Jerusalem*, is based on the understanding that the

problem in the Book of Ezekiel is the violation of the vassal oath by Zedekiah. Ezekiel argues against revolt. On this point, both Jeremiah and Ezekiel share the same conviction. They also argue against any hope of rescue
from Egypt, particularly from Psammetichus.[21]

In discussions of this era, scholars typically use the language of "pro-
Egyptian" or "pro-Babylonian" leanings. It is more accurate to think in
terms of survival than preference. The political reality of Judah, as a small
kingdom between rival imperial powers, each asserting a territorial claim
over Judah, was that it had no choice except to be a power subject. The
only choice was whether to choose vassal status to Egypt or vassal status
to Babylon. Given that choice, there were differences of opinion about the
best course of action. With the arrival of Psammetichus on the scene, some
leaders of the Palestinian vassal states thought they had the opportunity
to break free from Babylonian domination. This was the "pro-Egyptian"
faction. Both Jeremiah and Ezekiel counseled vigorously against reliance
on Egypt, and for continued compliance with Judah's vassal obligations to
Babylon. This stance surely indicates that they were better political ana-
lysts than those who counseled revolt; whether it makes them "pro-Babylonian" is another issue. What is clear in all of this is that Judah was a
power subject in its own land. Rather than use the language of
"pro-Babylonian" or "pro-Egyptian," it is more appropriate to use the language of accommodation. The choice was whether to accommodate to the
territorial claims of Babylon or the territorial claims of Egypt. The leaning
of the Rhetor was to accommodate to Babylon, rather than to depend upon
Egypt.

The Ending

The ending of the Book of Ezekiel is a city with a name that declares
the presence of YHWH.

> These shall be the exits (מוֹצָא) of the City:
> On the north side,

[20.] Matitiahu Tsevat, "The Neo-Assyrian and Neo-Babylonian Vassal Oaths
and the Prophet Ezekiel," *JBL* 78 (1959): 199; "On installation, Nebuchadrezzar
made Zedekiah swear an oath by YHWH his own deity, the western practice being
for such oaths to be in the name of the god of the subordinated state, supplement-
ing the name of the principal god of the sovereign power. The precise form of the
loyalty oath would have been a local variant to that used earlier by Assyrian kings,
with specific clauses the breaking of which would justify further action by the
overlord" (Wiseman, 33).

[21.] Bernhard Lang, *Kein Aufstand in Jerusalem: Die Politik des Propheten Ezechiel*
(Stuttgart: Verlag Katholisches Bibelwerk, 1978).

which is to be four thousand five hundred cubits by measure,
three gates,
the Gate of Reuben,
the Gate of Judah,
and the Gate of Levi,
the gates of the City being named after the tribes (שִׁבְטֵים) of Israel.
On the east side,
which is to be four thousand five hundred cubits,
three gates,
the Gate of Joseph,
the Gate of Benjamin,
and the Gate of Dan.
On the south side,
which is to be four thousand five hundred cubits by measure,
three gates,
the Gate of Simeon,
the Gate of Issachar,
and the Gate of Zebulun.
On the west side,
which is to be four thousand five hundred cubits,
three gates,
the Gate of Gad,
the Gate of Asher,
and the Gate of Naphtali.
The circumference of the City shall be
eighteen thousand cubits.
And the name of the City henceforth shall be,
YHWH is there (שָׁם)(48:30–35).

The name of the City is *YHWH Shammah*. Since both the pre-exilic First
Temple and the post-exilic Second Temple were located in Jerusalem, most
scholars immediately identify the City as Jerusalem, and move on to other
issues.

Scholars have noted several problems with this ending. Zimmerli
notes with surprise that the City is the place of YHWH's presence.[22] This
seems to be a direct contradiction of the earlier chapters which located
YHWH in the House of YHWH, apart from the City. Zimmerli identifies
the aim of these chapters as the representation of the glory of the city of
Jerusalem.

> Yahweh is in Jerusalem, so that the latter can in fact be called af-
> ter him, links up with 43:1ff, where Jerusalem has taken the place
> of the temple. The last sentence of the book of Ezekiel shows how

---

[22] Zimmerli, vol 2, 545.

the old tradition of the city of God has forcefully obtained justice for itself against the priestly reform project, which, through the separation of city and temple has robbed the city of much of its dignity."[23]

Another object of attention has been the impossibility of the physical geography. Cooke comments that:

> The new Jerusalem would be twice the size of the present city, the walls of which measure about two and half miles in circuit; again the facts of topography are ignored in this ideal reconstruction.[24]

However, just as the primary problem with the blueprint genre is the absence of vertical dimensions, the significant issue here is that this City is never called "Jerusalem" anywhere in Chapters 40–48. This omission of the name "Jerusalem" is either accidental or intentional. At the beginning of the vision, three elements of geography are identified: land, mountain, and the form of a city.

> And brought me in the visions of God into the Land of Israel,
> and set me down upon a very high mountain
> on which was a form like a city (40:2).

The Land is named Israel, but neither the city nor the mountain is named. If the Rhetor is assumed to be rhetorically competent, this non-use of Jerusalem is not an oversight but rhetorically significant. By identifying the City as the "new Jerusalem," scholars miss an important aspect of this rhetoric.

In *God and Temple*, Ronald Clements argues that there were "two pillars" of Judah's religious life before the exile.

> These were the belief in a covenant between Yahweh and the house of David, and the special position of Jerusalem as Yahweh's chosen dwelling-place.[25]

Clements' image of two pillars is an appropriate one. It uses architectural language to convey the necessary connection between the House of YHWH and the House of David, both joined together in Jerusalem.

Levenson also states that Jerusalem and King David were "inextricably associated. "

[23.] Zimmerli, vol 2, 547.

[24.] Cooke, 535.

[25.] Clements, *God and Temple*, 109.

It was he who conquered the city for Israel, who brought the Ark of the Covenant—the most potent symbol of YHWH—into the city, who made Jerusalem his capital, and laid the groundwork for the Temple which his son built on Mount Zion. That Temple was thus different from the other shrines throughout the land; it was a royal sanctuary, close to the king's palace, with which it shared a destiny. From the tenth century on, for the next four hundred years, until the destruction of the kingdom of Judah and the razing of Solomon's Temple by the Babylonians in 587 B.C.E., the fortunes of Jerusalem and the house of David were to rise and fall together.[26]

The "two pillars" represent a confluence of several discrete elements: YHWH, Jerusalem, temple, monarchy, David, and Zion theology. In turn, this ideology represents a synthesis of several strands of common Ancient Near Eastern and Canaanite ideology into this specifically Israelite synthesis. The characteristics of Baal and El, and their divine dwelling places, became associated with YHWH and Mount Zion. The territorial claim of Mount Zion as the dwelling place of YHWH was joined with the territorial claims of the Davidic dynasty in Jerusalem. Adoption of Canaanite ideology about divine ownership of land gave legitimacy to the Davidic claims to rule over the land.

...the doctrine of the joint election of David and Mount Zion was nothing short of a divine authorization and sanction for the whole Davidic state. Yahweh had chosen Mount Zion, which, in its religio-political meaning, entitled Israel to possession of the land of Canaan, and he had chosen David to rule over it.[27]

My question is this: Did the Rhetor of the Book of Ezekiel intend to maintain this synthesis of Jerusalem Temple and Davidic monarchy? The rhetoric of the Vision of Transformation answers this question with a strong, No. In the history of Israel, Jerusalem was the one city which was identified as the territory of the human king. David created an area within his own territory for the territory of YHWH. The House of David built (and controlled) the House of YHWH on Mount Zion. The concept of Zion, the mountain of the divine King, was joined to Jerusalem, the city of the human king. It is precisely this overlapping of territories which is the issue for the Book of Ezekiel. There is room for only one king in YHWH's territory. This is no longer Jerusalem, City of David; it is YHWH Shammah, the

---

[26.] Levenson, *Sinai and Zion*, 97.
[27.] Clements, 50–51.

City of YHWH, the territory of the King of Israel. The religious ideology of Israel was a process of innovation, borrowing, and blending. This means that these "two pillars" were constructed of various components. My point is that what can be put together can also be taken apart.

My thesis is that the Rhetor intended to undo the synthesis by offering the thoroughly radical notion of a temple society without a human king. The architectural language of the Vision of Transformation creates another social structure with only one pillar, the kingship of YHWH. The rhetoric of the Vision of Transformation represents a conflict between two opposing views of territoriality, the territorial claim of human kings and the territorial claim that only YHWH is King. The Vision of Transformation treats the monarchic era as an aberration from a social and political structure which had only one King in Israel, a disastrous experiment with human kingship which led to chaos in Israel.

The point of stasis in the Book of Ezekiel is a new political structure which has dis-*placed* the Davidic monarchy, and re-*placed* it with the monarchy of YHWH. This City named YHWH Shammah has twelve gates, one for each of the tribes of Israel. This language of twelve tribes is archaic language, recalling the society of Israel before the monarchy, before Israel and Judah, before the dispersion of the ten tribes of Israel. The vision of stasis is a unified entity called Israel, composed of twelve tribes, each with access to the City, and each living in its own land. It is the "New Israel" but not the "New Jerusalem. "

> Finally we learn the name of the future city, YHWH *šamma,* 'YHWH is there'; the infamous *y^erušalayim,* so excoriated in Ezekiel's prophecy—'polluted of name' he calls it (22:5)—will cease to be mentioned.[28]

Summary of Chapter Five

The beginning of the Book of Ezekiel identifies intrusion into the stasis of exile as an event in the fifth year of the exile of King Jehoiachin. This date coincides with the date of a meeting in Jerusalem of the various Palestinian vassal states in order to revolt against their Babylonian overlord, Nebuchadrezzar. The Rhetor identifies this action as a violation of Zedekiah's vassal treaty with Nebuchadrezzar, and the event which culminates in the destruction of the Jerusalem temple.

The ending is the new City which replaces the human monarchy with the kingship of YHWH, and restores Israel to a pre-monarchic social structure.

[28.] Greenberg, "Design," 233.

CHAPTER 6

Critique of Monarchy

MONARCHY

The language of demotion which is often applied to the Levites is more properly applied to monarchy. Monarchy was the pervasive social structure of the Ancient Near East. The common ideology of monarchy in the Ancient Near East was that the human king was the anointed of the god, who was the real king. According to this ideology, the human king was responsible for the well-being of the society. The judgment of the Book of Ezekiel is that the actual result of human kingship in Israel was chaos rather than well-being. It is an indictment of the monarchic system of government and the territorial claims of its human kings. The monarchic social system led to the destruction of the temple and city of Jerusalem, and caused the exile of Israel, by its violations of YHWH's territory. The territorial claim of the Vision of Transformation is simultaneously a critique of the monarchic social system and its territorial power relations and practices.

The territorial critique of the kings is explicit.

> and the House of Israel shall no more defile (טמא) my holy (קדש) name,
> neither they (המה),
> nor their kings,
> by their harlotry (זנות),
> and by the *monuments* (פגרים) of their kings,
> *in their death* (במותם)[1]

by setting their threshold (סַף) by my threshold (סַף)
and their doorposts (מְזוּזָה) beside my doorposts (מְזוּזָה),
with only a wall (קִיר) between me and them.
they have defiled (טמא) my holy (קֹדֶשׁ) name
by their abominations (תוֹעֵבוֹת) which they have *made* (עָשָׂה),
so I have consumed them in my anger.
Now let them *put far away* (רחק) their *harlotry* (זְנוּת)
and the *monuments* (פְּגָרִים) of their kings
from me,
and I will dwell (שׁכן) in their midst (בְּתוֹךְ) for ever (43:7b-9).

This speech describes the past practices of the House of Israel and its kings in locational terms. Although "harlotry," "idolatry" and "abominations" are usually understood by commentators in ethical and moral categories, my translation emphasizes the territorial and locational issues involved. The translation of פְּגְרֵי מַלְכֵיהֶם as "the monuments of their kings" instead of "dead bodies of their kings" follows Neiman's suggestion that the פְּגָרִים are royal stelae rather than corpses.[2] Allen also cites the suggestion by Ebach that the reference is to offerings for the dead set up in memory of deceased kings.[3] In either case, the issue is violation of YHWH's place by practices which memorialized the kings. It is significant that 43:7 uses the phrase שֵׁם קָדְשִׁי ("my holy name") rather than בַּיִת ("House") or מִקְדָּשׁ ("Holy Place") here when the issue is remembrance. These are the only occurrences of this phrase in the Vision of Transformation.

The last word of 43:7 in the MT is בְּמוֹתָם; which means "in their high places." My translation "in their death" is based on repointing the MT to בְּמוֹתָם. Not only is there some manuscript support for this slight revocalization, but it also makes sense in the context.[4] The issue is violation of the Holy Place, rather than the high places.[5]

Many of the details concerning the House, Portion, City, and Land gain added significance as an argument against the monarchy, when compared to other biblical narratives about analogous areas. A notable example is a comparison between the two temple descriptions of Ezekiel 40–42 and 1 Kings 6–8. Working under the assumptions of the blueprint genre, many scholars have compared Ezekiel 40–42 with the narrative of King Solomon's construction of the Jerusalem Temple in 1 Kings 6–8. Such com-

---

[1.] Omitted in RSV

[2.] David Neiman, "*PGR*: A Canaanite Cult-Object in the Old Testament," *JBL* 67 (1948): 58–59.

[3.] Allen, 257.

[4.] Manuscripts cited by the critical apparatus of the *BHS* are *Theodotion* and *Targum Ed.*

[5.] See also Zimmerli, vol. 2, 417.

parisons have been used to fill in the gaps of the description of the temple in Ezekiel 40–48, and to raise questions about its "missing" furnishings. However, from the perspective of territorial rhetoric, such comparisons miss the essential differences between these narratives. Such studies keep the discussion focused on issues of architecture and furnishings, rather than on the difference in rhetorical intent. The issue here is the relationship between temples, kings, social power, and rhetoric. In his analysis of the nineteenth century Sri Lankan kingdom of Kandy, James Duncan studied the relationship between Kandyan scriptural traditions, the material structures of the city, and the assertion of power by the king of Kandy.[6] Duncan uses the vocabulary of rhetoric to argue that the city itself is a text, created for rhetorical purposes, which can be "read" just as a written text can be read.[7] The fundamental insight of Duncan's work is that a public building such as a temple is more than a building; it is an expression of political power.[8]

The obvious and significant difference between Duncan's work and studies of the biblical temple narratives is that Duncan could travel to Sri Lanka and study the material remains of the city of Kandy, and relate them to scriptural texts. For biblical scholars, there are only texts about the temples described in Ezekiel and 1 Kings. Solomon's Temple and the visionary temple in the Book of Ezekiel exist only in textual form. This difference does not minimize the importance of Duncan's insight for studies of the biblical temple texts. A temple is more than a building; it is an expression of political power. 1 Kings 6–8 and Ezekiel 40–42 both describe temple buildings, but there is much more to these narratives than architectural detail. They reflect fundamentally different expressions of political power.

THE TEMPLE OF SOLOMON

1 Kings 6–8 describe the building of the Jerusalem temple by King Solomon. The house that Solomon builds for YHWH is sixty cubits long, twenty cubits wide, and thirty cubits high (1 Kings 6:2). It has three rooms, each twenty cubits wide. The vestibule is ten cubits long (6:3), the nave is forty cubits long (6:17).[9] The innermost room is a cube twenty cubits in

---

[6.] James S. Duncan, *The City as Text: The Politics of Landscape Interpretation in the Kandyan Kingdom* (Cambridge: Cambridge University Press, 1990).

[7.] Duncan, 19–22.

[8.] Duncan, 87–118.

[9.] This is another instance where Hebrew usage defines length as the longest measurement and width as the shortest. However, my convention continues to use "length" to refer to the dimensions of the house from north to south, and "width" to refer to the dimensions of the building from east to west.

each dimension (6:20). There is an annex structure around the side of the house with side chambers in three storeys, with beams which do not intrude into the walls of the house (6:5–6). In contrast to the Book of Ezekiel narrative, this narrative includes a measurement of height.

The rest of the description of the house describes the building materials: "costly stones" (אבנים יקרות)[10] and cedar, cypress, and olive wood. The decorative motifs are gourds (פקעים),[11] open flowers (פטורי צצים),[12] cherubim (כרובים), and palm trees (תמרה).[13] The narrative also describes the lavish use of gold and bronze. The pillars, Jachin and Boaz, at the vestibule of the house are made of bronze and decorated with pomegranate and lily motifs. The gold and bronze furnishings are also described in precise detail.

The narrative also describes the building of Solomon's own house: the "House of the Forest of Lebanon," the "Hall of Pillars," and the Hall of the Throne," as well as his own house, and house for his wife, Pharaoh's daughter (7:1–8). This building project takes thirteen years in contrast to the seven years required to build YHWH's house.

Throughout the narrative, the rhetoric makes the point that Solomon is the one responsible for building this house. The temple is referred to as "the house which King Solomon built for YHWH" (6:2). The active verbs refer to Solomon who "built" (בנה), "made," (עשה) "carved" (קלע), "prepared" (כון), "overlaid" (צפה), "covered" (ספן) and "finished" (כלה) the house and surrounding structures, and the furnishings. The only other person named is Hiram of Tyre who did the bronze work (7:13–46).

Solomon's speech at the dedication of YHWH's house makes clear that Solomon is the one who is providing a house for YHWH.

> Then Solomon said
> YHWH[14] said that he would dwell (שכן) in thick darkness (ערפל).
> I have built a *lofty abode* (זבל) for you,
> a *fixed place* (מכון) for you to dwell (שכן) in forever (8:12).

The speech goes on to recite the promise to David that his son would be the one to build a house (8:18–19). Solomon refers to the house he has built for the name of YHWH (8:20, 27, 43, 44, 48) as the basis for the future well-being of the society. Since the house will be the place of YHWH's dwelling forever, all future prayer directed toward the house will be heard

---

10. 1 Kings 7:9, 10, 11.
11. 1 Kings 6:18; 7:24, 24.
12. 1 Kings 6:18, 29, 32, 35.
13. 1 Kings 6: 32, 32, 35; 7:36.,
14. RSV adds: "has set the sun in the heavens, but… "

(6:27–53). Solomon offers his dedicatory prayer at the altar (8:22, 54) and offers the burnt offerings, cereal offerings, and well-being offerings (8:64). What is most remarkable about this narrative is how unremarkable it is. The narrative describes an Ancient Near East king who builds a house for the patron deity and a house for himself. In this instance, the king is King Solomon, the patron deity is YHWH, the house for the deity is the Jerusalem Temple, and the house for himself is the king's palace. In all of this, Solomon is carrying out the typical role of Ancient Near East kings as temple builders. Temples were lavish affairs, built with as much visible display of wealth as possible. The more imposing the structure, the more evidence that the deity had blessed the rule of the king.[15] A substantial portion of this narrative is devoted to a catalogue of the expensive building materials and furnishings. There is particular emphasis on the use of gold and bronze, including the hiring of a foreign craftsman to make bronze objects. In the economy of the Ancient Near East, these two metals were available only to the wealthy.

The building of a temple accomplished several goals. It was a visible display of the king's power and it was also a claim that the patron deity had chosen the king to serve as the deity's human counterpart. The legitimization of Solomon's rule by this building project is evident.

> Now the word of the YHWH came to Solomon,
> "Concerning this house which you are building,
> if you will walk in my statutes
> and obey my ordinances and keep all my commandments and walk in them
> then I will establish my word with you,
> which I spoke to David your father,
> And I will dwell *in the midst of* (בתוך) the children of Israel
> and will not forsake my people" (1 Kings 6:11–13).

This speech legitimates the rule of Solomon who built the focal point of the society, the place where YHWH dwells in the midst of Israel, and the place from which YHWH blesses the society.

> The entire ideology of the Jerusalem temple centered in the belief that, as his chosen dwelling-place, Yahweh's presence was to be found in it, and that from there he revealed his will and poured out his blessing upon his people.[16]

[15.] Keith W. Whitelam, "The Symbols of Power: Aspects of Propaganda in the United Monarchy," *BA* 49 (1986): 166–173.

[16.] Clements, 76.

This ideology also made the king the center of the society, so that well-being of the society depended upon the relationship between YHWH and the king.

> The dwelling place of the deity was restricted to the king and his cultic functionaries. This expressed more than anything else how the king was at the sacred center, while the rest of the population was only related to this through the monarch.[17]

This aspect of Ancient Near East temple-building ideology is evident in Solomon's dedicatory prayer. The presence of YHWH in the house would ensure the well-being of the society.

This description of the building project omits an important social reality, namely the fact that this temple was built by corvée labor. Despite the verbs which attribute the work to Solomon, the work was done by enforced labor, at enormous cost to Israel. Another significant aspect of this building project is that the house for YHWH was built next to the buildings for the king. (Also, the house for the human king was larger than the house for the divine King, and took longer to build.)

The obvious similarities between the descriptions of the House of YHWH in 1 Kings and Ezekiel are the size and shape of the house building itself. Both narratives describe a three-room house building with almost the same length and width dimensions.[18] They also describe—unclearly in both cases—a three-storeyed annex structure constructed so that its beams do not intrude into the house building.

There are also differences in building materials, decoration, and furnishings. Ezekiel's house has no gold, bronze, pomegranates, lily work, or decorative flowers. There is no mention of the many furnishings such as pots, shovels, lavers, snuffers, lamps, and basins. Nor is there mention of the Ark or the bronze "sea." While Ezekiel mentions only one table before YHWH, Solomon's house has both a golden altar and a golden table in the house (1 Kings 7:48). There have been many explanations offered for these differences. From a rhetorical perspective, the difference between these two narratives does not lie in the dimensions of structures, the use or non-use of metals or decorative motifs, or the presence or absence of particular items.[19]

[17.] Whitelam, 171–172.

[18.] The only difference is the length of the vestibule. It is 10 cubits for the Solomonic temple and 12 cubits (11 cubits according to the MT) for the Ezekiel temple. (See the discussion in Chapter 1.)

Rhetorical Purpose of the Temple Narratives

The rhetorical difference is that these are two conflicting claims to kingship. These two narratives accomplish the same rhetorical function. Each uses a divine house in order to legitimate the rule of a king. The difference is that the Solomon narrative recognizes two kings, the divine

---

[19.] The material about weights and measures is rhetorically significant, and deserves further study. It demonstrates the importance of proportion, Babylonian influence, and monarchic critique. The Book of Ezekiel is the only Old Testament book which defines units of weight in terms of proportion between units (45:10–12). It defines a system based on the Babylonian sexagesimal system (with sixty shekels to the mina) rather than the Palestinian quinquagesimal system (with fifty shekels to the mina). However, RSV has read 45:12 according to the LXX rather than the MT. The MT reads "twenty shekels, twenty-five shekels, fifteen shekels shall be your mina" (20 + 25 + 15 = 60). RSV reads "and your mina shall be fifty shekels. " (See Scott, 353–357.)

The cubit is also a matter of rhetorical significance. The Rhetor identifies the cubit as "a cubit and a handbreadth" (40:5; 43:13), which is seven handbreadths. Understanding of the cubit measure is complicated by terminology which refers to "short cubits," "medium cubits," and "long cubits." To complicate matters even further, scholars identify three "medium" cubits, including the "short cubit," the Cubit of Moses and the Builder's Cubit. The "medium" Builder's Cubit is longer than the Royal or Long Cubit, which originated in Egypt but which became a standard of measurement throughout the Ancient Near East, including Babylon. For three studies which attempt to sort out the differences, see: Scott, 345–349; Arye Ben-David, "The Hebrew-Phoenician Cubit," *PEQ* 110 (1978): 27–28; Asher S. Kaufman, "Determining the Length of the Medium Cubit," *PEQ* 116 (1984): 120–132.

There is a notice in 2 Chronicles 3:3 which identifies the cubit used by Solomon as the "former cubit." Although there are difficulties involved in using the Chronicles narrative as a historical source, the narrative indicates both that there were different standards for the cubit and that Solomon chose to use an earlier standard for construction of the temple. Kaufman argues that the Second Temple used different cubit standards depending on whether the area was considered holy or common (Kaufman, 121–122). Both of these examples indicate the existence of long-standing traditions which related the standard of cubit used to its function. They also indicate that choice of standard for the cubit was a matter of rhetorical intention. The Book of Ezekiel originated in the period between the First and Second Temples, and demonstrates its continuity with these traditions. My point is that the specification of the seven handbreadth cubit in the Vision of Transformation is not a neutral matter, but is rhetorically significant.

I offer two hypotheses for further study. The first is that the seven handbreadth cubit is further evidence of Babylonian influence on the Book of Ezekiel. The second is that it is part of the critique of the pre-exilic monarchy which used another cubit for the temple.

King YHWH, and the human King Solomon. In Ezekiel, there is only one
King, the divine King YHWH. At the heart of the Ezekiel vision is an assertion which can be expressed in rhetorical terms as a syllogism:

> Kings build temples.
> YHWH built this temple.
> YHWH is king.

The ideology of Ancient Near East temple building connects kings and
temples. Solomon builds a House for YHWH as a legitimization of his
kingship. The most important difference between these two narratives is
that there is no human king responsible for building the house for YHWH
in Ezekiel's vision. This House is already built. The point cannot be over-
stressed. YHWH builds this house as a claim to kingship. The temple in the
Book of Ezekiel serves the same functions which all temples serve in the
Ancient Near East. They legitimate the rule of kings, they serve as the focal
point of the society, they are the source of blessing and well-being. The difference is that there is no human king in the picture.

It is this rhetorical perspective which has been missed by the blueprint
genre, with its assumption that Ezekiel 40–42 is the building plan (תבנית)
of a temple. In her comparative study of temples and temple-building in
the Ancient Near East, Patton makes the point that there is no record anywhere of the plan for a temple being given to any one other than a king.

> ... until Ezekiel, every Near Eastern text that described the build-
> ing or restoration of a temple attributed the project to the glorifi-
> cation or shame of the reigning king. Not once in Mesopotamian
> literature does a priest or prophet receive the plan for the tem-
> ple.[20]

However, Patton's thesis is that "the overall purpose of the text is to provide a plan for the layout of the temple."[21] It is a "plan or *tabnit*" [sic] even
though the word תבנית is never used in Ezekiel 40–48.[22] She then concludes with the assessment that "the temple not only did not have to be
built, but that it should not be built."[23] Patton has provided an important
insight about this text, but has missed its significance because of her genre
assumption. The significant point is not that a prophet receives a building
plan, but that a human king does not build this temple.

[20.] Patton, 180.
[21.] Patton, 188.
[22.] Patton 184
[23.] Patton, 187.

The rhetorical purpose of Ezekiel 40–48 is the territorial claim of YHWH as the only King of Israel. What the prophet receives is not a building plan but a territorial claim, expressed through the vision of an already-built temple. The territorial design of the House complex has as its fundamental goal the separation of any human claim to royal power from the royal territory of YHWH as King. This rhetorical purpose explains a number of features about the Ezekiel vision which have generated substantial discussion in scholarship.

It explains the purpose of the mysterious Binyan behind the house building. Zimmerli provides an important clue in his comparison of the two narratives.

> … 1 Kgs 6f involves a temple building surrounded by a court which, in turn, is part of an extensive palace complex of Solomon enclosed within a "great court" (7:9, 12). There is no trace whatsoever of this surrounding palace complex in Ezekiel 40f.[24]

Later, Zimmerli discusses the Binyan.

> The enormous בנין ("building"), whose dimensions exceed quite considerably the great House of the Forest of Lebanon in Solomon's palace precinct (according to 1 Kgs 7:2, one hundred cubits by fifty) and whose roof would have to have been supported by a still greater number of rows of pillars than was the case there, is clearly the product of an embarrassing situation. Its intention is to forbid all access to the area behind the temple, that is behind the back of the Lord of the holy of holies who is facing forward i.e. eastwards. Hence there is never, even in the latest expansions, the slightest indication of the use of this, the most enormous structure in the whole temple area.[25]

Although Zimmerli does not follow through on his own clue, he has in fact identified the purpose of the Binyan. The Binyan takes the place of the palace. There is no room for the house of the human king in this territory. This is a sharp contrast with the Solomonic temple which set "their threshold by my threshold and their doorposts beside my doorposts, with only a wall between me and them" (43:8).

In contrast to Ezekiel 40–48, the narrative of 1 Kings has nothing about protecting the territory of YHWH. The whole vocabulary of gates, guards, walls, and separation is missing. Comparison of quantity of text leads to a difference of emphasis. In Ezekiel, half of the narrative in 40–42 refers to

---

[24.] Zimmerli, vol. 2, 359.
[25.] Zimmerli, vol. 2, 380.

gates. There is no mention of gates in 1 Kings. The material about the gate structures in Ezekiel constitutes an implicit critique of the monarchy's protection of YHWH's territory. The remarkable features of these gates are their enormous size and the three recesses on each side of the passageway. The problem for scholarship is that there is no archaeological evidence for such gateways in temples. However, there is archaeological evidence of such gates in the Solomonic era cities of Megiddo, Hazor, and Gezer.[26] This means that this temple has Solomonic era city gates, without the towers characteristic of city gates. In his discussion of these gates which "might thus appear as something new and revolutionary," Zimmerli once again provides an important clue but misses the territorial significance of his observation.

> The greatly enlarged gates, which have adopted the form of the old defensive gates of the royal city, in which in the three recesses on either side of the passageway the guards keep watch and ward off any enemy, proclaim God's exclusive and defensive holiness, which does not demean itself with human affairs, even with the governmental affairs of a human king.[27]

Although Zimmerli recognizes the implicit territorial claim here, with this description of royal gates, he does not recognize that these gates are part of a territorial critique of the monarchy.

The vision of Chapter 40 concerns a "form like a city." It is appropriate for a city to have city gates, with places for guards to control access into the city. In contrast, towers are not territorial features. They provide means of observation, but not means to control access. Therefore, they are not necessary for maintenance of boundaries. This is why it not really astonishing that the features of Solomonic city gates have been incorporated into this vision. In the conflict between the competing territorial claims of the human monarchy and YHWH, this temple vision uses the kind of gates Solomon used to protect his cities to ensure its own territorial defense. The size of the gates indicates the importance of guarding the boundaries, a task which the human monarchy failed to accomplish.

After his discussion of the "great guidance vision," and the differences between the temple of this vision and Solomon's temple, Zimmerli makes the following conclusion.

> Against the background of that earlier temple vision of chapter 8 what is revealed as new is a judgment on what has happened

---

26. Zimmerli, vol. 2, 352.
27. Zimmerli, vol. 2, 361.

and a summons to turn their whole mind and all their own resolve towards the new. The language in which this new factor is
enshrined is, moreover, unusual enough. It is the language of objective architectural forms and measurements. Its decipherment
and its translation into the word which addresses man as one
who is lost in the imprisonment of the exile, and at the same time
as one who is called to responsibility for himself, is not easy.[28]

This conclusion deserves comment for several reasons. Zimmerli has
missed the territorial significance of the "unusual enough" language. He
has also missed the social implications of this vision by spiritualizing the
discussion. What is intended as a vision for "the house of Israel" has become a word for "man."[29] This has changed a vision which is addressed to
a community into a message for individuals.

THE NASI

The figure of the Nasi in Ezekiel 40–48 has been the subject of intense
critical discussion on two questions: Is the Nasi the future king? What is
the relationship between this Nasi and David?

In the material about the future outside of Chapters 40–48, there are
two notices about the future role of David.

> And I will set up over them one shepherd,
> my servant David,
> and he shall feed them;
> he shall feed them and be their shepherd.
> (34:24):
> And I, YHWH, will be their God,
> and my servant David shall be Nasi (נשׂיא) *in their midst* (בתוך);
> I, YHWH, have spoken (34:23–24).

> My servant David shall be king (מלך) over them;
> and they shall all have one shepherd.
> They shall follow my ordinances and be careful to observe my statutes.
> They shall dwell in the land where your fathers dwelt that I gave to my
> servant Jacob;
> and they and their children's children shall dwell there for ever;
> and David my servant shall be their Nasi (נשׂיא) for ever (37:24–25).

In these two notices, David is called "king" one time and "Nasi" twice in
the MT. In the LXX, David is called ἄρχων (archōn), rather than βασιλεὺς

---

28. Zimmerli, vol. 2, 361.
29. My concern here is not so much with the gender exclusiveness of the language as with its individualism.

(*basileus*) in each instance. These notices in Chapters 34 and 37 identify the post-exilic leader of Israel as David. However, in Chapters 40–48, the Nasi is never identified with David, and is never called king. Such evidence can be used to argue both sides of the question, Is the Nasi Davidic? The same evidence has also been used to argue on both sides of the question, Is the Nasi a king? As with so many questions which harden into "either/or" categories, there is strong evidence to argue both sides of both of these questions. The issue has been argued on historical, redactional, and theological grounds.[30] My goal here is not to come down on one side or the other of these questions, but to look at the access rights of the Nasi to the House of YHWH, the City, and the Land in 40–48 as a critique of the pre-exilic monarchy.

In relation to the House of YHWH, the Nasi is a power subject whose access to the House is carefully defined. He is restricted from the Inner Court. He is also granted privileged access to the Outer East Gate (44:1–3) and the Inner East Gate (46:2, 11). Depending on whether one emphasizes the restriction or the privilege, this evidence too can be used to argue both sides of the question, Is the Nasi the king? Two studies which are particularly sensitive to the relationship between access to space and social structure are by John Wright and Jonathan Smith.[31]

Wright emphasizes the uniqueness of the Nasi's role. Wright throughout translates נשׂיא as "prince," a translation which is consistent with his understanding that the Nasi is a royal figure. He argues that the East Gate defines the royal sphere.

> The east gate legitimates the prince's power, equating him with the divine presence within the society.[32]

The role of the prince is to mediate the divine presence between the elders ("the people of the land") and the priests. In Wright's analysis, "the prince is alone on the top of the Judean temple community." His work on the role of gates is particularly significant. In Iron Age II Judean cities, the city gate functioned as the center of power. In the Neo-Babylonian era (in which he places Ezekiel 40–48), the center of power shifts from the perimeter of the city to the temple complex. He recognizes two locations of power: the center, where YHWH dwells, and where the priests exercise power; and the East Gate, where the prince exercises power as YHWH's royal representa-

---

[30] For a survey of scholarship on these issues, see Levenson, 57–62; C. R. Biggs, "The Role of *nasi* in the Programme for Restoration in Ezekiel 40–48," *Colloquium: The Australian and New Zealand Theological Review* 16 (1983): 46–57.

[31] John Wright, "A Tale of Three Cities"; Jonathan Smith, *To Take Place.*

[32] John Wright, 17.

tive. Wright sees a shared power between the Nasi and the priests, each in their respective power locations.[33]

In contrast, Jonathan Smith's study of Ezekiel 40–48 understands a complex interrelationship between maps of status and power.[34] He analyzes the material in Ezekiel 44:1–3 in terms of status. He argues that "the prince is no king" since he must enter the closed East Gate from the west, a direction opposite the direction of the royal path of YHWH. He is "at best, a mock king as in some saturnalian role reversal."[35] This is a status reversal which places the "king" outside the temple proper. Smith also divides the Holy Place into "three zones of relative sacrality." According to this division, the "central spine" is "the god's house." This central zone, from east to west, includes: the eastern steps; the Outer East Gate (40:6); the Inner Court stairs; the Inner Court gate (40:49); the Altar (40:47); the stairs to the Vestibule (41:3–4); the Vestibule, Nave, and Inner Room; the Restricted Area (41:12–13); and the Binyan (41:12). This central zone is "the god's house, centered on the throne room," in which "all of the sacred transactions of the temple occur." In addition, Smith identifies a zone of priestly domestic activity and a zone for the people.[36]

These arguments of Wright and Jonathan Smith represent the two sides of the argument. Wright emphasizes the royal function of the Nasi while Smith emphasizes the loss of status. Both use the language of "prince" to refer to the Nasi. In one the royal figure is honored; in the other, he is demoted. However, the situation is not quite so simple. Smith's identification of the central sacred spine gives strength to Wright's argument that the Nasi is serving a royal function by having access to both of the East Gates. In turn, Smith's argument that this access to the Outer Gate represents a loss of status is an important balance to Wright's argument which does not give sufficient attention to the restrictive nature of the Nasi's access. Both Smith's assessment of the Nasi as a "mock king" and Wright's assessment that the prince is equated with the divine presence seem excessive in both directions.[37]

An issue which neither Wright nor Smith addresses is the rhetorical significance of the title, "Nasi." In his study of the Nasi, Speiser argues that

---

[33.] Wright, 4, 10–19.

[34.] Smith's analysis of the structure of Ezekiel 40–48 will be considered more fully below.

[35.] Jonathan Smith, *To Take Place*, 61.

[36.] Jonathan Smith, *To Take Place*, 58–60.

[37.] It seems highly unlikely that the same text which addresses the prophet as בֶּן אָדָם ("Mortal"), an address which emphasizes his humanity in relationship to YHWH's divinity, would be likely to "equate" any human being with the divine presence.

the translation of Nasi as "prince" is not justified in any biblical context in which it is used. He suggests instead "chieftain" when the context is "clans and tribes" and "leader" or "president" when the context refers to political states.[38] Just as the city was not named "Jerusalem," this leader is not called "king." In both cases, the terminology is rhetorically significant, and needs to be taken seriously as part of the argument created by the Rhetor. In comparison with the pre-exilic kings of Judah, the role of the Nasi is a significant restriction. While Solomon stood at the altar and presided over the dedication of the Jerusalem Temple, the Nasi has no access to the Inner Court and Altar. The priests offer his sacrifices for him, while he stands at the doorpost of the Inner East Gate. In addition, the judicial function of the monarchy is given to the priests (44:24). The location of the Nasi's Possession is also significant. The Nasi has a Possession but it is located outside the area of the Portion. It is clear from this that the Nasi is one whose access is restricted. A possession (אֲחֻזָּה) is property given as a grant by the sovereign. In Israel's history, kings made land grants as rewards to their supporters. This language makes clear that YHWH is the king who grants possessions in Israel. Not only is the Nasi's Possession carefully defined, the grant comes with a justification based on past territorial practices of the monarchy which have oppressed the people.

> Thus says YHWH God:
> Enough, O Nasis of Israel!
> Put away violence (חָמָס) and oppression (שֹׁד)
> and execute (עֲשֹׂה) justice and righteousness
> cease (רִים) your evictions of my people,
> says YHWH God (45:9).

The matter of ceasing evictions has to do with territorial abuses, the process by which the monarchy evicted the people of Israel from their land.[39] The new practice is that the Nasis will give the land to the House of Israel according to tribes. This "new" practice is a return to pre-monarchic social structure and land division according to tribes.

46:16–18 concern the Nasi's disposition of land. This section brings together three important themes: inheritance, inalienability of inherited land, and the Jubilee. The important issue is that inherited property was inalienable, which means that it could not be removed from the family.[40]

[38.] E. A. Speiser, "Background and Function of the Biblical Nasi," *CBQ* 25 (1963): 25.

[39.] See: Lang, *Monotheism*, 114–127; Marvin L. Chaney, "Bitter Bounty: The Dynamics of Political Economy Critiqued by the Eighth-Century Prophets," in *Reformed Faith and Economics*, Robert L. Stivers, ed. (Lanham, Maryland: University Press of America, 1989), 15–30.

The distinction in this section is that the Nasi could give his land to his sons, but could not make permanent gifts of land to "his servants" (עבדיו). Whatever land grants the Nasi might give would return to his family at the year of liberty or Jubilee. These prohibitions are followed by a purpose clause.

> ... in order (למען) that none of my people shall be *scattered* (פוץ) from his *possession* (אחזה)(46:18b).

This language of "scattering" is the language of exile. RSV has translated as "dispossessed" which does not convey the centrifugal process of scattering. This language also connects the scattering with the whole process by which the monarchy confiscated inherited land from the people.

The Possession of the Nasi is outside the Portion and the Possession of the City. In contrast to the territorial situation of the Davidic monarchy, this is a significant change by means of displacement. Not only has the Nasi been separated from the Holy Area, he has also been separated from the City. Rather than Jerusalem, the city of the Davidic king, the City is YHWH Shammah, and is accessible to the whole House of Israel. Such comparisons make clear that the Nasi has restrictions that the pre-exilic kings of Israel did not have. These carefully defined territorial restrictions are framed as a critique of the pre-exilic monarchy.

SUMMARY OF CHAPTER SIX

The Vision of Transformation demotes the monarchy by changing access to the House of YHWH and the Land. The narratives concerning temples in 1 Kings and Ezekiel 40–48 are both the territorial claims of kings. However, Solomon was functioning in the typical role of Ancient Near Eastern kings as the temple builder for the patron deity. In contrast, the narrative in Ezekiel shows a temple which is already built by the divine King YHWH. The critique of past territorial violations of the kings of Israel is explicit, and provides the justification for displacing the human king in this new territory. This idea of a temple without a human king is a radical innovation in social structure. The territorial access and social role of the Nasi is very different from the role of the Davidic kings as power holders of the land and temple.

---

40. Christopher Wright, 55–65.

CHAPTER 7

Organization of the Text

WHAT MAKES IT HANG TOGETHER?

It is now time to return to the question of the organization of the text. Is the Vision of Transformation really a crazy-quilt of random scraps, or is there a pattern to the organization? Is a work based on the Priestly ideology of creating order out of chaos really so chaotic that there is no coherent structure to it? The words of Dale Patrick and Allen Scult in *Rhetoric and Biblical Interpretation* are particularly appropriate here.[1]

> An interpretation of a work must avoid internal contradictions, shifting premises, arbitrary thematic changes, and so forth. It is an interpretative maxim that any serious logical incoherence or conceptual oscillation renders an interpretation unviable. Consistency is essential to intelligible and intelligent discourse.
>
> Not only should interpretation be consistent, it should endeavor to find the work itself consistent. Since incoherence is fatal to an argument, a work which seeks to establish some proposition by argument would be a better work if it were coherent...The interpretation committed to grasping the text as the best text it can be will seek to discover how a work hangs together.[2]

[1.] Dale Patrick and Allen Scult, *Rhetoric and Biblical Interpretation*, JSOTSup, no. 80 (Sheffield: Almond Press, 1990).

What about defective works of art or argumentation? Obviously one of the tasks of interpretation is criticism. If the efforts to discern consistency fail, the interpreter should diagnose the defect and perhaps "reconstruct" the project imaginatively to remedy it. The critic, though, should exercise humility, for the detection of flaws may actually be his or her failure to discern what makes the work hang together.[3]

My goal is to read the whole of Ezekiel 40–48 as an intentionally rhetorical text by assuming that there is, in fact, a coherent structure lurking beneath the mass of detail of these chapters. My hypothesis is that "what makes the work hang together" is the topic of territoriality. The reason that scholars have not perceived the structure is that historically-oriented biblical scholarship has had no paradigm to recognize that almost every element of these chapters expresses some aspect of this definition of territoriality. The problem is a genre problem.

Moshe Greenberg

My analysis here begins with the work of four scholars who have read Ezekiel 40–48 as a coherent text: Moshe Greenberg, Jacob Milgrom, Susan Niditch, and Jonathan Smith. Moshe Greenberg's study of Ezekiel 40–48 is a rhetorical response to the work of Hartmut Gese, and those scholars— most notably Walther Zimmerli—who have been influenced by Gese.[4] Greenberg's assessment is that Gese's "thorough, disintegrating" analysis of these chapters demonstrated a complete disregard for the typical stylistic features of Ancient Near Eastern scribal practice. What Gese regarded as glosses, accretions, and strata, and thus evidence of different authors, Greenberg argues is consistent with other Ancient Near Eastern documents. He cites examples from the Qumran *Temple Scroll*, Hittite and Aramaic documents, as well the Mesopotamian "Laws of Hammurabi" as examples of shifts of style, juxtaposition of topics, repetitions, and gram-

---

[2.] The phrase, "the best text it can be" comes from Ronald Dworkin and is central to Patrick and Scult's work in *Rhetoric and Biblical Interpretation*. Dworkin calls the criterion of the best text the "aesthetic hypothesis" which attempts to interpret a work of art as the best text *it* can be [Ronald Dworkin, *A Matter of Principle* (Cambridge: Harvard University Press, 1985), 149]. The emphasis on the pronoun is the essence of the definition [Dworkin, 150]. A best text reading insists on the difference between explaining a work of art as it is and changing it into a different one. Patrick and Scult define a best text reading according to five criteria: comprehensiveness, consistency, cogency, plenitude, and profundity [Patrick and Scult, 84–87].

[3.] Patrick and Scult, 85–86.

[4.] Greenberg, "Design," 215–236.

matical inconsistencies which seem deficient by modern standards. Greenberg wants to argue that Ezekiel 40–48 is the work of one author, and that these chapters are designed to accomplish a single purpose. Composition by a single author to accomplish a single purpose does not mean that the whole text was written at once.

> His program does give the impression of composition in stages, with duplication, cross-reference, and separation of related matter all indicating editorial arrangement and several returns to a given subject.[5]

Greenberg's observation on the differences between the Pentateuchal material and Ezekiel deserves particular emphasis.

> The nonpriestly Mosaic legislation in Exodus and Deuteronomy regulates private, civil, criminal, and public administrative realms that lie outside Ezekiel's scope. His concerns, concepts, and terminology resemble those of the priestly legislation that comprises the central parts of the Pentateuch (end of Exodus, Leviticus, Numbers). The arrangement of his program is also like that of the priestly corpus: first a description of the sanctuary, then regulation of its personnel and ritual, and finally disposition of the tribes around the sanctuary and the land allotment. The major omissions in Ezekiel, when compared with the priestly legislation, are the whole system of purity and impurity, ethics and morality (e.g. sexual conduct), idolatry, and private life (e.g. vows)—in sum, all the prescriptions of lay conduct making Israel a holy nation! Since such omissions cannot imply annulment, we must suppose Ezekiel to be highly selective, treating only of those topics which he sought to effect revisions.[6]

The wisdom conveyed by this last paragraph brings an important, and frequently missed, perspective to discussions of Ezekiel 40–48. *The Rhetor selected topics which were rhetorically significant to his argument.* The whole list of "omissions" which scholars have identified by comparing the Ezekiel material with the priestly Pentateuchal material would only be omissions if the Rhetor's rhetorical purpose were to recreate an entire system of cultic regulations for life in the New Israel. With this implicit assumption, the interpretive task is to explain why significant elements of Israel's ritual life, such as Yom Kippur, are omitted in Ezekiel's program. If however, the Rhetor is engaged in a rhetorical argument, his purpose is not to

---

[5.] Greenberg, "Design," 235.
[6.] Greenberg, "Design," 233.

provide a complete catalogue of cultic regulations, but to argue against those he wants to change.

Here too, Greenberg points in the right direction by identifying the purpose of these chapters as an argument for more stringent regulations concerning public worship, and "keeping guard over the sanctuary and God's sacred things" than the regulations of the Pentateuch.[7] The main theme of the whole is "separation and gradations between the holy and the profane.[8] Although Greenberg does not use the word "territoriality," his analysis is a territorial analysis of Ezekiel 40–48.[9]

He divides 40–48 into three main divisions.

1. 40:1–43:12 is "the vision of the future temple.
   44:1–46:24 concern "'enterings and exitings'
   (—rules governing access to the temple and activity in it.")
2. 47:13–48:35 is "the apportionment of the land among the people."

In addition, two sections are "transitions." 43:13–27 concern the altar. It links "the static vision" of (1) with the activity prescribed in (2). 47:1–11 concern the water from the temple which links the temple (1) and (2) to the land (3).[10]

An issue which is intimately linked with Greenberg's territorial analysis is the relationship between the priestly material of the Pentateuch and Ezekiel 40–48. One of the earliest problems with Ezekiel 40–48 was its relationship to the cultic system of the Pentateuch. Many studies on Ezekiel refer to the Talmudic story that Rabbi Hananiah ben Hezekiah, in the first century C.E., burned the exorbitant quantity of three hundred pots of oil to resolve the contradictions between Ezekiel and the Pentateuch.[11] The relationship between Ezekiel and the Pentateuch has continued to be a source of contention ever since, involving controverted issues of dating, composition, and redaction of both P and Ezekiel.

[7.] Greenberg, "Design," 234.

[8.] Greenberg, "Design," 225.

[9.] There is no single study of the Book of Ezekiel which has shaped my understanding more than this article by Greenberg. This study first led me to question the usual genre assumption of "temple blueprint" and to think in spatial terms about this material. It was the impetus for beginning a journey into the unfamiliar terrain of human geography. Although I have come to disagree with Greenberg at a number of points, I want to acknowledge the influence of this work on my understanding of the fundamental importance of space in the Book of Ezekiel.

[10.] Greenberg, "Design," 222.

[11.] For example: Bodi, 11.

JACOB MILGROM

Wellhausen's Documentary Hypothesis has been an extraordinarily important paradigm in biblical scholarship. Wellhausen identified four written sources behind the Pentateuch as J, E, D, and P. According to the Hypothesis, P was the latest source, with Ezekiel prior to P. The issue of the Levites in Ezekiel 44 played an important role in this Hypothesis. In opposition to Wellhausen, Jacob Milgrom dates P as pre-exilic. In his study of Levitical terminology, he characterizes Ezekiel 44:14 as a "midrash on P's identification of Levitic duties..."[12] A *midrash* is a commentary upon scripture. By this characterization, Milgrom disputes the relationship order between P and Ezekiel which is foundational for Wellhausen. If Ezekiel 44 is midrash, then P must be prior to Ezekiel.

In his study on Levitical terminology, Milgrom briefly discusses Ezekiel's midrashic technique. "He states a change and then appends a paraphrase from P."[13] In his Anchor Bible commentary on Leviticus, Milgrom analyzes the difference between P and Ezekiel in terms of contagious holiness. The difference is that "*sancta are contagious to persons*" in Ezekiel but are only contagious to objects in P.[14] As proof, Milgrom argues that the outer Altar is the geometric center of the temple complex in Ezekiel. In contrast, the geometric center in P is the Ark in the inner room of the Tabernacle.

> By moving the focus of holiness to the altar, Ezekiel takes the position that the altar is of equal sanctity to the inner sancta and hence qualifies for the same degree of contagion, which bars lay access.[15]

Using this principle that the "sancta are contagious to persons," Milgrom explains the differences between P and Ezekiel. It "accounts for the unique floor-plan of his temple and the distribution of priests, Levites, and laymen within it."[16] In every case where Ezekiel differs from P, Ezekiel takes a stricter position. Ezekiel is the religious conservative, "a standard bearer of an older tradition, which has been rejected by P, but which he wishes to restore."[17] His midrash is "a continuing polemic against the prevailing practice of the Jerusalem Temple."[18]

[12.] Milgrom, *Studies*, 14.
[13.] Milgrom, *Studies*, 84.
[14.] Milgrom, *Leviticus*, 452. Italics in the original.
[15.] Milgrom, *Leviticus*, 452.
[16.] Milgrom, *Leviticus*, 452.
[17.] Milgrom, *Leviticus*, 453.
[18.] Milgrom, *Leviticus*, 453.

In the context of this study, I make no effort to assess the history of composition of either P or the Book of Ezekiel, or to attempt to argue for the priority of either one over the other. It is not necessary to accept Milgrom's arguments about dating, or his characterization of Ezekiel as a midrash on P, in order to recognize the usefulness of his principle. Both Milgrom and Greenberg have identified an important feature of Ezekiel 40–48 in comparison with the priestly Pentateuchal materials. The material in Ezekiel is more stringent regarding territorial access than the Pentateuchal material. I suspect that the P material of the Pentateuch and the Book of Ezekiel are the work of different priestly factions within the exile, who share similar world views on any number of issues, but also disagree on the issue of access to holy space. The Rhetor argues only those issues over which there is an argument. The central issue of argument seems to be access to the Altar. Other issues, such as Yom Kippur, are not matters of argument and therefore not mentioned in the Book of Ezekiel.

JONATHAN SMITH

Jonathan Smith analyzes the organizational structure of Ezekiel 40–48 as a social map of "an ideal cultic place."[19] He sees four homologous maps: Map 1 (40:1–44:3) is a "hierarchy of power built on the dichotomy sacred/profane"; Map 2 (44:4–31) is a "hierarchy of status built on the dichotomy pure/impure"; Map 3 (45:1–8) and (47:13–48:35) is "civic and territorial"; and Map 4 (46) is "orientational." In addition, Smith identifies an additional map (47:1–7) which cannot be homologized to the rest; therefore Smith omits it from his analysis.[20]

This is a complicated analysis according to social categories, based on the work of Louis Dumont. The hierarchy of power has the king at the apex, while the hierarchy of status has the priest at the apex. These are complementary systems in which "the king supports, protects, and preserves the power of the priests," while "the priest legitimates the power of the king."[21] Smith analyzes Map 1 as a power conflict within the royal function between YHWH as the King and the power claims of the human king. He analyzes Map 2 as a conflict within the priestly function between the Zadokites and the Levites. In each case, one party to the conflict triumphs and the other is reduced in status. YHWH is the only King, while the human "king is reduced to a "mock king"; the Zadokites are "promot-

---

[19.] Jonathan Smith, *To Take Place*, 48.
[20.] Jonathan Smith, *To Take Place*, 56.
[21.] Jonathan Smith, *To Take Place*, 54–55.

ed" while the Levites are "degraded."[22] Smith uses the "classic hierarchy of status" to analyze the results of these promotions and demotions.

1. priests
2. kings and warriors
3. providers of sacrifice
4. servants
5. those outside the system

According to these categories, the Zadokites are in class 1 at the apex, the king has been demoted from class 2 to class 3, the Levites have been demoted from class 1 to class 4, and the foreigners have been reduced from class 4 to class 5.[23] Smith then turns to the other two maps, by first asking why there are four maps. What function do Maps 3 and 4 play in this system? His answer is based on social theory. The first two maps are centripetal and hierarchical. The second two maps are a "rectification" of the first two maps. They are expansive and more egalitarian. Map 3 is a map of power using the idiom of sacred/profane, while Map 4 is a map of status based on the idiom of pure/impure.[24]

Susan Niditch

Susan Niditch identifies Ezekiel as a "spirit medium," who functions as a "bridge between heaven and earth."[25] She compares the detailed architectural plan of Ezekiel 40–48 with the mandala in Tibetan Buddhism, which creates a mirror of the cosmic realm.[26] She argues that Ezekiel 40–48 is cosmogonic; it orders a universe by making categories and the process of differentiation. She compares Ezekiel 40–48 with the priestly creation material in Genesis 1–11.

> The world is created and recreated, ordered and refined, distinguished and differentiated over and over again in the primeval history. Such is the nature of the cosmogonic process. It is one of division and subdivision, border-marking, year-counting, and hierarchical definition. An overview of Ezekiel's so-called architectural plan reveals the very cosmogonic, ordering, categorizing emphases found in Genesis 1–11: hierarchy and work roles; geo-

---

22. Jonathan Smith, *To Take Place*, 60–65.
23. Jonathan Smith, *To Take Place*, 62–63.
24. Jonathan Smith, *To Take Place*, 65–66.
25. Susan Niditch, "Ezekiel 40–48 in a Visionary Context," *CBQ* 48 (1986): 208.
26. Niditch, 216.

graphical loci and boundaries: the division between peoples and places which make for a map of reality.[27]

She argues effectively for the importance of place in the ordering of society. "One's place in this world is especially defined by one's role and place in the temple."[28]

> The temple is a microcosm, reflecting a larger reality and affecting it. Most interesting in the process of defining this world is the boundary drawn between "us" and "them" or, in the vision's own terms, the boundary drawn between those admitted to the temple and those excluded.[29]

Ezekiel 40–48 are the culmination of a mythic pattern of the *victory and enthronement* of the deity.[30] This traditional theme typically has several motifs.

1. a challenge to the deity
2. a battle
3. a victory
4. a procession
5. the enthronement/building of a house
6. a feast

She identifies these victory and enthronement motifs in the Book of Ezekiel.

38:10-13	challenge/hubris
39:1-10	battle, victory
39:11-16	establishment of order: peace and cleansing
39:17-20	feast
39:25-29	procession/return
40-48	building

The pattern of victory-enthronement deals with the establishment of order out of chaos.

ASSESSMENT

Each of these four analyses of Ezekiel 40–48 has a contribution to make to understanding the structure of the text. Both Greenberg and Milgrom

---

[27.] Niditch, 216–217.
[28.] Niditch, 219.
[29.] Niditch, 219.
[30.] Niditch, 220–223.

identify the difference between P and Ezekiel 40–48 as greater territorial restriction in Ezekiel. In addition, Greenberg treats the text as a unity. His evidence for different standards of organization and scribal practice in Ancient Near Eastern documents also provides an important clue for the organization of Ezekiel 40–48, particularly in the organization by subject matter in the Laws of Hammurabi. Smith treats the text as an indication of social conflict. Niditch analyzes the cosmogonic issues involved. Although I have specific points of disagreement with each of these scholars, my interest in their work here is to use their insights as part of my own analysis of the structure of Ezekiel 40–48. I draw several implications from their studies. The first is that the Rhetor of the Book of Ezekiel is engaged in an argument with the Rhetor of P concerning access to holy space, particularly the Altar. Comparison of P and the Vision of Transformation clarifies the points at issue. Comparison also makes clear that the P Rhetor and the Book of Ezekiel Rhetor share a similar world view. It is also clear that the territorial issues of the Vision of Transformation have both social and cosmic implications.

In addition to these Ezekiel studies, a recent study of P material in the Pentateuch provides an important model for understanding the structure of Ezekiel 40–48. Frank Gorman combines a study of the cosmic, social, and cultic aspects of the priestly ideology with the issues of space, time, and status. In his analysis of the construction of the Tabernacle, he identifies a pattern. First, the sacred space is constructed according to the pattern given by YHWH. Then, the instructions are given for the ritual activity which is to take place in the sacred structure. The pattern is to define the area before defining its function.[31]

Organization of Ezekiel 40–48

What then is the organizational structure of Ezekiel 40–48? There are four principles of organization. The first is that Sack's definition of territoriality provides a model for the order of the text: definition of area, communication of boundaries, and control of access. An area is first defined and its boundaries delineated. Then, there is a discussion of access which requires discussion of social roles. This general principle makes sense of much of the structure. It is also very similar to the pattern Gorman has identified in the P material. The second principle is that the concentric arrangement of the three areas determines the order in which the areas are discussed, from detail map of the House of YHWH, to area map of the Portion and Possession of the Nasi, to area map of the Land. The third princi-

---

[31.] Gorman, 48.

ple demonstrates the arrangement by subject matter which Greenberg identified as a characteristic of the Mesopotamian legal codes. The Rhetor gathers material according to social role in relation to place. The fourth principle is that the whole vision is the return and enthronement of YHWH as the King of Israel. It follows the pattern of a Mesopotamian *akitu* ceremony with YHWH taking possession of his House, followed by cleansing of the temple, and fixing of the cosmic order, in order to heal the disorders of the society.

The structure of these chapters can be defined as:

I. Holy Place:
   A. Renewal of Kingship
      1. 40–42: Definition of the area of the House of YHWH and its boundaries.
      2. 43: Return of Kabod YHWH, claim as king, and cleansing of the House.
   B. 44:1–16: Access to the House of YHWH
   C. Priests
      1. 44:16–28 Territorial ordinances
      2. 44:28–31 Provisions by inheritance

II. Portion: Inheritance returned to YHWH
   A. 45: 1–8: Definition of area, access by social role
   B. Nasi
      1. 45:9–25: Obligations of Nasi
      2. 46:1–10: Lay access to the House of YHWH
      3. 46:11–24: Offerings, land gifts

III. The Land: Inheritance given to Israel
   A. 47:1–12: Healing of the Land
   B. 47:13–23: Definition of area and boundaries of the Land
   C. 48: 1–29: Tribal access to the Land and Portion
   D. 48:30–34: Tribal access to the City

The tour begins and ends by defining the area of the House of YHWH by establishing its outer boundary (40:5, 42:15–20). The man defines the area and boundaries of the entire Outer East Gate (40:6–16) before the Narrator is allowed access through the gate to enter the Outer Court (40: 17). From that vantage point, the Narrator watches while the man defines area and boundaries of the Outer Court, first by defining the Chambers and pavement, and then by measuring from Outer Gate to Inner Gate three times (40:17–19, 23, 27). The man also defines the areas and boundaries of the other two Outer Gates (40:20–22, 24–26). This ends the first stage of the process of defining the territory. The man has defined the outer boundary, the means of access through the outer wall, and the area of the Outer

Court. After completing the whole process, the Narrator is then given access to the area of the Inner Court.

The next stage is the definition of the three Inner Gates. The man follows the same pattern of defining the area and boundaries of each gate (40:28, 32, 35). In the case of these Inner gates, the Narrator is allowed to enter the Inner Court before the man defines the area and boundaries of these gates (40:28, 32, 35). The Narrator then describes the area of the Inner North Gate (40:38–43). However, instead of measurements of the area, the Narrator gives specific information about the dimensions of the tables (including height), instruments, offerings, and the particular locations within the gate structure for each stage of preparation. How does this information relate to the territorial map which has been concerned to this point with areas, boundaries, and gates? Many scholars have argued on redactional grounds that this material is out of place here. In Zimmerli's words:

> The great harmonious plan, which in the guidance vision unmistakably intentionally tries to say something essential about the ordering of the future temple, is disturbed by the inclusion of vv 38–43. It is also unprecedented that a chamber is here described down to the smallest details of its furnishings.[32]

Zimmerli is absolutely correct that the style of this section is different from the material which has preceded it. However, such an assessment does not ask why it was inserted in this textual location. Rather than assume the incompetence of a redactor, it is more useful to ask how this material functions rhetorically. When the Rhetor raises an issue it is because it is a matter of dispute. One of the innovations of the Vision of Transforrnation is that the responsibility for slaughtering the sacrifices was taken away from the laity and given to the Levites. This location and these tables are significant details here because access to this area is restricted. In this section, the man is defining areas. This material occurs here because it concerns material structures organized in space at particular locations with particular territorial significance. The second reason is the understanding of holiness which differentiates between the offerings for the priests and the offerings for the laity. Even the offerings are to be kept separate to avoid communicating holiness.

40:44–46 describe the two chambers in the Inner Court for the priests who guard the Altar and the House. This is the first time the bronze-like man speaks during the measuring tour. This section has also raised questions concerning the organization of the text. Why is the silent process of delineating space interrupted by a speech? Why is the reference to social

---

[32] Zimmerli, vol 2, 365.

roles here rather than in Chapter 44 which is concerned with questions of access according to social role? Here, too, redaction critics point to the reasons why the text does not belong here. In Zimmerli's judgment:

> ... this premature statement by the man about the chambers destroys the effect of the statement about the holy of holies in 41:4, which clearly formed the conclusion and the real object of the visionary guidance scene.[33]

Once again, Zimmerli has correctly identified a portion of text which is different from the material around it. And once again, my question is, What is the rhetorical purpose of this insertion? This material has the same rhetorical function as the inserted material concerning the Inner North Gate. It restricts access to an area according to social role. The area is identified as the territory of the priestly class. The reference to the priests here serves as a label to identify the areas rather than to discuss the specific roles.

The man then completes the process of defining the area of the Inner Court. The Narrator notes that the Altar is located in the Inner Court in front of the House (40:47).

The Narrator is given access to the Nave. From there, he watches while the man defines the areas and boundaries of the Vestibule, Nave, and Inner Room (41:14). After defining the inner areas of the House building, the man then defines the external structures and spaces of the House building and the Binyan. In my earlier discussion of this material, I argued that the purpose of these complex measurements was to define the spaces of the House building (41:5–12) and the Binyan (41:5–15a) as perfect squares. The material in 41:15b-26 concerns the decorative motifs and building materials of the House, and the table in the Nave. Again, the inclusion of this material in this location is a problem for Zimmerli's redactional analysis.

> It is with a certain amount of surprise that one reads, in the continuation of chapter 41 from v 15b on, a precise description of the interior furnishings of the temple...The return to the temple interior once again is unexpected...From the point of view of form and style, too, the section 41:15b-26 does not fit its context.[34]

And once again, Zimmerli's form critical insights are valid, but I raise the question of the rhetorical function of this material here. Although this material does not fit neatly into the categories of area, boundaries, and access, it does represent an innovation, which Zimmerli notes.

---

[33] Zimmerli, vol. 2, 366.
[34] Zimmerli, vol. 2, 386.

...the variations between the description in Ezekiel and 1 Kings 6 with regard to ornamentation and materials show that the intention here is to describe something unique, something new.[35]

The pattern, both in the Vision of Transformation and in P, is to define an area before considering its function. Although the issue here is not function, but ornamentation, a similar pattern is evident in which the area of the House building is defined completely before considering the ornamentation of the area.

The pattern of defining the area before considering its function is evident in the next section. After completing the definition of the House building and Binyan, the man and Narrator begin to move outward. 42:1–12 define the area and boundaries of the chambers for the priests. Once again, Jonathan Smith's understanding of "zones of holiness" clarifies the logic of the text.[36] The dimensions given in the text clearly define the spaces of the central zone which includes the square spaces of the Inner Court, the House, and the Binyan. In contrast, neither the zone for the priests, nor the zone for the people has a square area. (The only square area to which the people have access is the Outer Court; however, part of the Outer Court lies within the holy inner zone belonging to YHWH.) The dimensions which are included are sufficient to define YHWH's zone, and YHWH's areas. On either side of this central zone, there are spheres of priestly domestic activities, which contain the priestly chambers (40: 44–46; 42:13). The measurements of one set of priestly chambers are given but not the other. On the other side of the priestly zone, there is the zone for the people. This zone contains the pavement (40:18), the chambers (40:17; 42:8), the kitchens (46:22). However, except for the dimensions of the cooking areas in the four corners of the Outer Court, there are no dimensions given for the places for the people. The shape of the cooking areas is the rectangle, the shape of the common, rather than the holy. This is one more indication that the purpose of these measurements is not to provide the measurements of a building plan, but to separate the holy from the common.

42:13–14 define the function of these areas. According to the principle that the Rhetor mentions what he wants to change, these details have rhetorical significance. The rhetorical motivation behind these instructions is the innovation Milgrom identifies as the concept that "the sancta are contagious to persons."[37] Contagious holiness can attach itself to persons as well as objects. He argues that the Vision of Transformation is a polemic

---

[35.] Zimmerli, vol. 2, 387.
[36.] Refer to the discussion in Chapter Two.
[37.] Milgrom, *Leviticus*, 452.

against the attitude in P that only objects attract holiness, which means that neither the priests, nor the vestments they wear while officiating at the Altar, can become holy and therefore contagious.[38] Milgrom argues that the conviction of the Rhetor of the Vision of Transformation is that everyone and everything which touches the Altar becomes holy: the priests, the offerings made on upon the Altar, and the clothing the priests wear while officiating at the Altar. The vestments worn by the priests have attracted the contagious holiness of the Altar, and must not be worn into the Outer Court.[39] Similarly, the offerings are the "most holy offerings" which are reserved for the priests. Since these offerings transmit holiness, they must be eaten in the priestly chambers.[40] This is one more instance where the rhetorical issue involves territorial restriction.

42:15–20 complete the outward movement to the outside of the House Complex, and define the whole area by measuring its outer boundary.

All of the definition of territory in chapters 40–42 is preliminary to the return of YHWH to take possession of the territory as the King. In Chapter 43, attention turns from definition of territory to the issue of access into the areas of the territory. One of Zimmerli's puzzles is the repetition involved in these chapters, expressed in these words: "One will simply have to accept the strange, repeated additions to the arrangement of this section as a whole."[41] The explanation for these "strange, repeated additions" is a changed purpose. In Chapters 40–42, the goal was to define areas; in these chapters, the goal is to define access to those areas. Even in the two sections which defined areas in terms of priestly access (40:45–46 and 42:13–14), the issue was to define areas for particular functions rather than to define social roles. This section begins with YHWH's access into the House, as the territorial power holder.

The structure of the text follows the order of the Babylonian *akitu* ceremony with the significant difference that there is no human king. The procession of the victorious returning king occurs in 43:1–6. It is followed by the claim to kingship (43:6–9) and the regulations for the future (43: 10–12).

43: 13–27 concern the Altar, a section which has created considerable difficulty for redaction critics. The Altar was mentioned in a very few words in 40:47. This return to the topic of the Altar in 43:13–27 is regarded as a problem of redaction. Zimmerli asserts that:

---

38. Milgrom, *Leviticus,* 452.
39. Milgrom, *Leviticus,* 448–449.
40. Milgrom, *Leviticus,* 446.
41. Zimmerli, vol. 2, 412.

The bald note about the altar [in 40:47]…was found to be unsatisfactory. In 43:13–17 precise details about the altar have been added, which admittedly do not answer the question about its more precise location in the court either.[42]

40:47 located the Altar in the Inner Court; 43:13–17 describe it. These are two different topics about the Altar.[43] 43:18–27 concern the ceremony to consecrate the Altar as part of the New Year ceremony.

Two factors are necessary for the community of Israel to experience the blessing of YHWH. The first is the presence of YHWH in the midst, accomplished by the return of the Kabod YHWH. The second is a means by which pollution and guilt can be removed. The social dimension of the priestly system has been well-developed in Gorman's study. The purpose of the Altar is not to appease an angry God, but to restore rupture in the community and the cosmos.[44] The narrative turns to the Altar in order to accomplish the second purpose. In the Babylonian New Year ceremony, the *akitu*, cleansing of the temple is a part of the ceremony, and occurs after the god Marduk takes possession of the house.[45] 43:18–26 describe the seven-day ritual for purification of the holy space. The function of the Altar is to purify the House from pollution caused by territorial violation. The purpose of the purification offering is not the forgiveness of sin but the purification of place. This is a one-time ritual so that the Altar may be used as an ongoing means of ensuring community well-being. After the seven days of purification are completed, the Altar will be ready for burnt offerings and well-being offerings. In addition to function, the ordinances (חקה), which are the rules of access, are defined. Only the Levitical priests who are descended from Zadok have access to the Altar. There is no re-ordination of the priesthood. The triumphal return of YHWH and the cleansing of the Altar are preliminary and one-time events which occur so that the normal operation of the House of YHWH may begin. In territorial terms, YHWH claims the territory and then requires that the territory be cleansed from all traces of territorial violation. From this perspective, the section makes perfect sense in this textual location.

Chapter 44 begins with rules of access for the House, starting again at the Outer East Gate (44:1). Commentators have noted the return and decided that the problem is bad redaction.[46] However, when the Narrator re-

---

[42] Zimmerli, vol. 2, 355.

[43] It is similar to the situation discussed earlier in which the interior of the House building was defined in 40:48–41:4 and described in 41:15b-26.

[44] Gorman, 37.

[45] Halpern, 59.

[46] See Zimmerli, vol. 2, 444.

turns to a location, the intention is different. Before, the goal was to measure the territory. Here, the instructions which follow from this point are normal operating procedure for the new House. The goal of these instructions is to detail the new rules of access which will ensure the continued presence of YHWH in the midst and the well-being of the society.

In 44:4, the Narrator is given access to the House area. This time, he enters through the Outer North Gate since the Outer East Gate is now closed. Once again the Narrator receives instructions about the new rules of access to replace the former practices of Israel. The list begins with the foreigners who are to have no access at all (44:9). The Levites are the ones who are responsible for the guard functions of the gates of the House of YHWH complex, but do not have access to the Altar or to the House building itself (44:10–14). The Zadokite priests have access to the Altar and the Holy Place, and are responsible for guarding the inner House (44:15–16).

44:17–27 is a collection of material gathered according to the subject matter of "priest. " What follows here are various ordinances for the priests concerning clothing, hair, wine, and suitable wives. Although I cannot explain the territorial basis for each of these terms, I suspect that the common issue concerning clothing, hair, and wine is the understanding that holiness is contagious to persons. While no reason is given for the restrictions about marriage, the most likely explanation is the relationship between marriage and inheritance of land. Priests were not allowed to inherit land. Marriage to a widowed woman from a non-Levitical tribe could complicate the prohibition against land inheritance. I also suspect that each of these issues was a matter of conflict among priestly factions in the exile, with the Vision of Transformation taking a restrictive position. 44:23–27 deal with other responsibilities of the priests. 44:28–31 deal with the issue of inheritance.

The topic of inheritance provides the link to the next section. Inheritance is also the topic which provides a structure to Chapters 45–46, the portion of text which critics have found the most unstructured of the entire Vision of Transformation. The key is the dual understanding of the concept of inheritance in Ancient Near Eastern ideology. The first meaning is cosmic in scope. All of the earth belongs to the god of the area who allows human beings to live on it and grow their crops in return for a tithe given back to the deity. This gift of land is the inheritance of the god. The second meaning is social, referring to the transfer of property rights within families, from generation to generation. Inherent in the territorial claim made by YHWH as King of Israel (43:7) is the territorial claim to ownership of the land, which is given as an inheritance to Israel. Israel's responsibility, as tenants on the Land, is to return a portion of the Land as an offering. This is the Portion (תרומה) which is apportioned to YHWH. Chapters 45–

46 detail the responsibilities of Israel to return to YHWH, as the territorial owner of the Land, a Portion of the Land and its produce to YHWH at YHWH's Holy Place. 45: 1–8 refer to the part of the Land which is to be returned to YHWH. According to the first principle of organization, the order of discussion begins with the definition of area. The areas are the Portion, subdivided into the Holy Portion and the Possession of the City, and the Possession of the Nasi. In terms of organization, 45: 18 define areas, but 48:9–22 define the boundaries of the areas. In addition, this section defines access according to social role: 45:4 gives the priests access to YHWH's Portion; 45:5 gives the Levites access to the Possession of the Levites; 45:6 gives the whole House of Israel access to the Possession of the City; and 45:7–8 give to the Nasi access to the Possession of the Nasi.

Just as 44:17–31 gathered material about the responsibilities of the priests, 45:9–46:18 gathers material about the responsibilities of the Nasi, as the representative of the House of Israel. The topic of inheritance continues to provide the unifying thread. 45:1–8 refer to the portion of Land which is returned to YHWH; 45:13–46:15 refer to the portion of the produce of the Land which the House of Israel returns to YHWH as offerings through the Nasi. The material about the offerings is preceded by regulations concerning correct balances (45:10–12). It is not necessary to choose whether the importance of this issue is the correct measurement of offerings for the House of YHWH, or a prohibition against fraudulent practices which cheat the people of their inheritance. Both are issues of inheritance and both depend on accurate measures. The responsibility of the Nasi is to ensure that the weights are correct. This discussion also defines the access rights of the Nasi and the people of the Land to the House of YHWH. 46:16 turns to the second kind of inheritance, the Nasi's inheritance of land, and the prohibition against abuse of the inheritance rights of the House of Israel. Even the section in 46:19–24, about the kitchens for cooking the offerings is consistent with the topic of inheritance. The topic of 45:13–46:15 is the offerings as inheritance, which defines how much, when, where, and by whom, they are to be offered. This section explains the final disposition of the offerings, by defining where they are to be cooked, and who actually gets to eat them. The reparation, purification, and cereal offerings are the inheritance of the priests. The sacrifices are eaten by the people. Thus the unifying theme is inheritance, according to the first meaning; this is "cosmic" inheritance which refers to the portion of the land and its produce which are to be returned to YHWH out of gratitude for YHWH's gift of the inheritance of the Land to Israel. Most of the section is focused on the role of the Nasi who is responsible for returning the appropriate portion of YHWH's inheritance to YHWH.

The third area of the territory is the Land. However, before there is the definition of the area of the Land, its boundaries, and access by social role to the various areas of the Land, there is a healing of the Land. This is the function of 47:1–12 in which the stream comes from the House to heal the Land. It serves a similar function in the text to the role of the Altar in Chapter 43. The Altar cleanses the House of the effects of chaos, while the stream heals the Land. The symbolism here is cosmic, involving a healing of the Land from the effects of chaos.[47]

After the healing of the Land, the Land is then defined according to area, boundaries and access. Once again, the topic of inheritance plays an important role in this section. 47:13–20 define the area of the Land by defining its outer boundaries. 47:21 begins the process of defining access to the Land by means of inheritance. This is the second meaning of inheritance; it is "social" inheritance which refers to land ownership through families. The purpose of Chapter 48 is to define the boundaries of the Land in order to grant access according to the tribes. 48: 1–7 define the access of the northern tribes to their areas; 48:8–22 reconsider the areas of the Portion and Possession of the Nasi; 48:23–29 define the access of the southern tribes to their areas; and 48:30–35 define tribal access to the City. Even though 48:8–22 appear to be redundant after the similar material in 45: 1–8, these are two different sections with different functions. 45: 1–8 define the area given back to YHWH as a type of tithe ("cosmic" inheritance); 48:8–22 consider access to these areas by tribes ("social" inheritance). 45:1–8 do not identify the boundaries of the tithed area; 48:8–22 define the boundaries of the whole Land, including this central section which is tithed to YHWH.

SUMMARY OF CHAPTER SEVEN

The concept of territoriality and the structure of the Babylonian *akitu* provide the means for understanding the organization of the text. It is a renewal of kingship, a territorial claim to the three places of House, Portion, and Land, a cleansing of the House and healing of the Land, and instructions for the maintenance of YHWH's territory for the well-being of the society and the cosmos.

[47.] The reason why Jonathan Smith could not include this section in his social mapping of Ezekiel 40–48 is that its scope is cosmic.

CHAPTER 8

Transformation

In my introduction, I expressed my goal for this study: To read the Vision of Transformation according to a single criterion: *Does my interpretation make sense of this text as an effort to tell the truth and bring about change in the situation of the Babylonian exile?* My study has been guided by a fundamental premise: *Assumptions about genre determine interpretation.* To this point, I have argued that the genre designation which makes sense of the text is *territorial rhetoric.* The question now is, How is this text which asserts the territorial claim of YHWH to be King of Israel a response to the situation of exile? My answer begins with the nature of rhetoric.

RHETORIC

Some of the most well-known words of English literature come from John Donne:

> No man is an island, entire of itself;
> every man is a piece of the continent,
> a part of the main;[1]

What Donne expressed about the interconnectedness of human lives can be re-expressed as the truth about all writing. No writer is an island, but is a piece of the continent, a part of the main. Every text is written by some-

---

[1] John Donne, "Devotions upon Emergent Occasions, XVII," in *Major British Writers* I, G. B. Harrison, ed. (New York: Harcourt, Brace & World, 1959), 392.

one in particular historical and social circumstances, who has been shaped by numerous factors such as temperament, capacities, development, experiences, education, language, gender, and world view. The island metaphor also expresses another reality about writers and the writings they produce. Writers are located, not just in time but also in place. The metaphors of island, continent, and main speak in the language of geography, a language which recognizes that we are spatial people, located, and defined by our places. No text is produced *ex nihilo* but results from the interplay between choices made by the writer and the constraints which restrict the writer's choices, in a particular time and place. This interplay between choice, constraint, and situation lies at the heart of Pred's work about "an emerging discourse" between history, human geography, and social science.[2]

> Women and men make histories and produce places, not under circumstances of their own choosing but in the context of already existing, directly encountered social and spatial structures, in the context of already existing social and spatial relations that both enable and constrain the purposeful conduct of life.[3]

In this, Pred reworks Marx's most famous dictum regarding the making of history: "Men [and women] make their own history, but they do not make it just as they please; they do not make it under circumstances chosen for themselves, but under circumstances directly encountered, given and transmitted from the past."[4] Pred modifies, expands, and disputes Marx's work in significant ways, but the truth of this insight is central to Pred's work and lies at the heart of his critique of social science which attempts to abstract social processes from their contexts.[5]

> The situation of human activity and interaction in time and space makes them dependent not upon universal conditions and laws, not upon essences, not upon the articulation and conjunction of transhistorical and transgeographical social forms but upon the actual now-here, upon the historically and geographically particular context of presences and absences.[6]

All of this is inherent in my assertion that the Book of Ezekiel is a rhetorical response to exile. By making this assertion, I intend to broaden the

---

[2] Pred, *MHCHG*, 1.

[3] Pred, *MHCHG*, 9

[4] Pred, *MHCHG*, note 11, 33.

[5] Pred, *MHCHG*, 229.

[6] Pred, *MHCHG*, 11.

sense of rhetoric beyond the two distinct uses of the term in contemporary biblical scholarship. The first refers to *rhetorical criticism* as a type of literary criticism which looks for stylistic devices in the text.[7] The second refers to the use of *classical rhetoric* as a means to analyze texts as persuasive discourse.[8] However, rhetoric is more than the use of style or persuasion; it also applies to exposition and motivation.

> Rhetoric is the art or the discipline that deals with the use of discourse, either spoken or written, to inform or persuade or motivate an audience, whether that audience is made up of one person or a group of persons.[9]

This definition identifies the three necessary elements of rhetoric: a rhetor, an audience, and a discourse. However, before there is a rhetoric, there is a precipitating *exigence* which the rhetor wants to change. In Bitzer's memorable and incisive phrase, an *"exigence* is an imperfection marked by urgency."[10]

The essential characteristic of rhetoric is that it is a response to an existing situation which the rhetor thinks can somehow be changed by addressing words to a particular audience.[11] Earlier, I referred to Ball's dramatic analysis which used the language of intrusion and stasis. The stasis at the beginning of a play is the rhetorical context, the intrusion is the exigence, the dialogue is the discourse which attempts to respond to the exigence, and the end of the play is the response the rhetor wants to produce.

---

[7] James Muilenburg's Society of Biblical Literature Presidential Address in 1968 is often cited as the beginning point for contemporary interest in rhetoric in biblical scholarship under the methodological designation of rhetorical criticism. See James Muilenburg, "Form Criticism and Beyond," *JBL* 88 (1969): 1–18.

[8] See George A. Kennedy, *New Testament Interpretation through Rhetorical Criticism* (Chapel Hill: University of North Carolina Press, 1984); Yehoshua Gitay, *Prophecy and Persuasion: A Study of Isaiah 40–48* (Bonn: Linguistica Biblica, 1981); Wilhelm Wuellner, "Where is Rhetorical Criticism Taking Us?," *CBQ* 49 (1987): 448–463.

[9] Corbett, 3.

[10] Lloyd Bitzer, "The Rhetorical Situation," *Philosophy and Rhetoric* 1 (1968): 6. (Italics in the original.)

[11] Bitzer defines a rhetorical situation as "a complex of persons, events, objects, and relationships presenting an actual or potential exigence which can be completely or partially removed if discourse, introduced into the situation, can so constrain human decision or action as to bring about the significant modification of the exigence" (Bitzer, 6).

The complication for rhetorical analysis of biblical texts is that they are composite texts, written, redacted, and transmitted over time, in various places, and used to accomplish various purposes. One of the criticisms Jon Levenson raises against biblical scholarship is the tendency to obscure theological differences by neglecting to consider context.

> It is never self-evident what the context is in terms of which a unit of literature is interpreted. In the case of the Hebrew Bible, the candidates are legion. They include the work of the author who composed the unit, the redacted pericope in which it is now embedded, the biblical book in which it appears, the subsection of the Jewish canon which contains the book (Pentateuch, Prophets, or Writings), the entire Hebrew Bible treated as a synchronic reality, the Christian Bible (Old Testament and New Testament), and the exegetical traditions of the church or the rabbis. Each of these locations—and there are more—defines a context; it is unfair and shortsighted to accuse proponents of any one of them of "taking the passage out of context." Rather, the success of an interpretation is relative to the declared objectives of the interpreter. The great flaw of the biblical theologians is their lack of self-awareness on the issue of context and their habit, in the main, of acting as though the change of context made no hermeneutical difference. In point of fact, it makes all the difference in the world.[12]

As the quotation from Levenson makes clear, there are multiple contexts for the Book of Ezekiel. My rhetorical analysis assumes the context identified by the text itself, the context of the Babylonian exile.[13] The text is presented as the Rhetor's response to this exilic context.

---

[12] Jon D. Levenson, "Why Jews are not Interested in Biblical Theology," in *Judaic Perspectives on Ancient Israel*, Jacob Neusner, Baruch Levine and Ernest Frerichs, ed. (Philadelphia: Fortress, 1987), 300.

[13] In contrast to my assumption, Davis works from a functionalist literary perspective. She assumes that the genre of the Book of Ezekiel is "archival discourse." In her words, "The essential quality of archival speech is that it preserves an utterance by dissociating it from a particular speaker or context of production. Furthermore, the utterance gains authority by being embedded in a context—tradition, historical, or ritualistic—where it appears in some way fundamental to the life of the community" (Davis, 82–83).

EXILE

There is no factor which is more important for the rhetoric of the Vision of Transformation than the experience of exile, which is fundamentally an oppressive experience. Exile is an extreme expression of territoriality. The purpose of territoriality is to control access by asserting control over an area. Exile accomplishes this control of access by forced relocation from one place to another. It is always an act of power in order to control access to an area. For the ones exiled, this assertion of territoriality means complete denial of access to the area of origin. It also means control of access in the area of exile. The exiles cannot go back to the place of origin. They are denied access permanently (or until the exile ends).

Exile is more than a matter of location; it is also a matter of identity. In his sociological study of the Babylonian exile, Daniel Smith argues that a Fourth World perspective is most appropriate for understanding the experience of exile, defined as:

> ... the view of social events and values that become operative for a minority in a conditions [sic] of forced removal and settlement under imperial control and power.[14]

Smith emphasizes that the exile was an act of empire, and a "punishing experience."[15] It was the experience of domination by an outside power.

A community in exile is subject to many conflicting forces, some external and some internal. All of these forces are threats to the community's identity. The means for this loss of identity can be active or passive, violent or peaceful, by assimilation or destruction. The central generic issue facing an exiled community is the continued existence of the community itself, as a community. Smith discusses the mechanisms by which exiled communities respond to the experience of exile, ranging from assimilation into the dominant power on one extreme, to mythologized nostalgia for home on the other. On the continuum between these two extremes, exiles create various means for survival as a distinct community within the dominant culture.[16] Another generic reality of exile is that exiled communities are factionalized, representing different responses along this continuum: active revolt or passive submission; assimilation or isolation; despair or hope.

[14.] Daniel L. Smith, *The Religion of the Landless: The Social Context of the Babylonian Exile*, with a Foreward by Norman K. Gottwald (Bloomington, Indiana: Meyer Stone Books, 1989), 10.

[15.] Daniel Smith, 29, 31.

[16.] Daniel Smith, 49–68.

In this situation of exile, in a factionalized community, faced with the threat of the disintegration of the community, the response of the Rhetor was to write a book. A book is a potent means of resistance against a dominant culture which threatens to swallow up a minority community. This is particularly true if the rhetorical strategy of the dominant culture is to force its ideology on a minority. Whatever the necessary requisites for imperial pretensions, Nebuchadrezzar had them in abundance. It was not enough to conquer the world; he wanted to remake it in Babylon's image. Exiles were brought to Babylon to build the canals and the buildings and the other material structures designed to demonstrate divine favor to Nebuchadrezzar as king of Babylon, and ruler of the world.[17] Some exiles were brought to Babylon to be trained in Babylonian culture, an educated corps which could be sent back home as missionaries for Babylon. As a priest, Ezekiel was one of Judah's educated elite, an obvious choice for training in Babylonian culture.[18] The fact that he was taken in the first exile in 597, along with King Jehoiachin, indicates his social status in Judah.

A book functions as a powerful means of resistance against the dominant culture. Rhetoric provides an alternative to violent rebellion.[19] The Book of Ezekiel is "words as weapons of the weak," a local struggle against forces which threaten the disintegration of the community.[20] Nebuchadrezzar's social strategy to train the educated elite of his conquered territories in the culture of Babylon provides an explanation for the evidence of Babylonian literature in the Book of Ezekiel.[21] The irony is that the Rhetor used these Babylonian materials to produce a book which claimed the supremacy of YHWH.

The book is also a rhetorical response to those who argue for revolt against Babylon, the point of Lang's study, *Kein Aufstand in Jerusalem*. Much of the explicit rhetorical force of the Book of Ezekiel is directed

---

[17.] The same social and theological realities which Duncan described for the building projects of the King of Kandy in Sri Lanka, and which Whitelam described for the United Monarchy, and which I described for Solomon's building of the temple in Jerusalem, motivated Nebuchadrezzar. The difference is that Nebuchadrezzar's pretensions operated on a larger scale.

[18.] It is also important to remember that these exiles from Judah were not the only ones brought to Babylon. Babylonian imperial policy (following the policies of the Assyrians before them) resettled many peoples throughout the Ancient Near East. The Judahites were not the only exiles working along the canals of Babylon, or being trained in Babylonian culture.

[19.] Cunningham argues that "persuasion is the only real alternative to violence." David Cunningham, "Theology as Rhetoric," 421.

[20.] Allan Pred, "Locally Spoken Word and Local Struggles," *Society and Space* 7 (1989): 219.

against those whose strategy is revolt, directed against the "pro-Egyptian" faction. It excoriates Zedekiah for his violation of covenant with Nebuchadrezzar, which is regarded as violation of his covenant with YHWH. The rhetoric also excoriates Egypt, and the vassal states of Palestine, for their roles in this revolt against Nebuchadrezzar. The Rhetor uses cosmic symbolism to describe the political realities of the time.[22] There is also another rhetorical response in this book. It is a strong antidote to nostalgia, to wishful thinking, to denial, to comforting memories of the good old days back home. If the Rhetor is harsh against Zedekiah and company, he is relentless against those who would take comfort in nostalgia. It has been common to use the language of "restoration" in writing about Ezekiel 40–48.[23] Re-storation refers to re-vival, re-turn, re-building, re-making, re-newing, re-pairing, re-formation—to making something the way it was. However, what the Rhetor sees is not re-storation or re-formation but trans-formation.[24] There is no trace of nostalgia in this Rhetor's view of the world. The goal of the ideology of the Book of Ezekiel is not restoration to what was, but transformation to a new thing. The power of a book is that it can create a new world.

TERRITORIAL RHETORIC

What is this new world which the Rhetor wants to create? To answer this question, I return to the matter of genre. The genre issue here is that this is not only rhetoric, it is *territorial* rhetoric. How is this text, which asserts the territorial claim of YHWH to be the King of Israel, a response to the situation of the exiles? To address this question, I raise others. Did the Rhetor of the Book of Ezekiel expect that postexilic Israel would use this

---

[21.] In addition to his study which relates the Book of Ezekiel to the Poem of Erra, Bodi discusses the many Babylonian influences on the book. See particularly, Bodi, 35–51.

Although Davis discusses the effect of Babylon's literary culture on Ezekiel, she does not consider how an exile, living in one of the settlement camps along the Chebar canal, could have become so well acquainted with this culture. She writes only that "...exile set Ezekiel in the midst of a long-established and highly sophisticated literary culture" and that "...it is likely that he received some encouragement from the value long attached to writing in the foreign culture which now dominated his own (Davis, 42).

[22.] To cite only one example: the Egyptian pharaoh is the chaos monster set loose upon the earth.

[23.] Three examples are: Jon Levenson, *The Theology of the Program of Restoration;* Peter R. Ackroyd, *Exile and Restoration* (Philadelphia: Westminster, 1968): 110–117; Greenberg, "The Design and Themes of Ezekiel's Program of Restoration. "

[24.] Ralph Klein also makes this distinction. See: Klein, 182–183.

document as the building plan for a new temple? That the Land would be divided this way? That the City would be built this way? That the society would be arranged this way? How scholars answer these questions is intricately connected with their assumptions about genre. Those who argue that the Rhetor intended to produce building plans for a future temple, and a surveyor's map for the division of the Land, operate with the assumption that the Rhetor expected these plans to be carried out. And since the post-exilic temple did not look like this, and the geography of post-exilic Israel did not take this shape, then the rhetoric must be judged a failure. It did not accomplish its rhetorical purpose.[25]

Much of my argument to this point has been directed against the assumptions of the building plan genre. The command to "measure the proportion," the identification of the text as a vision, the lack of vertical dimensions, the symbolic numbers, the territorial emphasis, the cosmic symbolism, the archaic social language, all taken together argue against the assumption that the Rhetor thought that he was providing a detailed building plan and surveyor's map for post-exilic Israel.

If Ezekiel 40–48 do not provide a construction blueprint for the post-exilic temple, is the temple intended to remain only a literary creation, a symbol for the universal presence of God?[26] Many of the arguments against the building plan genre are arguments for the temple as literary symbol. However, this interpretation of the temple as literary symbol for the presence of God creates another set of questions. How would a text which understands the temple as only a literary symbol function rhetorically in the context of exile? How does it answer the questions of exile? For twentieth century Christian readers, it is no great problem to read this text about a future temple as a literary symbol for the universal and transcendent presence of God. There is no need for an actual temple in Christian ideology. Not only is there no need, Christian ideology often sees the temple as the focal point of an old and out-dated religion. Christians can

---

[25.] Moshe Greenberg's assessment is: "Wherever Ezekiel's program can be checked against subsequent events it proves to have had no effect. The return and resettlement of postexilic times had nothing in common with Ezekiel's vision…" Greenberg, "Design," 235.

[26.] For two very different treatments of the text which both argue against any notion that the temple should be built, see Tuell and Patton. Tuell states that "…the temple vision is an experience of a present, on-going reality, " free from "historical and geographical limitations," rather than a program for the restoration of Israel following the exile (Tuell, 101–102).

Patton argues that "…the textualization of the building plan, which as all critics agree is not a secondary act in 40–48, had the effect that the temple not only did not have to built, but that it should not be built" (Patton, 187).

read the text of another vision which replaces the temple with the presence of God. The Book of Revelation has as its point of stasis a New Jerusalem with no temple (Revelation 21). It is not much of a leap for Christian readers to imagine that the vision of the Book of Ezekiel is taking the same stance, and calling for a future which has no need of an actual temple. Nor would it be much of a leap for twentieth century Jewish readers to read this text about a temple as a metaphor. Jewish history long ago required the transition to a world view without a temple. Jews became the people of the book, with a tradition focused on the synagogue rather than the temple.

Did the Rhetor intend this text about a temple to remain a literary symbol? What would be the rhetorical purpose of producing a text in the context of the Babylonian exile which organizes post-exilic Israel around a temple as the focal point of the society if the Rhetor did not expect post-exilic Israel to have a temple? I cannot prove it, of course, but I find it incomprehensible that the Rhetor of this text could imagine a society without an actual temple as the symbolic center of the society. Rather than a choice between a building plan for an actual temple or a metaphor for a symbolic temple, there is a third option, based on the particular role of temples in the Ancient Near East. The rhetorical power of this text about a society organized around a temple comes from the particular role of temples throughout the Ancient Near East, a role which was so well known to the audience of the Vision of Transformation that they did not need to have it made explicit in the rhetoric.

HUMAN GEOGRAPHY

The basic problem with both the building plan genre and the literary symbol genre is the failure to think socially. What can be missed so easily in the mass of detail and the morass of exegetical questions is that this text is the call for radical social change. It recognizes the profound truth that societies are spatial. To change the way a society is organized in space is to change the society. The spatial organization of a society is its *human geography*.[27] The House of YHWH, the Portion, the City, the Possession of the Nasi, and the tribal divisions of the Land are not just spaces; they are social spaces which define the society of Israel by creating a new human geography.

[27.] Human geography is a broad division in the discipline of geography which deals with the spatial aspects of societies. It is further subdivided into branches such as: demography,social and cultural geography, political geography, economic geography, urban geography, and historical geography.

While biblical scholars have devoted substantial attention to issues of geography, the particular genre of geography has been physical geography. They have drawn maps, identified boundaries, and discussed the impossibility of the physical geography of the Vision of Transformation, but the vocabulary and perspective of the discipline of human geography have generally been missing from studies of these chapters in Ezekiel.[28] Studies of Ezekiel 40–48 which have not recognized that the Vision of Transformation is a human geography have missed the rhetorical intention of the text.

The genre of territoriality is a concept from human geography. It is an effort to control the human geography of a society by controlling access to space to particular areas. And because societies are defined by their spatial organization, any change in spatial organization created by this changed access is necessarily a change in the human geography of the society. The intention of the Vision of Transformation is to change the society of Israel, by changing the way the society is organized in space.

This is why it is so important to use the language of the Rhetor rather than to assume continuity with the past. The City is no longer called Jerusalem; this is not restoration of the old Jerusalem. This City has a radically changed human geography. It is a transformed city, with YHWH in the midst, rather than the human king. It is no longer an enclave of Judah, but is the City for all of the tribes of Israel. Even if the physical geography of the new City were unchanged, with the same location as the preexilic city of Jerusalem, it would not be the same city because its human geography has been changed by new rules of access. In the same way, the human geography of this new Israel has changed the monarchic social system of pre-exilic Judah which had a Davidic king, located in his own territory and controlling access to the territory of House and Land. Even though the

---

[28.] Soja's study of postmodern geographies is based on the central theme of "the reassertion of a critical spatial perspective in contemporary social theory and analysis," and argues the following thesis. "For at least the past century, time and history have occupied a privileged position in the practical and theoretical consciousness of Western Marxism and critical social science. Understanding how history is made has been the primary source of emancipatory insight and practical political consciousness, the great variable container for a critical interpretation of social life and practice. Today, however, it may be space more than time that hides consequences from us, the 'making of geography' more than the 'making of history' that provides the most revealing tactical and theoretical world. This is the insistent premise and promise of postmodern geographies" (Soja, *PMG. 1*).

Pred's study, *MHCHG*, insists on the inseparable interrelationship between the historical, geographical, and social. Pred's work is a profound critique of social theory which ignores the constraints of time and space.

Nasi has substantial privilege and power in the new human geography, the Rhetor does not call him the king, a rhetorical strategy which emphasizes the disjunction between Old and New Israel. Whether or not the Nasi is a descendant of David, and whatever "royal" privileges he may have, the human geography of the Nasi is radically different from the human geography of the Davidic kings of Israel.

The function of the temple as the mediator between the social and the cosmic, between the earthly and the heavenly, between the actual and the symbolic, makes the House of YHWH the focal point of the new society. In the language of physics, it is place which concentrates the energy of both heaven and earth into one spot. It is a liminal place, a place where the energy of one world encounters and transforms the energy of the other. At the core of this radical vision of a new human geography which creates a new society, is a view of a world shaped by the temple as the place of mediation between these two realities. For this Rhetor, imagining a world without a human king was radical; imagining a world without an actual temple would be impossible. In a world in which kings were temple builders, the Rhetor imagined a temple that was not the territory of a human king.

The Book of Ezekiel is a critique of a social system which concentrated power into the hands of a few at the top of a monarchic system. Many of the abuses of the monarchy were abuses of power regarding space. These were real abuses which took inherited land from poor peasants and consolidated these subsistence plots into monoculture agriculture for international trade. The rich got luxuries, the poor got displaced. It is a book about the horrible injustices done by political structures as they assert power by controlling space. Exile itself is a prime example of the spatial abuse of human societies by imperial policies.

Those who argue that the Book of Ezekiel had no effect in post-exilic Israel, because the future temple did not get built according to this "plan," have missed the fact that post-exilic Israel was a society organized around a temple without a human king. It is impossible to know how much this changed society was the result of Persian imperial practice and how much the result of the Book of Ezekiel and other exilic priestly writing, but the radical change in social structure imagined by this vision actually occurred. There was a new Israel, a new temple, and no king.[29]

How then does this vision of the future speak to the exiles? Niditch notes the connection between the exile and the production of cosmogonic texts, such as Ezekiel 40–48 and Genesis 1–11:

[29.] In the world created by P, there was no temple, no king, and no city.

... the ancient chaos-to-order pattern was greatly revitalized in the exile, and afterward as a description of the process of human history and more specifically of Israelite history.[30]

However, beyond mentioning the "staying power" of "the Tradition," she does not consider why this revitalization might have occurred in exile.

THEOLOGY

If the basic problem with the building plan genre and literary symbol genre is the failure to think socially, a related problem is the failure to think socially in theological terms. The sociological dynamics of exile precipitated profound theological responses. In his book, *Self-Fulfilling Prophecy,* Jacob Neusner defines a "Judaism."

A Judaism is a system made up of a world view, a way of life, and a social group that defines its life through that world view and lives in accord with the descriptions of that way of life.

He goes on to say that there have been many Judaisms, but that each shares one defining experience.

But all Judaic systems have recapitulated a single experience: the exile and return suffered by some Jews between 586 and 450 B.C.[31]

This experience of exile defined Jews as "special, different, and select," as they asked, Who are we?, in the face of exile.[32] The exile was perceived as a theological catastrophe, which cut to the core of the identity of the people, and their understanding of God.

Disaster had struck the deepest possible blow, stabbing at the national *raison d'etre,* at the cosmological heart of the Israelite world-view. For if God's chosen people could be defeated, his chosen king deposed and exiled, his chosen house burned to the ground and his chosen city ravaged, what sense could life make any more?[33]

---

[30] Niditch, 223.

[31] Jacob Neusner, *Self-Fulfilling Prophecy: Exile and Return in the History of Judaism* (Boston: Beacon Press, 1987), 1.

[32] Neusner, 5.

[33] Robert L. Cohn, "Biblical Responses to Catastrophe," *Judaism,* 35 (1986): 263.

The Book of Ezekiel is an effort to answer this question, What sense could life make any more?, by first retelling the history and human geography of Israel as a society which did not acknowledge YHWH's territorial claim as the only King of Israel.[34] An adequate justification of this last statement would involve a substantial argument at this point. For now, I can only point in the direction such an argument would take. It would begin with the importance of the genre of human geography within the Book of Ezekiel. To cite one example, Chapter 20 is the Rhetor's recounting of the history of Israel. However, it is a history expressed in terms of human geography, as Israel rebelled against YHWH in various places. It begins with the promise to Israel of the Land, a promise made in Egypt (20:6). It continues with a long narration of Israel's violations in Egypt, and in the wilderness. Throughout, Israel's violations of YHWH's statutes and ordinances have the potential to cancel the promise of the Land. When Israel does receive the Land, the violations are expressed as spatial violations. Israel worships at "any high hill or any leafy tree" (20:28). These violations of YHWH's space are punished spatially by exile, which is called a "scattering among the countries." The future promise is first expressed as a claim to kingship.

> As I live, says YHWH God,
> surely with a mighty hand and an outstretched arm,
> and with wrath poured out,
> I will be king over you (אמלוך עליכם) (20:33).

Israel will be "brought out from the countries" (20:34) and brought into the wilderness (20:35) for judgment. The future is expressed in terms of worship at a single place.

> For on my holy mountain,
> the mountain height of Israel,
> says YHWH God,
> there (שם) all the house of Israel,
> all of them,
> shall serve me in the land;
> there (שם) I will require your contributions
> and the choicest of your gifts,
> with all your sacred offerings (20:40).

[34.] This terminology comes from the title of Pred's book, *Making Histories and Constructing Human Geographies*. Histories and human geographies can be written in books, but the categories of history and human geography are not confined to the pages of books. When Pred refers to histories and human geographies he is referring to the processes by which human beings define themselves as they live out their lives in time and space and society.

The future Israel will be a new society in the Land at this holy place (20:40–44).

The temple vision of Chapters 8–11 is a human geography of the violation of YHWH's territory by both cultic and social trespasses. Each of the "abominations" cited is a violation of YHWH's space. The "seat of the image of jealousy which provokes to jealousy" (8:3); the images on the wall and the elders who are violating priestly prerogative with their censers of incense (8:10–11); the women weeping for Tammuz (8:14); the men between the altar and the temple, with their backs to the temple, worshipping the sun (8:16); are all violations of YHWH's space. The issue is explicitly expressed in terms of territorial violation.

> And he said to me,
> "Mortal, do you see what they are doing,
> the great abominations that the House of Israel are committing here,
> to drive me far from my sanctuary? But you will see still greater abominations" (8:6).

These violations of YHWH's territory resulted in the unthinkable: YHWH abandoned the temple and Jerusalem to destruction.

The human geography which violated YHWH's territory resulted in exile, not just the exile of the people, but the exile of YHWH.[35] In the world view of the Ancient Near East, the presence of a god in the land ensured blessing; absence brought chaos. The scene in Ezekiel 11:22–23 of the Kabod YHWH, going up "from the midst of the city," is the scene of YHWH's flight into exile, the abandonment of Jerusalem to its destruction. The rhetoric of the Book of Ezekiel is an effort of the Rhetor to answer the question, Why? Contrary to those who argue against an exilic provenance for the Book of Ezekiel because of its emphasis on Jerusalem, the content and tone of the whole book make manifest sense as an effort to respond to exile perceived as chaos, because YHWH no longer dwells in the midst of Israel.

The ideology of holiness which characterizes the priestly ideology of the Book of Ezekiel and P is a theology defined within the experience of exile. Smith discusses the sociological mechanisms involved in the development of the Priestly ritual codes. The concern with separation into categories which both Gorman and Greenberg identify as characteristic of the Priestly world view serves a sociological function of group survival under minority conditions.

> It was not the *formulation* of laws of purity that represented the most creative response to Exile by the priestly writer, for we have

---

[35.] On the exile of God, see Jonathan Z. Smith, "Earth and Gods," in *Map is not Territory* (Leiden: E. J. Brill, 1978), 121.

seen that form-critical analysis reveals many of these laws to rest on older traditions. It was rather the *elaboration* of these laws to emphasize *transfer* of pollution and the association of holiness with *separation*. While the post-exilic community reflected the results of these concerns, the most logical *Sitz im Leben* for their primary function was the Exile itself. The presence of these ritual elaborations of the meaning of separation lends more weight to our thesis that the Exile represented a threat to the Jewish minority. In sum, what we see in the development of purity law is a creative, Priestly mechanism of social survival and maintenance. To dismiss this creativity as "legalism" is to forget, or ignore, the sociopolitical circumstances in which it was formulated. Majority cultures rarely understand, much less appreciate, the actions of minorities to preserve and maintain identity.[36]

The ideology of holiness expressed as separation is both a sociological and theological response to the experience of being a minority under imperial power, a community attempting to maintain its existence as a community. At the heart this ideology is a theology of the presence of God. If God dwells in the midst of the people, there is blessing; if God leaves, there is chaos.[37]

The Book of Ezekiel is the work of a visionary who creates this text of a future society as a social manifesto.[38] A visionary is one who is able to see the possibility of change in an existing society. This is different from the apocalypticist who can see no hope for such change within history itself. The stance of the visionary is surely different from the technician or contractor who can see only the possibility of what is, or the literary critic who can see only the possibility of metaphor. The visionary sees radical social change as a real possibility. This is political rhetoric, focused on the social reality of the future.

[36.] Daniel Smith, 149. Italics in the original.

[37.] See Gorman, 45.

[38.] Ezekiel 40–48 is identified as a visionary experience (40:2), a genre designation which has led to substantial discussion in the literature, and demonstrates my premise that genre assumptions determine interpretation. Interpreters evaluate the visionary character of the text on the basis of their own assumptions about what an "authentic vision" is supposed to be, whether the vision was a real experience or a literary fiction, whether authentic visions contain legislation, and so on. A complete discussion of this issue would take me far beyond the framework of my study here. My use of the term "visionary" here is intended to emphasize the social aspects of the vision, without denying the possibility of an ecstatic vision.

What about the characterization that these chapters are the work of a priestly group out to claim power for themselves? According to this understanding, the exiled elite in Babylon, with the resource of literacy, were able to rewrite their histories to provide texts which legitimated their own power.[39] There is no question that the Book of Ezekiel is the work of an elite social class. There is also no question that the new human geography of Israel places the priests in control of the territory of the House of YHWH. However, to acknowledge that the rhetoric of the Vision of Transformation is a claim to power, that it is a territorial claim by one group of the society's elites to control the space of the House of YHWH, that it reflects the world view of that particular elite social group, does not conflict with my assumption that the Book of Ezekiel is also a work of integrity and theological conviction.

What is truly remarkable about the priestly vision of the reorganized society of Israel is the balance of power inherent in it, and its concern for the well-being of everyone in the society. It is true that the priests are the ones who control access to the holy place. It is also true that the priests do not own land. I find that single fact extraordinary. Unlike the monarchy, which both controlled the temple and controlled the land, this social plan creates a balance of power. The very existence of the priests, their subsistence and livelihood, depends upon the support of the people who do possess land. It is a system which is characterized by justice, a reorganization of society in which everyone has enough. No one is displaced and no one is wronged by a rapacious central government out of control.

We must be careful here not to impose our notions of justice upon this system. This society probably does not appeal to many twentieth century readers. It is a hierarchical and patriarchal system, with God as king, and tribes headed by the sons of Israel. Priesthood is male and hereditary. A system of worship focused on the ritual slaughter of animals is probably offensive to most contemporary sensibilities. However, the probability that contemporary readers, in our contexts, with our constraints, would not choose this human geography, does not discredit the integrity of the Rhetor.

This concern for the well-being of the whole society is particularly evident in the intended audience as the "House of Israel," a designation which is sufficiently ambiguous to have generated substantial discussion about its meaning. At the very least, the term refers to a community, rather than to an individual. It includes the twelve tribes, the resident aliens, and rejoins the former kingdoms of Israel and Judah. The sign action of Chap-

---

[39.] For example, see: Robert B. Coote and Mary P. Coote, *Power Politics and the Making of the Bible* (Minneapolis: Fortress Press, 1990), 69–73.

ter 37:15–23 is a command to write on two "sticks" concerning "Judah" and "the children of Israel," and "Joseph" and the "House of Israel" in order to create one people.

> and I will make them one *people* (גוי) in the Land,
> upon the mountains of Israel;
> and one king shall be king over them all;
> and they shall be no longer two *peoples* (גוים)
> and no longer divided into two kingdoms (37:22).[40]

In all of this, the "House of Israel" is an inclusive and broad designation, and the goal of the rhetoric is to create a community, rather than to maintain divisions. Its genre is political rhetoric, for the benefit of a community, in the future.[41]

How then does this vision of the future speak to the exiles? For a factionalized, displaced, despairing people in exile, a minority under imperial domination, with its own king held captive, and its central worship site destroyed, the vision creates a new world. It is a healed world, a cleansed world, a holy world. The theology of separation is a sociology of unification. It is a world with one community in its own Land, with its own temple, and YHWH, the only King of Israel, in the midst. It expresses the conviction that Israel will have a future as a people. But in order to have a future, it must be an Israel shaped by a new human geography. The center of this new geography is a new temple, which fulfills the purpose of a temple as the focal point for social and cosmic well-being, a holy place where YHWH dwells in the midst of Israel. And so finally, what is the Vision of Transformation? It is an expression of hope: hope in the transcendent reality of God; hope in the continued existence of a people; hope that there is

---

[40.] In the context of my discussion here, I cite this text for what it claims about the future community, with YHWH as King. In this text, the "king" is David, not YHWH. Earlier, I referred to this text, and the exegetical difficulties of relating this text to the material about the Nasi in the Vision of Transformation, which has no place for a human king.

[41.] In their study of rhetoric and biblical interpretation, Patrick and Scult also argue that the existence of the community, as a community, is the goal of biblical narratives. They argue that the truth of the narrative is not in what actually happened but in the power of the narrative to define the community's identity. It is this "rhetorical truth" which is the purpose of the narrative. "Our best text reading, therefore, does not deny that these narratives might reference actual events, but merely recognizes that this dimension is ancillary to the most important truth they have to tell—the truth contained in the narratives' rhetorical power to create and define a community's identity" (Patrick and Scult, 51).

a future; hope that exile is not the last word. The last word is that YHWH is in the midst. YHWH is there.

Summary of Chapter Eight

The genre of the Vision of Transformation is territorial rhetoric. Territoriality is a concept from human geography, which concerns the spatial organization of societies. Ezekiel 40–48 is the work of a visionary who changes the society of post-exilic Israel by changing access to space. The concern is not to provide a building plan for a building but to restructure the society from pre-exilic monarchy to a post-exilic temple society without a human king.

Summary and Conclusions

The Book of Ezekiel is the answer to profound questions. Why has this happened to us? Who are we? Do we have a future? Will we go home again? In all of these questions, the most basic question is, Where is God in all of this? The question, Where?, is the motivating question of the book. However, most modern studies of the book of Ezekiel have been shaped by a different question, the question, when? When was the book written? What was the history of composition? Is it historically reliable? All of these When? questions are valid questions. The Book of Ezekiel itself is manifestly interested in questions of history. It is unique among the prophetic books in its precise attention to dates. It has been a matter of emphasis. Scholars have tended to concentrate on temporal questions without giving equal attention to spatial matters. History has prevailed over geography.

Human geography has to do with the social organization of space. Contemporary human geographers have argued that this priority of history over geography has been a pervasive blind spot in social science disciplines, beginning in the nineteenth century and continuing to the present. One of the strongest voices from this perspective is that of Allan Pred who argues that there can be no history without geography and no geography without history. This perspective from human geography plays a dominant role in this study of Ezekiel in the topic of *territoriality*. Territoriality is the effort to control social space, by defining areas, communicating boundaries, and attempting to control access.

Ezekiel 40–48 is territorial rhetoric. A rhetorical text is one written to persuade, to accomplish a purpose in a specific context. The Rhetor perceives an exigence—an imperfection marked by urgency—in the Rhetor's context, and attempts to argue for some sort of response in the intended audience. These chapters in Ezekiel were written as a rhetorical response to the social and theological crises of a community in exile. These crises threatened the destruction of the community, as a community. In order to grasp the urgency of the exigence, and the passion of the response, it is necessary to understand the exile as a shattering social and theological crisis.

The urgency of the crisis focused on the question of the location of God. And it is here that contemporary readers of Ezekiel have the greatest blind spot. For most contemporary readers, the question, Where is God?, brings the response, God is everywhere. Yet it is precisely this worldview which sets modern readers apart from the worldview and understanding of the Rhetor and the exiles in Babylon. They shared the pervasive worldview of the Ancient Near East that gods were located in place.

In rhetorical terms, the question, Where is God?, creates several rhetorical constraints. Rhetoric is characterized by choice. It is the effort of a Rhetor to persuade an audience to choose a particular response. However, even before there is the possibility of choice, there are constraints. Constraints are whatever interferes with choice. Constraints have many forms: histories, human geographies, worldviews, prior life experiences, intellectual capacities, personalities, psychological temperaments, and social status. All rhetors and all audiences are constrained by some factors. Most contemporary readers bring to the book of Ezekiel two constraints which interfere with our capacity to grasp the rhetorical intent of the book. The first is a theological constraint which assumes the omnipresence of God. If the human geographers are correct, the second is a constraint of scholarship which tends to overlook matters of human geography in favor of historical questions. These two cultural constraints have interfered with the capacity of contemporary readers to grasp the rhetorical intention of the book, particularly in terms of the final vision, Ezekiel 40–48.

To come to a book such as Ezekiel, and especially to the material of chapters 40–48, is to enter a strange and foreign world. It is full of minutiae, about topics and items which seem irrelevant to our lives. We read seemingly endless measurements, descriptions of gates, details about offerings, and the boundaries of land, all written in confusing and often redundant detail. And we decide that this is a strange way to do theology.

In order to read Ezekiel 40–48 as a rhetorical response to a situation of crisis, it is necessary to operate with the assumption that the Rhetor did not set out to write an irrelevant book. If this is indeed rhetoric, it was written out of a sense of urgency, because the Rhetor cared passionately about the theological significance of such details which we tend to dismiss as irrelevant. From our perspective, the book of Ezekiel can too easily be dismissed as the legalistic restrictions of a disturbed individual. What we miss in this kind of characterization is that this book is a creative response to the experiences of a disturbed community. It was a disturbed community because it was exiled by an imperial power, and its homeland devastated. The most significant devastation was the ruin of the temple—the nexus of the cosmos and the society, and the dwelling place of YHWH—whose presence provided the well-being of the community. The rhetorical purpose of the book was to give hope to a community in exile. It does this by creating a vision of a future restructured society, a society centered around the temple of YHWH, a society at home in its own land, a society with YHWH in its midst.

Ezekiel 40–48 is territorial rhetoric, produced in the context of the Babylonian exile to restructure the society of Israel by reasserting YHWH's territorial claim as the only king of Israel. Many of the problems of interpretation concerning Ezekiel 40–48 are problems of genre, most notably the assumption that Chapters 40–42 are the "blueprint" for the post-exilic temple in Jerusalem. The argument that this is territorial rhetoric rather than a blueprint depends on the definition of territoriality and a conceptual shift from structures to spaces. The rhetorical purpose of the guided tour is to measure the proportion of the House of YHWH, in order to claim territory, not to provide a building plan for a temple. The dimensions given define spaces rather than structures, a process which explains the omission of most vertical dimensions of the structures. Territoriality includes definition of area, communication of boundaries and means of access to territory. The measurements defined three concentric spaces: the House of YHWH, or Holy Place; the Portion; and the Land of Israel. A shift of focus from structures to spaces reveals the importance of the square shape of the House complex, the Outer Court, the Inner Court, the area of the House building, the area of the Binyan, and the Altar. The emphasis on the square shape continues in the description of the Portion, which includes the Holy Portion, made up of YHWH's Portion and the Possession of the Levites, and the Possession of the City.

A particular spatially-oriented ideology of holiness motivated this definition of space. This ideology of holiness located the Altar as the concentric center of House, Portion, and Land to be the place of mediation between the society and the cosmos. The Altar is the place of purgation of the effects of impurity. The purpose of territorial systems is to control access to space, by means of boundaries. Comparison of Ezekiel with P shows that both shared a similar understanding of holiness, but that access to

holy space was more restricted in Ezekiel than P, particularly in terms of access to the Altar.
Ezekiel 40–48 is the territorial claim of YHWH to be the only King of Israel. The rhetoric claims that YHWH is the only power holder; all others are power subjects in YHWH's territory. The date of the vision as the tenth day of the month at the beginning of the year corresponds to a significant date in the Babylonian New Year ceremony, the *akitu*. The vision of the Kabod YHWH coming to take possession of the House of YHWH is YHWH's claim as power holder of the territory and the renewal of YHWH's claim to kingship. All others are power subjects, with varying degrees of access. The priests have maximum access to the territory of YHWH's House. The Levites have lesser access, and the laity have the least access to the House. The rhetoric did not intend to demote the Levites to a secondary status by this territorial claim. The rhetorical intention was to restrict the laity of Israel from access to the Inner Court and the Altar.

The theme of inheritance is an essential aspect of territorial access. Cosmic inheritance refers to the gift of the Land to Israel from YHWH. Social inheritance refers to the transmission of land from father to son. In the Vision of Transformation, access to the Land, the Portion, and the House is determined by social role. The role of cosmic inheritance is evident in the material concerning the Portion and the offerings. They are a type of tithe returned to YHWH. Social inheritance refers to access to land ownership. Eleven tribes have access to Land by ownership but restricted access to the House of YHWH. The Levitical tribe has access to the House of YHWH but restricted access to Land. The Nasi receives a portion of Land as a grant from YHWH.

The structure of drama provides a tool for identifying the intrusion into stasis at the beginning of the book, and the resolution of stasis at the end. The intrusion was an event in the fifth year of the exile of King Jehoiachin, a date which coincided with a meeting in Jerusalem of the various Palestinian vassal states in order to revolt against their Babylonian overlord, Nebuchadrezzar. The Rhetor characterized this action as a violation of Zedekiah's vassal treaty with Nebuchadrezzar, and the event which would culminate in the destruction of the Jerusalem temple. The new stasis of the ending is the new City which replaces the human monarchy with the kingship of YHWH, and restores Israel to a pre-monarchic social structure.

The Vision of Transformation intended to demote the monarchy by changing access to the House of YHWH and the Land. The narratives concerning temples in 1 Kings and Ezekiel 40–48 are the territorial claims of kings, with significant rhetorical differences between these two descriptions. Solomon was functioning in the typical role of Ancient Near Eastern kings as the temple builder for the patron deity. In contrast, the narrative in Ezekiel shows a temple which is already built by the divine King YHWH. The critique of past territorial violations of the kings of Israel is explicit, and provides the justification for displacing the human king in this new territory. This human geography of a temple without a human king is a radical innovation in social structure. The territorial access and social role of the Nasi is very different from the role of the Davidic kings as power holders of the land and temple.

The concept of territoriality and the structure of the Babylonian *akitu* provide the means for understanding the organization of the text. Rather than a chaotic jumble of disjointed elements, this is a coherent, purposeful text, with a discernible organizational structure. It is a renewal of kingship, a territorial claim to the three places of House, Portion, and Land, a cleansing of the House and healing of the Land, and instructions for the maintenance of YHWH's territory for the well-being of the society and the cosmos.

The Vision of Transformation is the work of a visionary who creates a vision of a future society as a response to current reality, based on a particular spatial view of holiness. The rhetorical intention of the vision is not to provide a building plan but to restructure the society from pre-exilic monarchy to a post-exilic temple society without a human king. In the Rhetor's analysis of the exigence, the crisis facing the exiled and scattered community is the threat of assimilation by the dominant Babylonian imperial culture. The Rhetor offers the hope of a future as a healed and transformed community, a holy community in its own land, with the presence of YHWH in the midst.

What is the value of such a book for contemporary readers? Its value is not in the specifics, but in the raising of the questions. The Rhetor is a true creator, who responds to a contemporary crisis with a vision of what can be, without ever losing sight of current reality. The Rhetor offers a vision of a radically restructured society. It is a book of resolute honesty, deep convictions, and profound courage. It challenges us to recreate our theologies with the same passionate honesty, conviction, and courage, to ask ourselves, Who are we? Do we have a future? Are we in exile? Where is home? And most importantly and profoundly, it challenges us to ask, Where is God?

Selected Bibliography

Abba, Raymond. "Priests and Levites in Ezekiel." *VT* 28 (1978): 1–9.

Ackroyd, Peter R. *Exile and Restoration: A Study of Hebrew Thought of the Sixth Century B. C.* OTL. Philadelphia: Westminster Press, 1968.

Allan, Nigel. "The Identity of the Jerusalem Priesthood During the Exile." *HeyJ* 23 (1982): 259–69.

Allen, Leslie. *Ezekiel 20–48.* WBC, no. 29. Dallas: Word Books, 1990.

Anderson, Bernhard W. *Creation Versus Chaos: The Reinterpretation of Mythical Symbolism in the Bible: With a New Afterword on the Cosmic Dimensions of the Biblical Creation Faith.* Philadelphia: Fortress, 1987.

Andrew, M. E. *Responsibility and Restoration: The Course of the Book of Ezekiel.* Dunedin, New Zealand: University of Otago Press, 1985.

Avigad, Nahman. "The Inscribed Pomegranate from the 'House of the Lord'" *BA* 53 (1990): 157–66.

Ball, David. *Backwards and Forwards: A Technical Manual for Reading Plays.* With a Foreword by Michael Langham. Carbondale, IL: Southern Illinois University Press, 1983.

Bechtel, Lyn M. "Shame as a Sanction of Social Control in Biblical Israel: Judicial, Political, and Social Shaming." *JSOT* 49 (1991): 47–76.

Ben-David, Arye. "The Hebrew-Phoenician Cubits *PEQ* 110 (1978): 27–28.

Biggs, C. R. "The Role of *Nasi* in the Programme for Restoration in Ezekiel 40–48." *Colloquium: The Australian and New Zealand Theological Review* 16 (1983): 46–57.

Bitzer, Lloyd F. "The Rhetorical Situation." *Philosophy and Rhetoric* 1 (1968): 1–14.

Blenkinsopp, Joseph. *Ezekiel.* IBC. Louisville: John Knox Press, 1990.

———. *A History of Prophecy in Israel: From the Settlement in the Land to the Hellenistic Period.* Philadelphia: Westminster Press, 1983.

Block, Daniel I. "The Prophet of the Spirit: The Use of *RWH* in the Book of Ezekiel." *JETS* 32 (1989): 27–49.

Bodi, Daniel. *The Book of Ezekiel and the Poem of Erra.* Orbis Biblicus et Orientalis, no. 104. Freiburg, Schweiz: Universitätsverlag, 1991.

Bowman, John. "Ezekiel and the Zadokite Priesthood." *Glasgow University Oriental Society* 16 (1955–6): 1–14.

Brownlee, William H. *Ezekiel 1–19.* WBC, no. 28. Waco, TX: Word Books, 1986.

Brueggemann, Walter. *The Land: Place as Gift, Promise, and Challenge in Biblical Faith.* OBT. Philadelphia: Fortress Press, 1977.

Cagni, Luigi. *The Poem of Erra.* Sources and Monographs: Sources from the Ancient Near East, Vol. 1. Malibu: Undena Publications, 1977.

Carley, Keith W. *The Book of the Prophet Ezekiel.* Cambridge: Cambridge University Press, 1974.

Chaney, Marvin L. "Bitter Bounty: The Dynamics of Political Economy Critiqued by the Eighth-Century Prophets." In *Reformed Faith and Economics,* ed. Robert L. Stivers, 15–30. Lanham, MD: University Press of America, 1989.

Chen, Doren. "Cubit of the Temple, Cubit of Qumran." In *Proceedings of the Tenth World Congress of Jewish Studies,* Jerusalem. August 16–24 1989, 9–14. Jerusalem: World Union of Jewish Studies, 1990.

Clements, R. E. "The Ezekiel Tradition: Prophecy in a Time of Crisis." In *Israel's Prophetic Tradition: Essays in Honour of Peter R. Ackroyd,* ed. Richard Coggins, Anthony Phillips, and Michael Knibb, 119–36. Cambridge: Cambridge University Press, 1982.

———. *God and Temple.* Oxford: Basil Blackwell, 1965.

———. "Temple and Land: A Significant Aspect of Israel's Worship." *Glasgow University Oriental Society: Transactions* 19, (1961–2): 16–28.

Clifford, Richard J. *The Cosmic Mountain in Canaan and the Old Testament.* Cambridge, MA: Harvard University Press, 1972.

Cody, Aelred. *Ezekiel: With an Excursus on the Old Testament Priesthood.* OTM. Wilmington, DE: Michael Glazier, 1984.

———. *A History of Old Testament Priesthood.* AnBib, no. 35. Rome: Pontifical Biblical Institute, 1969.

Cohn, Robert L. "Biblical Responses to Catastrophe." *Judaism* 35 (1986): 263–76.

———. *The Shape of Sacred Space: Four Biblical Studies.* American Academy of Religion Studies in Religion. Chico: Scholars Press, 1981.

Cook, Stephen L. "Innerbiblical Interpretation in Ezekiel 44 and the History of Israel's Priesthood." *JBL* 114 (1995): 193–208.

Cooke, G. A. *The Book of Ezekiel.* ICC. Edinburgh: T. & T. Clark, 1937 <1985>.

Coote, Robert B., and Mary P. Coote. *Power. Politics and the Making of the Bible: An Introduction.* Minneapolis: Fortress Press, 1990.

Corbett, Edward P. J. *Classical Rhetoric for the Modern Student.* 3d ed. New York: Oxford University Press, 1965 < 1990>.

Cross, Frank Moore. "The Priestly Houses of Early Israel. " In *Canaanite Myth and Hebrew Epic: Essays in the History of the Religion of Israel,* 195–215. Cambridge: Harvard University Press, 1973.

————. "The Priestly Tabernacle in Light of Recent Research. " In *Temples and High Places in Biblical Times: Proceedings of the Colloquium in Honor of the Centennial of Hebrew Union-Jewish Institute of Religion*, 169–80. Jerusalem, Israel: Hebrew Union College-Jewish Institute of Religion, 1977.

Cunningham, David S. *Faithful Persuasion: In Aid of a Rhetoric of Christian Theology* Notre Dame: University of Notre Dame Press, 1990, 1991.

————. "Theology as Rhetoric." *TS* 52 (1991): 407–30.

Darr, Katheryn Pfisterer. "The Wall Around Paradise: Ezekielian Ideas About the Future." *VT* 37 (1987): 271–79.

Davies, Eryl W. "Land: Its Rights and Privileges." In *The World of Ancient Israel: Sociological, Anthropological and Political Perspectives: Essays by Members of the Society for Old Testament Study*, ed. R. E. Clements, 349–69. Cambridge: Cambridge University Press, 1989.

Davies, W. D. *The Territorial Dimension of Judaism*. Minneapolis: Fortress Press, 1991.

Davis, Ellen F. *Swallowing the Scroll: Textuality and the Dynamics of Discourse in Ezekiel's Prophecy*. JSOTSup, no. 78. Sheffield: Almond Press, 1989.

Dijkstra, Meindert. "The Altar of Ezekiel: Fact or Fiction?" *VT* 42 (1992): 22–36.

Douglas, Mary. *Purity and Danger: An Analysis of the Concepts of Pollution and Taboo*. London: Ark Paperbacks, 1966 <1984>.

Duguid, Iain M. *Ezekiel and the Leaders of Israel*. VTSup, no. 56. Leiden: Brill, 1994.

Duke, Rodney. *The Persuasive Appeal of the Chronicler: A Rhetorical Analysis*. Bible and Literature Series, no. 25. Sheffield: Almond Press, 1990.

————. "The Portion of the Levite: Another Reading of Deuteronomy 18:6–8." *JBL* 106 (1987): 193–201.

————. "Punishment or Restoration?: Another Look at the Levites of Ezekiel 44:6–16." *JSOT* 40 (1988): 61–81.

Duncan, James S. *The City as Text: The Politics of Landscape Interpretation in the Kandyan Kingdom*. CHG. Cambridge: Cambridge University Press, 1990.

Eichrodt, Walther. *Ezekiel: A Commentary*. Translated by Cosslett Quin. OTL. Philadelphia: Westminster Press, 1970.

Eliade, Mircea. *The Sacred and the Profane: The Nature of Religion*. Translated by Willard R. Trask. New York: Harcourt Brace Jovanovich, 1959.

Ellul, Danielle. "Ezechiel 40,1–41,4: Le Nouveau Temple: Un conglomérat confus de prescriptions sacerdotales, ou l'épure prophetique d'une création sanctifiée." *Foie et Vie* 85 (1986): 9–17.

Eph'al, I. "The Western Minorities in Babylonia in the 6th-5th Centuries B. C.: Maintenance and Cohesion." *Orientalia* 47 (1978): 74–90.

Everson, A. Joseph. "Ezekiel and the Glory of the Lord Tradition." In *Sin, Salvation, and the Spirit: Commemorating the Fiftieth Year of the Liturgical Press*, ed. Daniel Durken, 163–76. Collegeville, MN: Liturgical Press, 1979.

Fiorenza, Elisabeth Schussler. "Rhetorical Situation and Historical Reconstruction in 1 Corinthians." *NTS* (1987): 386–403.

Freedy, K. S., and D. B. Redford. "The Dates in Ezekiel in Relation to Biblical, Babylonian and Egyptian Sources." *JAOS* 90 (1970): 462–85.

Friedman, Richard Elliott. *Who Wrote the Bible*. New York: Harper & Row, 1987.

Galambush, Julie. *Jerusalem in the Book of Ezekiel: The City as Yahweh's Wife.* SBLDS, 130. Atlanta: Scholars Press, 1992.

Gammie, John G. *Holiness in Israel.* OBT. Minneapolis: Fortress Press, 1989.

Gitay, Yehoshua. *Prophecy and Persuasion: A Study of Isaiah 40–48.* Forum Theologiae Linguisticae. Bonn: Linguistica Biblica, 1981.

Gorman, Frank H. Jr. *The Ideology of Ritual: Space. Time and Status in the Priestly Theology.* JSOTSup, no. 91. Sheffield: JSOT Press, 1990.

Gowan, Donald E. *Eschatology in the Old Testament.* Philadelphia: Fortress Press, 1986.

Greenberg, Moshe. "The Design and Themes of Ezekiel's Program of Restoration." In *Interpreting the Prophets,* ed. James Luther Mays and Paul J. Achtemeier, 215–36. Philadelphia: Fortress Press, 1987.

———. *Ezekiel 1–20.* AB. Garden City, New York: Doubleday & Company, 1983.

———. "Ezekiel 17 and the Policy of Psammetichus II." *JBL* 76 (1957): 304–09.

———. "The Vision of Jerusalem in Ezekiel 8–11: A Holistic Interpretation. " In *The Divine Helmsman: Studies on God's Control of Human Events, Presented to Louis H. Silberman,* ed. James L. Crenshaw and Samuel Sandmel, 143–64. New York: KTAV Publishing House, 1980.

Greenfield, J. C. "Cherethites and Pelethites." In *IDB,* 557, vol. 1. Nashville: Abingdon Press, 1962.

Halpern, Baruch. *The Constitution of the Monarchy in Israel.* HSM, no. 25. Chico, Scholars Press, 1981.

Hals, Ronald M. *Ezekiel.* FOTL, vol. XIX. Grand Rapids: William B. Eerdmans Publishing Company, 1989.

Haran,Menahem. "Temple and Community in Ancient Israel. " ed. Michael V. Fox. In *Temple in Society,* 17–25. Eisenbrauns: Winona Lake, 1988.

———. "Temples and Cultic Open Areas as Reflected in the Bible." In *Temples and High Places in Biblical Times: Proceedings of Coloquium in Honor of the Centennial of Hebrew Union College-Jewish Institute of Religion. Jerusalem, Israel:* Hebrew Union College-Jewish Institute of Religion, 1977.

———. *Temples and Temple-service in Ancient Israel: An Inquiry Into the Character of Cult Phenomena and the Historical Setting of the Priestly School.* Oxford: Clarendon Press, 1978.

Hauge, Martin Ravndal. "On the Sacred Spot: The Concept of Localization Before God." *SJOT* 1 (1990): 30–60.

Hauser, Gerard A. *Introduction to Rhetorical Theory.* Speech Communication Series. New York: Harper & Row, 1986.

Helberg, J. L. "Land in the Book of Lamentations." *ZAW* 102 (1990): 372.

Hurvitz, Avi. *A Linguistic Study of the Relationship Between the Priestly Source and the Book of Ezekiel: A New Approach to an Old Problem.* CahRB. Paris: J. Gabalda et Cie, 1982.

Hutchens, Kenneth D. "Defining the Boundaries: A Cultic Interpretation of Numbers 34:1–12 and Ezekiel 47:13–48:1;28." In *History and Interpretation: Essays in Honour of John H. Hayes,* ed. M. Patrick Graham, William P. Brown, and Jeffrey K. Kuan, JSOTSup, no. 173. Sheffield: JSOT Press, 1993, 215–230.

Jenson, Philip Peter. *Graded Holiness: A Key to the Priestly Conception of the World.* JSOTSup, no. 106. Sheffield: Almond Press, 1992.

Joyce, Paul. *Divine Initiative and Human Response in Ezekiel.* JSOT, no. 51. Sheffield: JSOT Press, 1989.

Kapelrud, Arvid S. "Temple Building, a Task for Gods and Kings. " *Orientalia* 32 (1963): 56–62.

Kaufman, Asher S. "Determining the Length of the Medium Cubit." *PEQ* 116 (1984): 120–32.

Kennedy, George A. *New Testament Interpretation Through Rhetorical Criticism.* Chapel Hill: University of North Carolina Press, 1984.

Kenyon, Kathleen M. *Jerusalem: Excavating 3000 Years of History.* New York: McGraw-Hill Book Company, 1967.

Kiuchi, N. *The Purification Offering in the Priestly Literature.* JSOTSup, no. 56. Sheffield: JSOT Press, 1987.

Klein, Ralph. *Ezekiel: The Prophet and His Message.* Studies on Personalities of the Old Testament. Columbia: University of South Carolina Press, 1988.

Klein, Ralph W. *Israel in Exile: A Theological Interpretation.* Philadelphia: Fortress Press, 1979.

Klimkeit, Hans -J. "Spatial Orientation in Mythical Thinking as Exemplified in Ancient Egypt: Considerations Toward a Geography of Religions." *HR* 14 (1975): 266–81.

Knibb, Michael A. "The Exile in the Literature of the Intertestamental Period." *HeyJ* 17 (1976): 253–72.

Knight, G. A. F. "The Concept of Chaos." *Glasgow University Oriental Society: Transactions* 16 (1955–6): 14–17.

Kort, Wesley A. "'Religion and Literature' in Postmodernist Contexts." *JAAR* 58 (1990): 575–88.

Kuhrt, Amélie. "Usurpation, Conquest and Ceremonial: From Babylon to Persia." In *Rituals of Royalty: Power and Ceremonial in Traditional Societies,* ed. David Cannadine and Simon Price, 20–55. Past and Present Publications. Cambridge: Cambridge University Presse, 1987.

Lang, Bernhard. *Ezechiel: Der Prophet und das Buch.* Erträge der Forschung. Darmstadt: Wissenschaftliche Buchgesellschaft, 1981.

———. *Kein Aufstand in Jerusalem: Die Politik Des Propheten Ezechiel.* Stuttgart: Verlag Katholisches Bibelwerk, 1978.

———. *Monothesism and the Prophetic Minority.* SWBA, no. 1. Sheffield: Almond Press, 1983.

Lenski, Gerhard E. *Power and Privilege: A Theory of Social Stratification.* Chapel Hill: University of North Carolina Press, 1966 < 1984> .

Levenson, Jon D. *Creation and the Persistence of Evil: The Jewish Drama of Divine Omnipotence.* San Francisco: Harper & Row, 1988.

———. "From Temple to Synagogue: 1 Kings 8. " In *Traditions in Transformation: Turning Points in Biblical Faith,* ed. Baruch Halpern and Jon D. Levenson, 143–66. Winona Lake, IN: Eisenbrauns, 1981.

———. *Sinai and Zion: An Entry Into the Jewish Bible.* San Francisco: Harper & Row, 1985.

————. "The Temple and the World." *JR* 64 (1984): 275–98.

————. *Theology of the Program of Restoration of Ezekiel 40–48.* HSM. Missoula, MT: Scholars Press, 1976.

————. "Why Jews Are not Interested in Biblical Theology. " In *Judaic Perspectives on Ancient Israel,* ed. Jacob Neusner, Baruch Levine, and Ernest Frerichs, 281–307. Philadelphia: Fortress Press, 1987.

Levine, Baruch A. "The Language of Holiness: Perceptions of the Sacred in the Hebrew Bible." In *Backgrounds for the Bible,* ed. Michael Patrick O'Connor and David Noel Freedman, 241–54. Winona Lake, IN: Eisenbrauns, 1987.

————. *In the Presence of the Lord: A Study of Cult and Some Cultic Terms in Ancient Israel.* Studies in Judaism in Late Antiquity. Leiden: E. J. Brill, 1974.

Long, Burke O. "Social Dimensions of Prophetic Conflict." *Sem* 21 (1981): 31–53.

Lundquist, John M. "What is a Temple?: A Preliminary Typology. " In *The Quest for the Kingdom of God: Studies in Honor of George E. Mendenhall,* ed. H. B. Huffmon, F. A. Spina, and A. R. W. Green, 205–19. Winona Lake, IN: Eisenbrauns, 1983.

Lust, J., ed. *Ezekiel and His Book: Textual and Literary Criticism and Their Interrelation.* Leuven: University Press, 1986.

McConville, J. G. *Law and Theology in Deuteronomy.* JSOTSup, no. 33. Sheffield: JSOT Press, 1984.

————. "Priests and Levites in Ezekiel: A Crux in the Interpretation of Israel's History." *TynBul* 34 (1983): 3–31.

McKeating, H. *Ezekiel.* Old Testament Guides. Sheffield: JSOT Press, 1993.

————. "Ezekiel 'The Prophet Like Moses'?." *JSOT* 61 (1994): 97–109.

McKenzie, John L. "Mythological Allusions in Ezekiel 28:12–18." *JBL* 75 (1956): 322–27.

Maier, Johann. "The Architectural History of the Temple in Jerusalem in Light of the Temple Scroll. " In *Temple Scroll Studies: Papers Presented at the International Symposium on the Temple Scroll.* Manchester. December 1987, ed. George J. Brooke, 23–62. Sheffield: JSOT Press, 1989.

Malamat, A. "The Last Kings of Judah and the Fall of Jerusalem: An Historical-chronological Study." *IEJ* 18 (1968):137–56.

Mays, James Luther. *Ezekiel. Second Isaiah.* Proclamation Commentaries. Philadelphia: Fortress Press, 1978.

Mazar, Benjamin. *The Mountain of the Lord.* Garden City, New York: Doubleday & Company, Inc., 1975.

Milgrom, Jacob. "Israel's Sanctuary: The Priestly 'Picture of Dorian Gray' *RB* 83 (1976): 390–99.

————. *Leviticus 16: A New Translation with Introduction and Commentary.* AB. New York: Doubleday, 1991.

————. *Studies in Cultic Theology and Terminology.* Leiden: E. J. Brill, 1983.

————. *Studies in Levitical Terminology,* I. Berkeley: University of California Press, 1970.

Miller, J. Maxwell, and John H. Hayes. *A History of Ancient Israel and Judah.* Philadelphia: Westminster Press, 1986.

Miller, James E. "The Thirtieth Year of Ezekiel 1:1." *RB* 99 (1992): 499–503.

Muilenburg, James. "Form Criticism and Beyond." *JBL* 88 (1969): 1–18.

Neiman. David. "*PGR*: A Canaanite Cult-Object in the Old Testament." *JBL* 67 (1948): 55–60.

Nelson, Richard D. *Raising Up a Faithful Priest: Community and Priesthood in Biblical Theology.* Louisville: Westminster/John Knox Press, 1993.

Neusner, Jacob. *Self-Fulfilling Prophecy: Exile and Return in the History of Judaism.* Boston: Beacon Press, 1987.

Niditch, Susan. "Ezekiel 40–48 in a Visionary Context." *CBQ* 48 (1986): 208–24.

Oded, Bustenay. "Judah and the Exile." In *Israelite and Judean History,* ed. John H. Hayes and J. Maxwell Miller, 435–488. Philadelphia: Westminster Press, 1977.

Odell, Margaret S. "The City of Hamonah in Ezekiel 39:11–16: The Tumultuous City of Jerusalem." *CBQ* 56 (1994): 479–489.

———. "The Inversion of Shame and Forgiveness in Ezekiel 16:59–63." *JSOT* 56 (1992): 101–112.

Ollenburger, Ben C. *Zion the City of the Great King: A Theological Symbol of the Jerusalem Cult.* JSOTSup, no. 41. Sheffield: JSOT Press, 1987.

Ottosson, Magnus. *Temples and Cult Places in Palestine.* Uppsala: Acta Universitatis Upsaliensis, 1980.

Patrick, Dale, and Allen Scult. *Rhetoric and Biblical Interpretation.* JSOTSup, no. 80. Sheffield: Almond Press, 1990.

Patton, Corrine L. *Ezekiel's Blueprint for the Temple of Jerusalem.* Ph. D. Diss. Yale University, 1991.

Pred, Allan. "The Locally Spoken Word and Local Struggles." *Society and Space* 7 (1989): 211–33.

———. *Making Histories and Constructing Human Geographies: The Local Transformation of Practice, Power Relations and Consciousness.* With a Foreword by Charles Tilly. Boulder, CO: Westview Press, 1990.

Rooker, Mark F. *Biblical Hebrew in Transition: The Language of the Book of Ezekiel.* JSOTSup, no. 90. Sheffield: JSOT Press, 1990.

Rowley, Harold H. "The Book of Ezekiel in Modern Study." *BJRL* 36 (1953–4): 146–90.

Runnalls, Donna. "The *parwar*: A Place of Ritual Separation." *VT* 41 (1991): 324–31.

Sack, Robert David. *Human Territoriality: Its Theory and History.* Cambridge Studies in Historical Geography. Cambridge: Cambridge University Press, 1986.

Schiffman, Lawrence H. "Architecture and Law: The Temple and Its Courtyards in the 'Temple Scroll'" In *From Ancient Israel to Modern Judaism: Intellect in Quest of Understanding: Essays in Honor of Marvin Fox,* ed. Jacob Neusner, Ernest S. Frerichs, and Nahum M. Sarna, 267–84. Brown Judaic Studies. Atlanta: Scholars Press, 1989.

Scott, R. B. Y. "Weights and Measures of the Bible." In *BAR,* 345–58. Garden City, New York: Doubleday & Company, 1970.

Smith, Daniel L. *The Religion of the Landless: The Social Context of the Babylonian Exile.* Bloomington, IN: Meyer-Stone Books, 1989.

Smith, Jonathan Z. *Map is not Territory: Studies in the History of Religions.* Studies in Judaism in Late Antiquity, no. 23. Leiden: E. J. Brill, 1978.

———. *To Take Place: Toward Theory in Ritual.* Chicago Studies in the History of Judaism. Chicago: University of Chicago Press, 1987.

Smith, Mark S. *The Early History of God: Yahweh and the Other Deities in Ancient Israel.* San Francisco: Harper & Row, 1990.

Smith, Morton. "The Common Theology of the Ancient Near East." *JBL* 71 (1952): 135–37.

Soja, Edward W. *The Political Organization of Space.* Resource Paper, no. 8. Washington, D.C.: Association of American Geographers, 1971.

———. *Postmodern Geographies: The Reassertion of Space in Critical Social Theory.* New York: Verso, 1989.

Speiser, E. A. "Background and Function of the Biblical Nasi." *CBQ* 25 (1963): 111–17.

Stinespring, W. F. "Temple, Jerusalem." In *IDB*, 534–60, vol. 4. Nashville: Abingdon Press, 1962.

Strange, John. "Architecture and Theology." *SEA* 54 (1989): 199–206.

Tkacik, Arnold J. "Ezekiel." In *JBC*, ed. Raymond E. Brown, Joseph A. Fitzmyer, and Roland E. Murphy, 344–65. Englewood Cliffs, New Jersey: Prentice Hall, 1968.

Tsevat, Matitiahu. "The Neo-Assyrian and Neo-Babylonian Vassal Oaths and the Prophet Ezekiel." *JBL* 78 (1959): 199–309.

Tuell, Steven Shawn. *The Law of the Temple in Ezekiel 40–48.* HSM, no. 49. Atlanta: Scholars Press, 1992.

———. "The Temple Vision of Ezekiel 40–48: A Program for Restoration?" *Proceedings Eastern Great Lakes Biblical Society* 2 (1982): 96–103.

Vawter, Bruce, and Leslie J. Hoppe. *A New Heart: A Commentary on the Book of Ezekiel.* International Theological Commentary. Grand Rapids: Wm. B. Eerdmans Publishing Company, 1991.

Watson, Duane F., ed. *Persuasive Artistry: Studies in New Testament Rhetoric in Honor of George A. Kennedy.* JSNTSup, no. 50. Sheffield: JSOT Press, 1991.

Wellhausen, Julius. *Prolegomena to the History of Ancient Israel: With a Reprint of the Article "Israel" from the Encyclopaedia Britannica.* Translated by J. S. Black and A. Menzies. With a Preface by W. Robertson Smith. New York: Meridian Books, 1957.

Wevers, John W., ed. *Ezekiel.* Century Bible. London: Thomas Nelson and Sons, 1969.

Whitelam, Keith W. "Israelite Kingship: The Royal Ideology and Its Opponents." In *The World of Ancient Israel: Sociological, Anthropological, and Political Perspectives*, ed. R. E. Clements, 119–39. Cambridge: Cambridge University Press, 1989.

———. *The Just King: Monarchical Judicial Authority in Ancient Israel.* JSOTSup, no. 12. Sheffield: JSOT Press, 1979.

———. "The Symbols of Power: Aspects of Royal Propaganda in the United Monarchy. " *BA* 49 (1986):166–73.

Wiseman, D. J. *Nebuchadrezzar and Babylon: The Schweich Lectures of the British Academy 1983.* Oxford: Oxford University Press, 1985.

Wright, Christopher J. H. *God's People in God's Land: Family, Land, and Property in the Old Testament.* Grand Rapids, MI: William B. Eerdmans Publishing Company, 1990.

Wright, John. "A Tale of Three Cities: Urban Gates, Squares, and Power in Iron Age II, Neo-Babylonian, and Achaemenid Israel." Paper Presented to Society of Biblical Literature Annual Meeting. New Orleans, 1990.

Wuellner, Wilhelm. "Where is Rhetorical Criticism Taking Us?" *CBQ* 49 (1987): 448–63.

Wyatt, Nicholas. "There and Back Again: The Significance of Movement in the Priestly Work" *SJOT* 1 (1990): 61–80.

Zimmerli, Walther. *Ezekiel 1: A Commentary on the Book of the Prophet Ezekiel, Chapters 1–24*. Translated by Ronald E. Clements. Hermeneia. Philadelphia: Fortress Press, 1979.

———. *Ezekiel 2*. Translated by James D. Martin. Hermeneia. Philadelphia: Fortress Press, 1983.

———. *I Am Yahweh*. Translated by James D. Martin. With an Introduction by Walter Brueggemann. ed. Walter Brueggemann. Atlanta: John Knox Press, 1982.

Index

Authors

Scripture Index